英语国际人

留学英语
情景会话50主题

50 Campus Conversation Topics

Martin Boyle 于戈 著

FOREWORD

Do you know under what circumstances friends in the UK shake hands or hug?

Do you believe that you can cope with heated debates in the seminar rooms of British universities?

Do you know what films British students watch, what songs they listen to and what video games they play?

The book you are about to read is not a boring textbook for spoken English, nor is it a travel guide for overseas study in the UK. The unique feature of this book is the demonstration of conversational English techniques through dialogues based on British campus culture. It enables readers who intend to study in the UK to improve their spoken English as they read through amusing situations which take place on British campuses.

Language is a tool of communication which can only be improved through practice. We are all aware of the importance of "speaking" in the learning of English, but spoken English is also a weak point for most Chinese students. The speaking exercises provided by school textbooks are often out of touch with young people's lives. Using materials that are irrelevant to our own lives to practice English is not "using language" at all. In order to use the language, the speaker must have the urge to communicate and express himself. The content of what you say must also make you feel that speaking English is fun and cool.

This is what originally inspired us to write this book. The authors, Ge Yu and Martin Boyle, have carefully picked 50 topics that are closely related to the lives of overseas students in the UK, such as "Habits and Customs", "Interviews and Applications", "Shopping in the Supermarket", "Seminars", "Essays and Presentations", "Sports Talk", "Part-time Jobs", "Pubs and Parties" and "Campus Romance". We have also included some topics that are taboo in English education in China, but very commonly discussed in British universities—topics such as "Sexual Health" and "Student Union Politics".

Every topic begins with an interesting "Background Knowledge". In the "Background Knowledge", you will learn about the cultural and linguistic similarities and differences between China and Britain on this topic. The second part of the topic is "Dialogue". These dialogues are collected from various corners of British campuses and are guaranteed to be idiomatic, stylish and practical. Every topic ends with a list of "Phrases" and a "Glossary", so that the readers can absorb the language points more formally and systematically. The language points in the background knowledge, the entire dialogues, phrases and glossaries are all Chinese-English, so that the readers can fully grasp the language environment.

Martin and Ge: one is British, the other is Chinese; one is a teacher, the other is a student. This arrangement has made this book a perfect combination of English linguistic authenticity and Chinese academic empathy. No longer will speaking English feel daunting and alien. Rather, it will feel friendly and addictive.

前　言

你知道在英国朋友见面时，什么时候握手，什么时候拥抱吗？
你相信自己能应付英国大学课堂里唇枪舌剑的辩论吗？
你了解英国大学生看什么电影，听什么歌，玩什么电脑游戏吗？

你面前的这本书不是一本单调的英语口语教科书，也不是一本旅游手册似的留学指南。这本书的独到之处是通过介绍英国校园文化来演示英语口语技巧，使准备去英国留学的读者们能在阅读英国校园趣谈的同时提高英语口语水平。

语言是交流的工具，只有在使用中才能得到锻炼。大家都知道"说"英语对英语学习的重要性。口语也是大多数中国学生的弱项。学校课本里的口语练习大多都离青年人的生活太远。用跟自己生活没有关系的材料练习口语，根本不能算是"使用语言"。要使用语言，说话的人必须有沟通和表达的欲望；所说的内容也必须是"不（用英语）吐不快"。

这就是这本书的创作初衷。作者于戈和马丁·博伊尔（英国），精心选择了50个和留学生活息息相关的话题，包括"习惯与风俗"、"面试与申请"、"超市购物"、"讨论课"、"论文与演讲"、"闲聊体育"、"业余打工"、"酒吧与晚会"、"校园浪漫"等等。许多中国英语教育界羞于讨论，但在英国校园里司空见惯的问题，我们也有所涉及，比如"性健康"和"校园政治"。

每个话题都以一段有趣的背景常识为开头。在背景常识里，你将了解到中英文化和语言习惯在这个话题上的区别与共同点，以及最可能涉及的词汇和表达方式。话题的第二部分是情景对话。这些对话都是从英国校园的各个角落采集来的，原汁原味、风趣实用。每个话题还都附有一个短语表和一个词汇表，使读者能够系统化地掌握语言点。所有背景常识里的语言点、情景对话和短语词汇表都为中英双语，以便读者体会完整的语言环境。

马丁与于戈两人，一英一中，一师一生，如此一来，这本书完美地结合了地道准确的表达方式和为中国学生量身定做的语言内容，保证让你觉得英语不再遥远和陌生，反而一见如故、"爱不释口"。

目 录

第1章	习惯与风俗　Habits and Customs	1
第2章	说完"你好"以后　After Hello	9
第3章	申请与面试　Application and Interview	13
第4章	理想与计划　Ambitions and Plan	17
第5章	旅行信息　Travel Information	21
第6章	联系住宿　Searching for Accommodation	27
第7章	新生周　Freshers' Week	33
第8章	校方官员　University Bureaucracy	39
第9章	见导师　Meeting Your Personal Tutor/Adviser	43
第10章	银行、诊所与警察局　Bank, Clinic and Police	47
第11章	图书馆与信息服务　Library and IT Services	51
第12章	实验室和工作室　Laboratory and Studio	55
第13章	签手机合同　Signing a Mobile Phone Contract	59
第14章	点　菜　Ordering a Meal	63
第15章	超市购物　Shopping in the Supermarket	69
第16章	买衣服　Buying Clothes	73
第17章	购　书　Buying Books	77
第18章	课程和学分体制　Modules and the Credit System	81
第19章	安排课程表　Arranging Your Timetable	87
第20章	上课第一天　First Day in Class	91
第21章	提问题　Asking Questions	95
第22章	敷衍搪塞　Hedging Answers	101
第23章	对比和比较　Contrast and Comparison	107
第24章	引用与转述　Quoting and Paraphrasing	111
第25章	教中文　Teaching Chinese	115

第26章	讨论课　Seminars	119
第27章	论文与演讲　Essays and Presentations	123
第28章	考试与复习　Exams and Revision	127
第29章	请一天假　Take a Day Off	133
第30章	像科学家一样说话　Sounding Like a Scientist	139
第31章	像哲学家一样说话　Sounding Like a Philosopher	143
第32章	像艺术家一样说话　Sounding Like an Artist	147
第33章	学生会与政治　The Student Union and Student Politics	151
第34章	辅导与建议　Counselling and Advice	157
第35章	加入一个社团　Joining a Society	163
第36章	闲聊体育　Talking Sport	169
第37章	义务劳动　Volunteering	175
第38章	业余打工　Part-Time Jobs	181
第39章	谦虚地展示技能　Demonstrating Skills Humbly	187
第40章	酒吧与晚会　Pubs and Parties	191
第41章	电影院和剧院　Cinema and Theatre	195
第42章	圣诞节与新年　Christmas and New Year	199
第43章	中国春节　Chinese New Year	205
第44章	谈中国　Talking about China	211
第45章	外国留学生　Other Overseas Students	217
第46章	校园浪漫　Campus Romance	221
第47章	学生性健康　Student Sexual Health	229
第48章	成年学生　Mature Students	235
第49章	游历英国　Travelling in the UK	241
第50章	告别英伦　Leaving the UK	245

第1章
习惯与风俗
Habits and Customs

背景常识

中国朋友之间打招呼(greet)，一般就是招招手(wave)。而在英国大学里，人们有时握手(shake hands)，有时拥抱(hug)，有时亲吻(kiss)对方的脸(cheek)。

握手(handshake)通常显得过于正式(formal)。要好的朋友(close friends)之间，互相拥抱更为常见。性别不同的人之间(between opposite sexes)拥抱也很正常。但是，由于拥抱是一个如此亲热的(intimate)举动(gesture)，如果你一天内三次见到某个朋友而次次拥抱他，就显得过于热情(overwhelming)了。英国人在见面和分别时经常亲吻脸颊，不过英国男人通常是不互相吻脸的。亲吻只在一对异性或两个女性间发生。说到吃饭，在中国，如果吃米饭的时候不把饭碗端起来，会显得(appear)没有食欲(appetite)。在英国，碗碟离桌是很不礼貌的(impolite)。喝汤(eat soup)和喝咖啡(drink coffee)的时候，喝出动静来也是粗鲁的(rude)。吃完饭以后打嗝儿(burp)是忌讳，但是发出 mmm 的声音来表示饭菜好吃则是对主人的尊重(respect)。至于穿着，学生们一般穿得都很随便(laid back)。不少中国人以为在英国不能穿白袜子(socks)，这其实是讹传(myth)。穿皮鞋的时候不能穿白袜子，而穿运动鞋时穿白袜子是很普遍的(common)。

这些还只是中英习俗差异的冰山一角(the tip of the iceberg)。面对异国风情，你不必总是入乡随俗(be assimilated)；由于英国盛行文化多元主义(multiculturalism)，有文化个性(individuality)的留学生是很受欢迎的。然而，融入(integrate)和感悟西方文化也是留学的任务和乐趣之一。读了万卷书，行了万里路的人应该有包容和理智的文化观，既不崇洋也不守旧。

Outside the Lecture

Wang: Hi Ping… how's things? You know, I had a bit of a run-in with the lecturer today.

Ping: Why? What happened?

Wang: Well①, she said I was being rude and making her stomach turn!

Ping: What? Why?

Wang: I had a runny nose and I was just, like, sniffing, you know.

Ping: Were you just sniffling a little bit or were you actually sniffing it all up and making a noise?

Wang: I thought it was just normal.

Ping: The thing is that in the West they really hate it when you do that in a noisy way… especially if you keep on doing it without blowing your nose… you know②… or you swallow the phlegm. They find that really disgusting.

Wang: Yeah… but blowing your nose is worse, surely!

Ping: Not in Europe. In fact, it's more polite to blow your nose and make a noise than it is to sniff noisily and swallow the catarrh. That's a big "no, no".

Wang: I didn't know that… they must think I'm a pig! You know, there was this Italian guy in our seminar, and he was always blowing his nose really loudly into this big white cotton handkerchief… like a foghorn… then stuffing it up his sleeve. All the Japanese and Chinese looked really embarrassed.

Ping: I know… it's difficult, isn't it? There was this Japanese guy in our class and he was so scared to blow his nose even though he had a massive cold and his nose was running like mad. He had five packets of paper hankies on the table in front of him, and he just kept wiping his nose, and sniffing. Anyway③, one of the other students picked up the hankies and asked him why he had Japanese hankies as he'd been in England for six months. You know what he said?

Wang: What?

Ping: He said, "Oh, my mum sent them to me because English hankies are too rough."

Wang: Hahahaha! What a sissy!

Ping: Yeah… and he was wearing a pink jumper as well… haha.

Wang: Yeah! Mummy's boy!

Ping: You see, they find us weird the same way we find them. I guess there are loads of things like that that we have to watch out for… you know, habits and customs and things.

Wang: Yeah… my teacher told me that when he was in China, he just couldn't get used to the way people didn't queue up. He knew that it wasn't the custom and that he should just jostle and shove, but he couldn't get used to it.

在课堂外

1. 王：嗨，萍，你好吗？你猜怎么着，我今天和我的讲师发生了点儿小摩擦。
2. 萍：为什么？怎么回事？
3. 王：她说我没礼貌，让她不舒服！
4. 萍：什么？为什么？
5. 王：我流鼻涕了，不过就是抽了几下。
6. 萍：你是就抽了几下还是抽到底？而且弄出动静了？
7. 王：我觉得流鼻涕很正常嘛。
8. 萍：问题是，在西方人们很讨厌抽鼻子出声，尤其是如果你总不擤鼻子，或者吞痰。他们觉得那很恶心。
9. 王：那，当众擤鼻子更过分，不是吗？
10. 萍：在欧洲就不是。实际上，大声擤鼻子要比抽鼻涕和吞鼻涕强。这后两个行为是绝对忌讳的。
11. 王：我不知道有那么回事。他们一定认为我很蠢！你知道吗，我们讨论课里有个意大利男生，他总是用自己的白棉手绢大声地擤鼻涕，像吹号似的，然后又把手绢掖回他的袖子里。所有中国人和日本人都很尴尬。
12. 萍：我知道，真拿这样的事没办法，是不是？我们班里有一个日本男生，他总不敢大声擤鼻子，即使他得了重感冒而且疯狂地流鼻涕。他面前的桌上总摆着五包纸巾，他就总是擦和抽。另外，一个同学拿起他的纸巾，问他为什么来英国6个月了还在用日本纸巾，你猜他说什么？
13. 王：什么？
14. 萍：他说："噢，这是我妈妈寄来的，因为英国手巾太粗了。"
15. 王：哈哈哈！太娘娘腔了！
16. 萍：就是，他还穿粉红毛衣呢，哈哈！
17. 王：对啊，整个一个乖宝宝！
18. 萍：你看，他们看我们就跟我们看他们一样奇怪。我估计还有很多类似的事情我们要小心，我是说，习惯和风俗之类的东西。
19. 王：是，我的老师告诉我，当他在中国的时候，他对人们不排队很不适应。他知道中国人不像英国人那么爱排队，而且他应该跟大家一块儿挤，但是他就是适应不了。

Ping: Well, you know what they say… "when in Rome…" I think if you just show good will, smile and say sorry… then most people understand, don't they?

In the Classroom

Teacher: I was reading in the *Economist* the other day that, since the easing of visa restrictions on Chinese tour groups, loads of Chinese tourists have been coming to England to go shopping in factory outlets and buying the oddest④ products.

Li: Like what kinds of things?

Teacher: Well, it said in the article that Clarks shoes were a real draw.

Li: Yeah… they're really famous in China. We think they're high quality.

Teacher: That's really strange to us here… we see Clarks as being a bit old-fashioned… you know—sensible shoes for school children. They are certainly not cool.

Li: That's weird… we think they are really fashionable.

Madina: Yeah… my neighbour told me the other day that I looked like a chav because I was wearing a Burberry baseball cap. It was really expensive… we think Burberry is really high-end stuff.

Teacher: That's the odd thing. There seems to be a gap in perception between us here about the products you think are archetypally British. I mean, you think Burberry is high class, but at the end of the 1990s it actually became associated with certain sections of British society… football hooligans, single mothers and so on… that word chav, you used… it refers to a particular kind of poor person who dresses in a way she thinks looks classy but is actually viewed as cheap and tacky by some others… cheap jewellery and big hooped earrings—known as bling—are another feature of chav dress. The company is trying to change its image through changing its marketing strategy. The problem is that most East Asians who buy these products are not aware of the negative connotations.

Li: But some of these names are really good brands. I mean Abercrombie and Barber and so on.

Teacher: Yes… but they can sometimes be seen as a bit preppy… you know… like Pringle, Ralph Lauren, Polo, Tommy Hilfiger—although some of these are not British—they are seen as indicative of someone who is not really cool—especially if you are a student. Most British students prefer to dress down. And you don't want to be labelled as spoiled rich kids by the British students, do you?

Madina: Well, I love my brand names… I couldn't be seen out in anything that wasn't good quality!

萍：就像他们说的，入乡随俗嘛。我想只要你表示友好，微笑并说声对不起，大多数人还是不会介意的，对吗？

在教室里

老师：我前两天在《经济学家》杂志上看到，由于对中国旅行团的签证限制放宽，现在有大批中国游客来到英国。他们到折扣商店购物，而且买的都是些稀奇古怪的商品。

丽：都是些什么呢？

老师：噢，文章里面说其乐牌的鞋非常畅销。

丽：是的，它们在中国非常有名。我们认为它们质量很好。

老师：对我们来说就很奇怪了。我们觉得其乐有点儿老土，对中小学生倒很合适。它们绝对算不上酷。

丽：那就怪了，我们觉得它们挺时髦的。

玛迪娜：对啊，我邻居前两天说我臭美，因为我戴了顶巴宝利的棒球帽。那帽子很贵呢。我们觉得巴宝利是高级东西。

老师：怪就怪在这儿了。我们之间，在对什么是英国的象征这个问题上，似乎有意识鸿沟。我的意思是，巴宝利的确高级，不过在上世纪90年代末，有人开始把它与英国社会的个别群体联系起来，足球流氓、单身母亲之类的。"臭美"，你用的这个词，就表示那种喜欢过分打扮的穷人，自以为上档次，但在别人看来却显得小气且虚荣。廉价的首饰和大圈耳环——穿金戴银——是臭美装束的另一个标志。这家公司正试图通过改变营销战略来改变自己的形象。问题是，大多数东亚地区的人对这一消极形象一无所知。

丽：但是，这些名字中还是有很不错的品牌。比如，艾伯克克龙比和巴伯等等。

老师：是的，但它们有时也被视为一种炫耀。比如普林格、拉尔夫·劳伦、马球、汤米——当然，这些不全是英国牌子——它们并不真是新潮的标志，尤其对学生来说。大部分英国学生更倾向于简朴一些的着装。你总不希望被别的英国学生看作纨绔子弟吧？

玛迪娜：哼，我就是喜欢名牌，我是不能穿着低档衣服出门见人的！

Teacher: Do you know, last year we had a group of Chinese lawyers here on a law course. We took them to Oxford on a day trip to visit the Bodleian Library, the famous colleges and museums and so on, and they were annoyed... they thought we were planning to take them to Oxford St⑤!

Li: That's not fair! Not all of us are like that!

Teacher: I know... I think this is just a cultural gap. I mean, take music for instance. Who are your favourite singers and groups?

Madina: Oh... I like Christina Aguilera and Jennifer Lopez.

Li: Yeah... and I like, you know, R&B and boy bands like Westlife.

Teacher: Well there's a big difference there! Do you know who the most popular groups are among British students? Have you heard of the Arctic Monkeys? The Zutons? The Scissor Sisters? No? Well, there you go!

Li: Hey! That's not fair! How many Chinese singers do you know? Have you heard of Beijing punk?

Teacher: Well, each to his own, I used to like Heavy Metal and Hard Rock when I was your age....

Li: Oh no, a sad old rocker!

注释

① well 这里是感叹词,不是"好"的意思。
② you know 没有实际意义,是英语口语中的感叹词。
③ anyway 这里是语气词,表示转换话题,没有实际意义。
④ oddest 这里不是 odd 的最高级,只表示"极度奇怪"。
⑤ Oxford St 牛津街,伦敦的购物中心。

老师：你们知道吗，去年有一批中国律师来这儿进修法律。我们带他们去牛津玩了一圈，参观了牛津大学图书馆，还有那些著名的学院和博物馆。可他们却很不满，他们本来以为我们要带他们去牛津街呢。

丽：别这么说！不是所有外国人都这样。

老师：我知道，我觉得这只是文化差异。比如说音乐吧，你们都喜欢哪些歌手和乐队？

玛迪娜：噢，我喜欢克莉丝汀·阿奎莱拉和詹尼弗·洛佩兹。

丽：还有，我喜欢节奏布鲁斯和诸如西城男孩一类的男声组合。

老师：你看，在这个问题上我们就有很大的区别！你们知道在英国学生中最流行的组合是哪些吗？有没有听说过北极猴？祖特斯？剪刀姐妹？都没听说过？看，我没说错吧！

丽：嘿！这不公平！你又知道几个中国歌手呢？你听过北京朋克吗？

老师：萝卜白菜，各有所爱。我像你们这么大的时候也喜欢重金属和硬摇滚。

丽：噢，好一个可怜的老摇滚迷啊！

实用短语

- ◆ Hi... how's things?   嗨，你怎么样？
- ◆ I had a bit of a run-in with...   我跟……发生点儿小摩擦。
- ◆ I didn't know that.   我不知道有那么回事。
- ◆ They must think...   他们一定认为……
- ◆ What a...!   真是个……!
- ◆ Well...   那么……
- ◆ It said in...（that）...   ……里面说……
- ◆ The problem/thing is that...   问题是……
- ◆ They can (sometimes) be seen as...   它们也可能被视为……
- ◆ You don't want to be labelled as...   你不希望被看作……
- ◆ Do you know who... are?   你知道……是谁吗？

词汇表

archetypally 最典型地
baseball cap 棒球帽
big "no no" 大忌讳
bling 夸张的装扮/穿金戴银
blow one's nose 擤鼻子
Bodleian Library 牛津大学图书馆
boy band 男声组合
catarrh 鼻涕
chav 爱臭美的人
cheap and tacky 小气而虚荣
classy 经典/上档次
cotton handkerchief 棉手绢
disgusting 恶心的
dress down 简朴打扮
each to his own 萝卜白菜，各有所爱
easing of visa restrictions 对签证限制的放松
embarrassed 尴尬的
factory outlet 折扣店/厂家直销店
football hooligan 足球流氓
gap in perception 意识差异

good will 好意
high-end 高级的/高档的
hooped earrings 圈形耳环
jostle and shove 推搡/挤
label 给…贴上标签/起外号
like mad 疯狂地/严重地
make one's stomach turn 让人讨厌、恶心
massive cold 重感冒
mummy's boy 没长大的孩子
negative connotations 贬义的口吻/消极形象
odd 奇怪的
Oxford St 牛津街
paper hankies 纸巾
phlegm 痰
pink jumper 粉红色毛衣
preppy 爱炫耀的
queue 排队
R&B（Rhythm and Blues）节奏布鲁斯
rough 粗糙的

rude 粗鲁的/不礼貌的
run-in 摩擦/误会
runny nose 流鼻涕的鼻子
sad old rocker 可怜的老摇滚/往事不堪回首
sensible 合适的
single mother 单身母亲
sissy 娘娘腔
sniff 抽涕
sniff it all up 把鼻涕全吸回去
sniffle 轻轻抽鼻子
spoiled rich kid 被宠坏了的有钱人家的孩子
stuff... up one's sleeve 把…掖回袖子里
swallow 吞
the Economist《经济学家》杂志
tour group 旅行团
watch out for 注意/小心
when in rome... 入乡随俗
wipe one's nose 擦鼻子

第 2 章
说完"你好"以后
After Hello

背景常识

几乎所有的英语课本的第一课都是 Hello。其实打招呼的词还有很多,比如 Hi、Hey 和 Heya。How are you? 也可以用 How is it going? 或 Are you all right? 来代替。What's up. 也是问候,不过太美国化了。在回答的时候,不要总用 I am fine, thank you, and you? 这样的教科书规定动作。你可以说 Not bad, yourself? 或者 Very well, how about you? 大多数情况下,英国人问"你好吗"只是一种形式上的礼节(formality)。至于你真的好不好,他们并不在乎。

在说完"你好"以后,仍然有很多讲究。作为一条基本原则(a general rule of thumb),英国人初次见面时的谈话(conversation)通常局限在诸如天气(weather)和交通(traffic)这样的中性话题上。有些时候,这些话题可能会让中国人感觉很无聊(boring),但是,对无聊的话题表示兴趣往往是英国绅士淑女们的必修课。不熟的人之间是不谈论家庭(family)、年龄(age)、体重(weight)与收入(income)的。谈论时事新闻(current affairs)很正常,不过有些人不愿意表露自己的政治观点(political view)和宗教信仰(religion)。

陌生的中国人互相介绍时,通常一方会告诉另一方自己的姓(surname)或者全名(full name);而英国人通常只介绍自己的名(forename)。另外,直呼一个人的姓通常是不礼貌的。几乎所有的中国学生都给自己取英文名字。其他国家来英国的留学生很少这样做,他们一般只把自己的名字直接音译成英文。由于很多中国字的发音外国人发不了,给自己取个英文名也未尝不可。只是小心不要给自己取一些如 Cloud 或 Angel 之类的有实际意义的名字。这些名字的本义可能很酷,但是作为人名就很可笑了。

In Flight

Ali: Hi, I think I'm sitting next to you. Seat 35B.
Wei Wei: Oh, sorry. I'll just move my things. Hold on a minute.
Ali: Thanks. Phwoo... I've been waiting in departure for ages.
Wei Wei: Mmm... The flight was delayed leaving Beijing. Security checks, you know.
Ali: Yeah. Same here.①
Wei Wei: Are you going to London, then?
Ali: Yes, I'm going to the LSE to do a master's in International Relations.
Wei Wei: Really? That sounds interesting. You must be really clever.
Ali: So are you going to London too?
Wei Wei: Well actually, I'm going to the University of Middlesex to do Business Studies.
Ali: That sounds interesting.
Wei Wei: Well actually,② it's my parents who want me to do Business Studies. I'd rather study Philosophy, but my dad wants me to take over the family business. He thinks Business Studies will make me rich.
Ali: Well, nobody wants to be poor... ah, here's the drinks trolley. What would you like?
Wei Wei: A Coke, please. I'm sorry... I don't know your name....
Ali: Oh, sorry. I forgot... Ali.

The Queue for the Registry

Kim: Hi there. Are you Korean?
Lu: No. I'm Chinese. I'm from Shanghai.
Kim: Oh, Sorry. I was just looking for the registry. I need to register for my course. Look... is this the right place?
Lu: Yes. That's right. I think it's going to take a while though.
Kim: Mmm... and I have to get my accommodation too... it's a bit complicated, isn't it?
Lu: Brrr... the weather's cold for September, isn't it?
Kim: Yes... I didn't think it'd be so cold at this time of year.
Lu: Mmm... which course are you doing?
Kim: Development Studies.
Lu: Wow. So am I. So I guess we'll be seeing more of each other.
Kim: Yes, I suppose we will. Is that an "A to Z" you've got there? Could I borrow it, please? I need to find out where my accommodation is.
Lu: Sure... here you are.
Kim: My name's Kim, by the way. I'm from Seoul.
Lu: Oh... ha... I'm Lu, nice to meet you.

在飞机上

阿里：你好，我想我是跟你坐在一起的，座位是35B。
薇薇：哦，对不起。稍等，让我把东西挪一挪。
阿里：谢谢。嘘，可算登机了。我在候机厅里等了半天。
薇薇：是啊，这飞机离开北京时就晚点了。安检，别提了。
阿里：可不，我们也是。
薇薇：这么说，你也去伦敦？
阿里：是啊，我去伦敦政经学院读国际关系硕士。
薇薇：是吗？听起来很有意思。你一定很聪明。
阿里：你也去伦敦吗？
薇薇：其实，我是去密德萨克斯大学读商学。
阿里：有意思。
薇薇：实际上，读商学是我父母的主意。我更喜欢学哲学，但是我父亲想让我将来接手家族产业。他觉得学商比较挣钱。
阿里：对啊，没什么别没钱嘛！哈，饮料车过来了。你想喝什么？
薇薇：可乐，谢谢。不好意思，我还不知道你叫什么呢。
阿里：哦，对不起，我忘了。我叫阿里。

排队注册

金：你好。你是韩国人吗？
陆：不，我是中国人，从上海来的。
金：哦，对不起。我在找学籍注册办公室。我得登记我的课程。你看是这儿吗？
陆：对，就是这儿。但我估计排到窗口还得有一会儿呢。
金：可不，而且我还得去办理住宿手续，真够复杂的。
陆：是啊！这儿9月的天气可够冷的，对吧？
金：是啊，我没想到一年的这个时候会这么冷。
陆：嗯，你是学什么的？
金：发展学。
陆：哇，我也是。看来我们会经常见面了。
金：嗯，我想我们会的。你拿的是"新生指南"吗？能借给我看看吗？我想要看看我的宿舍在哪儿。
陆：当然可以，给你。
金：顺便介绍一下，我姓金，来自首尔。
陆：嗯，我姓陆，很高兴见到你。

注释
① same here 表示"拥有相同的情况或在相同状态下"。
② well 是一个常用的语气词，表示正在思考。

实用短语

- Hi, I think I'm sitting next to you...　嘿,我想我是跟你坐在一起的……
- Hold on a minute. Let me move my things.　稍等,让我把我的东西挪一挪。
- Same here.　我也是。
- Yes, I suppose we will.　是,我想我们会的。
- Sure. Here you are.　当然,给你。
- The weather's cold for... isn't it?　对于……来说这天气够冷的,对吗?
- It's a bit complicated, isn't it?　真够复杂的,不是吗?
- I guess we'll be seeing more of each other.　看来我们会经常见面了。
- Really? That sounds interesting.　真的吗?这听起来很有意思。
- Well actually...　其实……
- Is that an A to Z you've got there?　你拿的是一本指南吗?
- My name's Kim, by the way.　顺便介绍一下,我姓金。
- I'm sorry I still don't know your name.　不好意思,我还不知道你的名字呢。
- Oh, sorry. I forgot...　哦,对不起,我忘了……
- Sorry. I didn't catch your name.　对不起,我没听见你的名字。
- I'm so sorry I haven't introduced myself.　对不起,我忘了介绍我自己了。

词汇表

A to Z 指南
accommodation 住宿
clever 聪明的
complicated 复杂的
Business Studies 商学
delayed 晚点的
departure 候机厅
Development Studies 发展学(国际关系学或经济学的分支,研究国家或地区发展的原因和障碍)
drinks trolley 装饮料的手推车
for ages 很长时间(夸张)
hold on 等等
I'd rather... 我宁可…/我更喜欢…
International Relations 国际关系学
philosophy 哲学
phwoo 嘘(感叹词,表示紧张后的放松)
register 注册
security check 安检
take over 继承/接管
then... 那么

第3章
申请与面试
Application and Interview

背景常识

一个留学生要经历很多申请和面试。面试你的人可能是你所申请学校的录取老师（admissions tutor）、英国使馆的移民官（immigration officer）、麦当劳的人事经理（human resource manager）或者一个有浓重西非口音（West African accent）的房东（landlord）。幸好，虽然不同的申请要求你展示自己不同的侧面（aspects），英语面试中还是有一些普遍规律（common rules）可寻的。

比如（for example），预先设想可能会被问到的问题是一个不错的战术，但不要死记答案。许多学生站在英国大使馆的面试窗前滔滔不绝（giving a monologue），眼睛却盯着（stare）天花板。面试是一个互动的（interactive）过程，不要把它变成了诗朗诵（poetry recital）。而且，面试与雅思口语考试也不一样，言简意赅（be concise）才是上策。

你可能经常会遇到你不懂的问题或者需要时间反应。学会使用一些词句，例如：Pardon?（对不起？）和 Sorry, could you say that again?（对不起，您能再说一遍吗？）

然而，与课堂上的讨论和非正式的闲聊不同（unlike），你应该时刻表现得积极（positive）而且准备充分（prepared）。如果你在某一个领域里缺乏信心（lack confidence），试着改变话题。你可以通过主动（active）提问来改变话题。被面试并不表示要一味（always）被动（passive）。能够提出尖锐（sharp）的问题证明（prove）你已经仔细地考虑（consider）过你申请的目的（purpose），这将给你的面试者留下更深的印象（impression）。

Visa Interview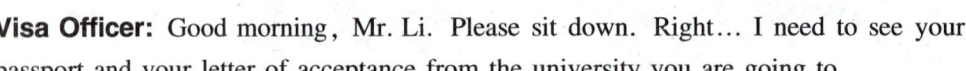

Visa Officer: Good morning, Mr. Li. Please sit down. Right... I need to see your passport and your letter of acceptance from the university you are going to.

Li: Here you are.

Visa officer: Thank You. OK. It says here that you have been accepted to do an MSc in International Finance at the University of Reading....

Li: That's right.

Visa Officer: OK. I need to see confirmation that you have paid the deposit for your fees as well. Have you got any proof?

Li: Yes. Here's the bank transfer details... you can see that I transferred the money three weeks ago and here's an email from the registry at Reading confirming receipt.

Visa Officer: That's great. Thanks. Hmm... I'll also need to see financial proof. I mean, how do you intend to pay for tuition, accommodation, food and living expenses while you are in the UK? I need to be sure that you will have enough to cover you for the next year without either working or having recourse to public funds.

Li: Sorry, what do you mean?

Visa Officer: What I mean is, we have to make sure that you have enough money to support yourself during your course without claiming state benefits.

Li: Well, here are my most recent bank statements... you can see that there's enough to cover me for the next year. My parents are acting as[①] guarantors... I mean they are paying for me to study there. Also, I have a credit card on my father's account for emergencies.

Visa officer: OK... that's fine... when does your course begin?

Li: Well, I have to be there by 30th September for the orientation programme[②] and to get settled in.

Visa officer: Hmm... well, it's already 20th September and flights are pretty full at this time of year... have you bought your ticket yet?

Li: Not yet. I want to get the visa sorted out first. Besides, I've got an uncle who works for the airline, so it should be OK.

Visa Officer: OK, well I can give you a one-year student visa.

Li: Thank you ever so much....

Visa Officer: You're welcome. Leave your passport with me and come back in three days. You can pick your visa up from the window over there. Good luck.

签证面试

签证官：早上好，李先生。请坐。好的，我需要看看你的护照和你准备就读的大学的录取通知书。

李：都在这儿呢。

签证官：谢谢。嗯，这上面说里丁大学录取你攻读国际金融的理科硕士。

李：对。

签证官：我还需要看看证明你付过入学押金的确认材料。你带证明了吗？

李：带了，这是银行的汇款单据。这上面可以证实我三个星期前就已经将钱汇过去了。还有，这是里丁学籍办公室发来的电子邮件收据。

签证官：很好，谢谢。嗯，我还得看看你的财政证明。我是指，你准备如何支付你在英国的学费、住宿、饮食以及其它生活开销？我需要确认你能在没有工作收入和公共资助的情况下有足够的资金来支付明年一年的费用。

李：抱歉，你是指什么？

签证官：我是说我们得确认你学习期间在没有政府福利的情况下你是否有足够的钱支付你的开销。

李：噢，这是我最近的银行账单。你可以看到，这上面有足够的金额支撑我下一年的消费。我父母是我的担保人。我的意思是，他们承担我在英国学习的费用。而且，我有一张设在我父亲账户下的信用卡，以备不时之需。

签证官：好的，可以。你的课程什么时候开始？

李：嗯，我必须在9月30号之前到达，以便参加入学简介并安顿下来。

签证官：嗯，那么，今天已经是9月20号了。而且航班在每年的这段时间都很紧张，你买到机票了吗？

李：还没有，我打算先拿到签证再买。再说，我有个在航空公司工作的叔叔，所以应该没问题。

签证官：好吧，那我就给你一个一年的学生签证。

李：太谢谢您了。

签证官：不用谢。把你的护照留下，三天后来取。取护照在那边的窗口，祝你好运！

注释

① are acting as 表示"承担某种行为"。
② orientation 是"方向、定位"的意思，学校或单位为新人组织的介绍活动通常称为 orientation 或 induction。

实用短语

- Please sit down.　请坐。
- Right… I need to see…　好的，我需要看看……
- Here you are.　都在这儿呢。
- It says here that …　这上面说……
- That's right.　对。
- Have you got any proof?　你带任何证明了吗？
- Yes. Here's the…　带了，这是……
- You can see that… and here's …　这上面是……还有……
- That's great.　很好。
- I mean…　我是指……
- I need to be sure that…　我需要确认……
- Sorry, what do you mean?　抱歉，你是指什么？
- What I mean is, …　我是说……
- Well, here are …　噢，这是……
- When does your course begin?　你的课程什么时候开始？
- Well, I have to be there by…　我必须在……之前到达。
- I want to get the visa sorted out first.　我打算先拿到签证再说。
- OK, well I can give you …　好吧，那我就给你……
- Good luck.　祝你好运！

词汇表

accommodation 住宿
account 账户
act as 起…作用
bank statements 银行账单
bank transfer 银行汇款
confirmation 确认／确认信
claim state benefits 要求政府福利
credit card 信用卡
fee 学费／费用

financial proof 财政证明
for emergencies 紧急情况／以备不时之需
get settled in 安顿下来
guarantor 保证人
have recourse to public funds 申请公共资助
International Finance 国际金融
letter of acceptance 录取通知书
living expenses 生活费

orientation programme 新人介绍活动
pick up 领取
pretty 很／挺
proof 证明
registry 学籍办公室
student visa 学生签证
support 证明（观点）／支持／担负
tuition 学费

第4章
理想与计划
Ambitions and Plan

背景常识

你为什么要来英国？为什么要去牛津？为什么要攻读硕士学位？如果你曾经问过自己类似的（similar）问题并有了明确的答案，那么你的留学生涯就算有了个好的开头（You are off to a good start.）。现在，你要做的就是把它们大声说出来（say them out loud）。英国大学极其倾向于选择那些有明确目标和可行（viable）计划的学生，而不喜欢那些漫无目的（aimless）的人。对于硕士生和博士生尤其如此。录取老师、你的导师和雇主，几乎所有的人都会问你这样的问题：Where do you see yourself will be in 2, 5, or 10 years?（你能看到未来2年、5年或10年后的自己吗？）

根据名气（reputation）选择大学，或者根据金钱选择工作，这些都没什么不对。毕竟金钱（cash）与名誉（fame）是现代生活中的基本构件。但是一个成功的学生在选择其课程和职业（career）时要考虑更多一些。你喜欢一门关于"项目管理模拟游戏"（simulated project-management）的课程，可能是因为这门课能给你提供很多实践经验（hands-on experience），而实践经验对于未来的企业主管（executive）来说是十分关键的。你想要上伦敦政经学院也许是由于它处于英国政治经济中心的地理位置（location），以及它师资力量的丰富背景（diverse background）。你所选择的工作可能工资不高，但作为刚刚毕业的学生，你把经验和晋升（promotion）机会看得比财政回报更重要。

正是这样的解释（elaboration）才能使你以一个奋发（motivated）坚定（resolute）的学生形象脱颖而出（be distinguished）。所以，仔细思考你的理想与计划，并练习用英语阐述它们。

University Interview

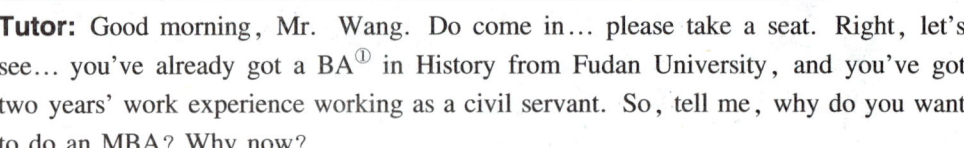

Tutor: Good morning, Mr. Wang. Do come in... please take a seat. Right, let's see... you've already got a BA① in History from Fudan University, and you've got two years' work experience working as a civil servant. So, tell me, why do you want to do an MBA? Why now?

Wang: Well, I feel that it'll help me to develop in terms of my career. I am interested in how organisations work... you know, the psychology and dynamics behind them. In fact, History has helped me a lot in my job. It gave me the ability to analyse the past. As I am sure you know, the actual subject you study at BA level doesn't really need to be in the same area as your job or your master's degree. The important thing is that it trains you to think critically and analyse things.

Tutor: Hmm... that's interesting. I agree with you. It's very important to have a critical awareness of things. Organisational theory is a big area though, isn't it? I mean it covers everything from psychology to law and politics. What aspects are you particularly interested in? I mean, what have you read about the subject?

Wang: Well, I like those books by famous CEOs, and I subscribe to *Business Week* online....

Tutor: Yes... well... I'm not talking about airport books②... I'm more interested in what you know about the theory itself. I mean... what academic texts have you read?

Wang: Well, I did a couple of Business Studies modules as part of my BA, and we looked at Kotler and Erskine... *Business Management*... that was the standard text... oh, yes and Handy... Charles Handy's book, *Understanding Organisations*. Yes....

Tutor: Ah... good. Handy is a standard text. Well, that's good... erm... could you tell me why you've applied to this university?

Wang: Well, your MBA has a good reputation and the thing I really like about it is that it concentrates on China and East Asia. I'm Chinese, and that's where my experience is.

Tutor: Well, we see ourselves as being at the cutting-edge here as far as that is concerned. Yes. Erm, Mr. Wang... I'd like to know how you feel you would cope in an international classroom. Our programme is very international here... 50% of our students come from East Asia, India, South America, The Middle East and Eastern Europe... add these to the home students... and....

Wang: Well, I admit it will be a challenge, but I think I'm up to it. The government department I worked for was heavily③ involved in facilitating foreign direct investment in China, so I have had plenty of experience of dealing with foreigners using English....

Tutor: Hmmm, and where④ do you see yourself in, say⑤, five years' time after you have your MBA?

Wang: Well, there are two ways of looking at this, I think. I could aim to progress through the government and end up in charge of a large department, using what I have learned on my MBA, or I might move over to the private sector⑥ and do something else... perhaps doing this programme will present me with opportunities I hadn't thought about before.

大学面试

老师： 早上好，王先生。快请进，请坐。那么，让我们看看……你获得了复旦大学历史学的文科学士，而且你还有两年的作为公务员的工作经验。既然这样，跟我说说，你为什么想学工商管理学硕士呢？又为什么选在现在呢？

小王： 嗯，我觉得这对我职业方面的发展会有帮助。我对组织机构的工作原理很感兴趣。比如，它们背后的心理学和动力。实际上，历史对我的工作帮助很大。它赋予了我分析过去事物的能力。我敢肯定你也知道，一个人在本科阶段的学习科目不一定要与这个人未来的工作和硕士学位挂钩。关键是要锻炼批判思维和分析事物的能力。

老师： 嗯，很有意思。我同意你的看法。对事物有批判的意识是十分关键的。组织理论可是一个很广的领域哦。我是说，它涵盖心理学、法律、政治等一系列科目。你对哪个方面特别感兴趣呢？你以前读过关于这个科目的书籍吗？

小王： 读过。我喜欢那些著名的首席执行官们写的书，而且我还在网上订阅《商务周刊》。

老师： 嗯，我指的不是消遣读物，我更想知道你对这个理论本身的见解。你看过任何学术资料吗？

小王： 嗯，我在本科阶段的时候选过一两门商学课程。当时我们看的是科特勒和厄斯金的《工商管理》，那是标准的教材。噢，对了，还有汉迪，查尔斯·汉迪的《解读组织》。

老师： 啊，很好。汉迪是标准教材，这很好。嗯，你能告诉我你为什么要申请这所大学吗？

小王： 嗯，你们的工商管理学硕士很有名。而且我非常喜欢的是，这个课程十分关注中国与东亚地区。

老师： 对，这个方面我们自认为是领先的。对了，王先生，我想知道，你觉得你能应付一个国际化的课堂环境吗？我们的课程是非常国际化的。50%的学生都来自东亚、印度、南美、中东和东欧，再加上本土学生。

小王： 我承认这会是一个挑战，不过我自信能够应付。我工作过的那个政府部门经常涉及到辅助外商来华投资的业务，所以我在应付外国人方面还是有一定经验的。

老师： 嗯，那么你认为，比如说，5年以后自己将是什么样？在你拿到工商管理学硕士以后？

小王： 我认为，有两种可能。通过我在 MBA 中学到的知识，我可以选择继续在政府部门中发展并最终主管一个大部门，或者我可能跳槽去私营企业做些别的。说不定学习这个课程会给我在就业机会上有新的启发。

注释

① BA, Bachelor of Arts 文科学士。
② airport books 在飞机场卖的书，指供人消遣的读物。
③ heavily 的原义是"严重的，重的"，这里可以表示"频繁"。
④ where 并不一定表示"哪里"，这里指"境况"。
⑤ say 表示"比如说"。
⑥ private sector 私营经济。

实用短语

- So, tell me, why do you…? 既然这样,跟我说说,你为什么……?
- Well, I feel that it'll… 嗯,我觉得这……
- In fact, … has helped me a lot in my job. 实际上,……对我的工作帮助很大。
- As I am sure you know,… 我敢肯定你也知道,……
- The important thing is… 关键是要……
- What aspects are you particularly interested in? 你对哪个方面特别感兴趣呢?
- I mean, what have you read about the subject? 你以前读过关于这个科目的书籍吗?
- Well, I like those books by… 我喜欢……写的书。
- What academic texts have you read? 你看过任何学术资料吗?
- Could you tell me why you've applied to this university? 你能告诉我你为什么要申请这所大学吗?
- I'd like to know how you feel you would… 我想知道,你觉得你能……吗?
- Well, I admit it will be a challenge, but I think I'm up to it. 我承认这会是一个挑战,不过我自信能够应付。
- Where do you see yourself in, say, five years' time after you have your MBA? 那么你认为自己,比如说,……年以后将是什么样子?
- Well, there are two ways of looking at this, I think. 我认为,有两种可能。

词 汇 表

academic texts 学术书籍、材料
actual 真的/实在的
airport books 消遣读物
analyse 分析
apply to 申请
as far as… is concerned 就……而言
be heavily involved 经常涉及
be up to… 能够
CEO 首席执行官(chief executive officer)
challenge 挑战
concentrate on 集中精力于
critical awareness 批判意识
cutting-edge 最先进的/前沿的/领先的
dynamics 动力
foreign direct investment 直接外国投资/外资
in charge of 主管/负责
law 法律
module 课(module 表示"单个一门的课";而 course 既可以表示"单独的一门课",也可以表示"整个的课程";class 既表示"单独的一门课",也可以表示"单独的一节课")
move to the private sector 跳槽去私人企业
organisational theory 组织理论
politics 政治
psychology 心理/心理学
see oneself as… 将自己视作……
standard text 标准教材
subscribe to 订阅
theory 理论
think critically 批判性地去思考

第5章
旅行信息
Travel Information

背景常识

英国,我来啦!(Here I come!)11个小时的空中旅行终于结束。希思罗(Heathrow)机场的空气中弥漫着(smell)新鲜(refreshing)、兴奋和少许的恐慌(terrifying)。你的留学生涯从现在起就开始了(The clock starts ticking.)。这可能是你有生以来第一次在英格兰说英语。不过,繁忙的英国海关(customs)大概不是凭栏感叹(enjoy the moment)的地方。

首先,你要向边检人员出示护照和入境卡。他们会问你 What is your reason for travelling? 之类的问题。入关以后,你可能得询问机场工作人员如何领取(claim)你的托运行李(check-in luggage)。然后,你还要决定到底是打的(taxi/cab)进伦敦,还是乘坐著名的地铁(underground/tube)。如果伦敦还不是你的终点站,你还得打听如何转机和转火车。

Ladies and gentlemen, may I have your attention please?(女士们、先生们,请注意。)这是机场通知(announcement)国际通用的开场白。当你从广播(tunnel)里听到这句话的时候,最好集中注意力。

Where、how 和 when,是你需要掌握的关键词。另外,当你在听你所需的信息时,注意捕捉这些词:left(左)、right(右)、straight(直走)和 turn(拐弯)。对时间、号码和地名也要留心一些。如果你没听明白,别不好意思说 pardon(对不起),然后再问一次。其实英国人也经常听不懂对方在说什么。最后,别忘了在开口询问时先说 excuse me(原谅我)或 sorry(对不起),并在询问结束时说 thank you(谢谢你)或 cheers(谢谢)。

At the Travel Agency

Travel Agent: Hello, can I help you?

Adrian: Oh yes, hello. I was looking for a cheap flight to Barcelona during the Easter holiday.

Travel agent: One-way or return?

Adrian: Return.

Travel Agent: And when do you want to go?

Adrian: Erm... 3rd April... returning on 10th... but I'm quite flexible with the dates. I could go a day or so early if my lecturer lets me skip the last seminar.

Travel Agent: Ok... let's see what we've got on the computer... right, there's a direct flight to Barcelona from Stansted with Easy Jet for £120 return... but it's at seven in the morning. I don't think you'd be able to get to the airport in time. The first train to the airport is at six from Liverpool St, and it takes about 40 minutes.

Adrian: Oh... have you got anything else?

Travel Agent: Well, there's another flight from Stansted direct to Barcelona at 10, but it's £250....

Adrian: Oh no... that's too much. What about other airports... or, I can change flights as well.

Travel Agent: Well, KLM are doing a special offer. If you are a student, you can fly to Barcelona from Heathrow for £105 return, but you have to change flights in Amsterdam....

Adrian: Oh... Well, what time would I get to Barcelona?

Travel Agent: Well, if you leave Heathrow at ten O five, you'd get the half past one pm flight from Amsterdam to Barcelona, and you'd be in Barcelona at half past four. That would give you plenty of time to get to where you're staying and get settled in before you hit the town....

Adrian: Cool. Could you book it for me? I also need a hotel for the time I'm there... could you recommend a nice one... not too expensive... quite cheap in fact...?

Travel Agent: Sure, if you are staying for more than three nights, I can do you a special deal £140 for seven nights at the Hotel Valls in Barcelona... it's the cheapest deal you'll find....

Adrian: Well... at that price, I can't argue, can I? I'll take it.

Travel Agent: All right... I just need your passport to book the flight and the hotel, and you'll need to leave a 20% deposit now.

Adrian: OK... here you are....

Travel Agent: I'll just give you a printout of your itinerary... here you are... leaving Heathrow on 3rd at 10.05, arriving Amsterdam at 12.10, leaving Amsterdam at 13.30 and arriving Barcelona at 16.00... then returning Barcelona-Amsterdam-London at 15.00 on 10th... getting into Heathrow at 20.30... remember the time difference... the UK is an hour behind Spain. Come back with your passport and visa and the rest of the money and we'll issue the ticket here.

Adrian: OK... cool. Erm, by the way... what's the quickest way to Heathrow?

在旅行社

旅游中介： 您好，我能帮您吗？

阿德里安： 哦，对，你好。我正在找复活节期间去巴塞罗那的机票。

旅游中介： 单程还是往返？

阿德里安： 往返。

旅游中介： 您准备什么时间出发呢？

阿德里安： 嗯，4月3号出发，10号回来，但是我在日期上是比较灵活的。如果我的讲师允许我旷掉最后一节讨论课，我就能早一天走。

旅游中介： 好的，让我们看看电脑上有什么信息。有了，易捷航空公司有一班从斯坦斯特德机场直飞巴塞罗那的航班，120英镑往返，但是要在早上7点起飞。我估计你可能没法及时赶到机场。最早的去机场的火车是早上6点，从利物浦街火车站出发，需要大约40分钟才能到机场。

阿德里安： 哦，那还有别的吗？

旅游中介： 从斯坦斯特德直飞巴塞罗那的还有10点的航班，不过要250英镑。

阿德里安： 不，那太贵了。其他机场怎么样？或者，我也可以转机。

旅游中介： 荷兰皇家航空公司有一个优惠活动。如果你是学生，你可以从希思罗飞巴塞罗那，105英镑往返，但是必须在阿姆斯特丹转机。

阿德里安： 嗯，那我什么时候能到巴塞罗那？

旅游中介： 如果你10点零5分从希思罗起飞，你将搭乘下午1点半的航班从阿姆斯特丹去巴塞罗那，4点半时到达巴塞罗那。这样在你进城去玩之前，你能有充足的时间赶到住的地方并安顿下来。

阿德里安： 酷！你就给我订这个吧。我还需要订个宾馆，在那儿住几天。你能给我推荐一个好的吗？不要太贵，最好是比较便宜的宾馆。

旅游中介： 可以。如果你要住3晚以上，我能给你个特殊优惠。在巴塞罗那的沃儿斯宾馆7个晚上140英镑。这是我能找到的最便宜的价格了。

阿德里安： 这个价位，我也没什么好争辩的。我就要这个了。

旅游中介： 很好，我只需要您的护照来订机票和酒店。而且您现在得付20%的押金。

阿德里安： 好，给你。

旅游中介： 我这就给您一份打印的清单。给，3号10点零5分离开希斯罗，12点10分到达阿姆斯特丹，13点半离开阿姆斯特丹，16点到达巴塞罗那。回程，巴塞罗那-阿姆斯特丹-伦敦，10号15点整起飞，20点30分到达希斯罗。别忘了时差，英国比西班牙慢一个小时。我们从这里出票，您来取票的时候别忘了带着护照和签证。

阿德里安： 好的，酷。嗯，顺便问一下，去希思罗最快的办法是什么？

Travel Agent: Well, the quickest option is the Heathrow Express from Paddington Station. It takes 30 minutes, and it's very comfortable, but it's quite expensive. It's cheaper to get the Piccadilly Line direct to Heathrow Terminals 1, 2, 3. Or, you could get the Airport Bus, the A2, from King's Cross. Here's a timetable. Remember that you need to check in an hour before the flight.

At Check-in   *Dialogue*

Clerk: Good morning. May I see your ticket and passport please?
Adrian: Of course... Here you are.
Clerk: Have you got any check-in luggage?
Adrian: No... just this bag. Can I take it as carry-on baggage?
Clerk: Yes... that should be OK. Would you like an aisle seat or a window seat?
Adrian: Window seat, please. Oh... and could I sit near the front?
Clerk: Of course. You've got a transfer to Barcelona. So I'll issue both your boarding cards now. Seat 12A, Gate 22 for your flight to Amsterdam, and Seat 10F, Amsterdam-Barcelona... Departure is that way... Just follow the signs for transfer when you get to Amsterdam. OK? Have a nice flight.
Adrian: Thanks.

At Spanish Passport Control   *Dialogue*

Immigration Officer: Good afternoon. Where are you coming from?
Adrian: London.
Immigration Officer: What's the purpose of your visit to Spain?
Adrian: Oh... I'm here on holiday... I really want to see the Sagrada Familia and the Gaudi Museum... oh and the Ramblas, of course. I'll be here for a week.
Immigration Officer: Where will you be staying?
Adrian: At the Hotel Valls... it's there on the landing card... by the way, could you tell me how to get to the Metro station?
Immigration Officer: Sure... it's outside, down the ramp to the right.

At UK Customs   *Dialogue*

Customs Officer: Do you have anything to declare, sir?
Adrian: Just this wine and these cigarettes.
Customs Officer: Let's see... two litres of Spanish red table wine... mmm, lovely. And... how many cigarettes?
Adrian: Twenty packets of Marlboro Lights.
Customs Officer: Gosh... that's a lot for a young man! I'm afraid the limit is two hundred and eighty, duty-free... you'll have to pay duty on the rest.
Adrian: Oh... they aren't for me... they're for my teacher and friends... I'm a student here.
Customs Officer: Sorry. Rules are rules, I'm afraid. You'll have to pay £12 plus VAT... that's £14.80 altogether.

旅游中介：最快的办法是从帕丁顿地铁站坐希思罗特快，全程 30 分钟，很舒服，但是费用比较贵。乘皮卡迪里线地铁到希思罗的 1、2、3 号站台。或者，你还可以从国王十字地铁站乘坐机场大巴，A2。这里有一份时间表。记住，您需要在飞机起飞前一个小时办理登机手续。

在登机手续办理台

工作人员：早上好。您能让我看看您的机票和护照吗？
阿德里安：当然可以，给。
工作人员：您有要托运的行李吗？
阿德里安：没有，就这么一个包。我能把它当手提行李吧？
工作人员：嗯，应该可以。您想要靠走道还是靠窗口的座位？
阿德里安：请给我窗口座位。嗯，还有，我能坐得靠前一点儿吗？
工作人员：当然。您还得转机去巴塞罗那。我现在就把两张登机牌都给您。去阿姆斯特丹时的座位是 12A，22 号登机口；从阿姆斯特丹到巴塞罗那的座位是 10F。候机厅在那边。在阿姆斯特丹转机时跟着标志走就行了。可以了吗？祝您旅行愉快。
阿德里安：谢谢。

在西班牙边检站

边检官：下午好。您从哪儿来？
阿德里安：伦敦。
边检官：您来西班牙的目的是什么？
阿德里安：嗯，我来度假。我想去看圣家堂和高迪博物馆。噢，当然还有河渠大道区。我会在这儿待一周。
边检官：您要住哪里？
阿德里安：住沃尔斯宾馆。我的入境卡上写了。顺便问一下，去地铁站怎么走？
边检官：就在外面，下了坡道然后右拐。

在英国海关

海关人员：您有要报关的东西吗，先生？
阿德里安：就这些葡萄酒和烟。
海关人员：让我们看看。两升西班牙晚餐红酒，嗯，很好。还有，多少香烟？
阿德里安：20 条特醇万宝路。
海关人员：天哪，对一个年轻人来说，这可真不少啊！不好意思，免税的限量是 280 英镑，其余的价值都要付税。
阿德里安：哦，这些不是给我自个儿的，是给我的老师和朋友们的。我是个学生。
海关人员：对不起，规矩就是规矩。您还得付 12 英镑，再加上增值税，一共是 14 英镑 80 便士。

实用短语

- Have you got anything else? 你还有别的吗?
- Could you book it for me? 你能帮我订这个吗?
- Can I take it as hand/carry-on baggage? 我能拿它当手提行李吗?
- One-way or return? 单程还是往返?
- When do you want to go? 您准备什么时候出发?
- Where are you coming/travelling from? 您从哪儿来?
- What's the purpose of your visit to…? 您去……的目的是什么?
- Do you have anything to declare? 您有要报关的东西吗?
- Where will you be staying? 您会住在哪里?
- There's a direct flight to… 这儿有一趟直飞的航班飞往……
- I can do you a special deal. 我可以给你特价。
- Would you like an aisle seat or a window seat? 您要靠走道还是靠窗口的座位?
- Well, the quickest option is the… 最快的选择是……
- How do I get there? 我怎么才能到那儿?
- Well, what time would I get to…? 那么,我到那里应该是几点?
- Can I pay by credit card? 我能用信用卡付款吗?
- Could you tell me how to get to…? 你能告诉我去……怎么走吗?
- Just follow the signs for… 想要去……跟着标志走就行了。
- Enjoy your stay. 祝您旅途愉快。
- I'm afraid you'll have to pay duty on… 恐怕您不得不为……付关税。
- Sorry. Rules are rules, I'm afraid. 对不起,规矩是规矩。

词 汇 表

altogether 一起/一共
Amsterdam 阿姆斯特丹
argue 论证/持某观点
boarding card 登机卡
carry-on baggage 手提行李
cheap flight 便宜机票
check in 办理登机手续/托运
check-in luggage 托运行李
declare 申报
direct flight 直飞航班
duty-free 免税
Easy Jet 易航(英国一家国内航空公司的名字)
fully comprehensive insurance 全面保险
get settled in 安顿下来
Heathrow Express 希思罗特快
hit the town 去城里
itinerary 行程安排
King's Cross 国王十字地铁站
landing card 入境卡
limit 限制
Liverpool St 利物浦街地铁站
Marlboro Lights 特醇万宝路
metro station 地铁站
one-way 单程
packet 包裹
Paddington 帕丁顿地铁站
pay duty on 为…付税
Piccadilly Line 皮卡迪地铁线
plenty of time 很多时间
printout 打印出来的
purpose 目的
ramp 斜坡/坡道
red table wine 宴用红酒
return 往返/返回
special offer 优惠/特惠
take 乘(交通工具)
terminal 站台
time difference 时差
vacation 假期

第6章
联系住宿
Searching for Accommodation

背景常识

对英国大学生来说,6人合住的中国式宿舍是不可想象的。英国大学的住宿大都是公寓(flat)式的,通常称为 hall of residence。在那里学生们有自己的卧室并与其他人共用厨房和卫生间。性别隔离是中国大学宿舍的又一特色。在英国大学里,男女同住一个公寓是很正常的。如果你的 hall 是 self-catering 的,这表示那里没有饭堂(cafeteria),你得自己做饭。en-suite 表示卧室里带有卫生间,也就更贵一些。另外,你还得考虑房间里是否有互联网接口(Internet connection),hall 里有没有洗衣房(laundry)和活动室(common room)。大部分宿舍是 smoke-free 的,这表示你不能在里面吸烟,而不是 free to smoke。

一般来说,私人住宿(private accommodation)要比学校的房子便宜很多,但是校园周边的住房一般很快就会被租出去。所以你可能不得不用距离来交换价格。跟房东做交易的时候,有几件事情你要注意。第一,你要考虑房租(rent)。如果房租是不包账单(bills excluded)的,你就必须另付电费、供暖费和煤气费。第二,要看房间是否有家具(furnished)。第三,别忘了检查室内安全设施(household safety),比如查看烟火警报器(fire alarm)是否运转正常。第四,要考虑租期长度(length of lease)。对照学校日历来确定你需要这个房间的具体时间。最后,一定要仔细阅读合同(contract)并索要押金(deposit)的收据(receipt)。

所有这些可能听起来很烦琐,但是当你最终安顿下来并建立起自己的"海外根据地"的时候,一种成就感会油然而生。找房子也是出国学习的重要一课。

● On the Phone

Landlord: Hello, 937 5464.

Jack: Hello. I'm calling about the flat.

Landlord: Oh… right. Where did you see it advertised?

Jack: On the Student Union notice board at Imperial.

Landlord: Oh right, that's the studio apartment in Earl's Court, yes?

Jack: Yes, that's right. When can I come and see it?

Landlord: You can come around at six o'clock this evening if you like. I'll meet you there. What's your name?

Jack: Jack… I'll see you then.

● At the Flat

Jack: Hello, there. I'm Jack.

Landlord: Hello there[①], mate. Well. This is it. As you can see, it's fully furnished. You've got your TV… cable TV and broadband Internet is included in the rent. You can plug your laptop in over there. The kitchenette is over here… all fully fitted… nice new fridge and cooker, kettle, toaster, microwave… all your mod-cons. The bathroom[②] is through there… box shower unit… sink… all new from B&Q. There's a nice view of the park from the window too.

Jack: Hmm… it's smaller than I thought. How much is the rent again?

Landlord: £200 a week, plus of course, you're responsible for utilities, council tax and all that stuff.

Jack: It said £160 in the ad[③].

Landlord: Yeah, but that was for the small room upstairs and that's already gone.

Jack: Well, £200 is a bit too much for me.

Landlord: Well this is London, mate. Know what I mean?[④] If you want cheap… move to Leeds or Leicester or somewhere crap like that, ha ha! It's a good place for the price… you're not going to find anywhere cheaper, and I've had three people round today already… know what I mean? And it is your own place… good location, near the Tube.

Jack: Yeah, but the ad said £160.

Landlord: Take it or leave it, mate.

Jack: Look[⑤]… I can stretch[⑥] to £180 a week… I can't afford £200 plus all the other bills.

Landlord: All right, mate. £180 a week… one month's rent in advance, plus a month's deposit. That'll be £1440 cash… you'll get the deposit back as long as everything's in good nick when you leave. The rent's due on the first of the month. Let's sit down and go through the forms… right. OK. This is the contract… read

电话里

房东：你好，这里是 9375464。

杰克：你好。我打电话是询问关于公寓的事情。

房东：噢，你在哪儿看见的广告？

杰克：在帝国理工的学生会通知栏。

房东：哦，你说的是在厄尔斯考特一带的那个工作室，对吗？

杰克：对，我什么时候能去看看房子呢？

房东：你可以今天晚上 6 点来，如果你愿意。我在那儿等你。你叫什么名字？

杰克：杰克。到时候见。

在公寓

杰克：你好，我就是杰克。

房东：你好，哥们儿。这就是。你看，全套家具，有电视……有线电视和宽带网都包括在房租里。你能在那儿连接你的手提电脑。厨房在这边，设施齐全，新冰箱和炉灶、烧水壶、烤面包机、微波炉……所有你需要的电器。卫生间在那边，淋浴房……脸池……都是从百安居新买的。从那边的窗户还能看到公园的风景。

杰克：嗯，这个房子比我想象的要小。房租是多少来着？

房东：200 英镑一周。另外，你得自己付物业费、地税之类的。

杰克：广告上说是 160 英镑。

房东：没错，可那是楼上那间小一点儿的房子。那间已经租出去了。

杰克：嗯，200 英镑对我来说有点儿太贵了。

房东：这可是伦敦，哥们儿。明白吗？想要便宜的，去利兹或莱斯特之类的烂地方吧，呵呵！这房间物超所值，你再也找不到更便宜的了。我今天已经接待 3 个感兴趣的人了，明白吗？你完全拥有自己的空间，地点好，离地铁站又近。

杰克：是啊，可广告上说的是 160 英镑。

房东：要就要，不要就拉倒，哥们儿。

杰克：我勉强能接受 180 英镑一周。我是绝对负担不起 200 英镑外加账单的。

房东：好吧，哥们儿。就 180 英镑一周。先交一个月的房租，加上等同于一个月房租的押金，一共是 1440 英镑现金。如果在你走的时候所有东西都完好无损，你就能把押金拿回去。每个月交房租的时间是 1 号。咱们坐下把这些表填了吧。这是合同，好好看看，在每页上都写上你的名字缩写，然后在最后一页签字。一式两份，你我各一份。你还得签这些，把煤气、电、水和地税转到你名下。

through it, initial each page and then sign at the bottom... there are two copies—one for each of us. Then you need to sign these ones... these are to transfer the gas, electricity, water and council tax over to you.

Jack: OK....

Landlord: Right, Jack. Here's the keys... front downstairs door and flat door. Hope you enjoy yourself here. Once you close that door behind you, you're in your own little palace. Don't make too much noise, eh.

Accommodation Office

Clerk: Hello. What can I do for you?

Maggie: I heard that you have some information on private accommodation, besides the university halls. I'm looking for a flatshare... somewhere near the university.

Clerk: All right. How much were you looking to pay?

Maggie: Well, about £100 a week maximum, really.

Clerk: OK. Let's see what we've got... there's a shared four-bedroom house in Selby Road, Chapeltown... there's three other girls there already... three students... erm... one English, one Turkish and one Nigerian... so they need someone for the fourth bedroom... it's got a double bed, study table, chest of drawers, wardrobe, etc. There's a shared living room with TV, and a shared fully-fitted kitchen and bathroom with a proper bath as well as a shower. It's just been renovated. The rent is £100 a week plus bills... you split them with the other residents, so you'd be responsible for working that out with them. Do you want me to call the landlord?

Maggie: All right.

注释

① there 无实际意义,语气词,表示亲切。
② bathroom 也有"卫生间"的意思,尤其在美语中。
③ ad 是 advertisement 的缩写和简称。
④ Know what I mean? 伦敦人的口头禅,跟 you know 一样,没有什么实际意义。
⑤ Look 也是语气词,表示要对方注意。
⑥ stretch 原义为"拉伸",这里表示"勉强地让步"。

杰克：好的。

房东：好了，杰克。给你钥匙，楼下前门的和公寓门的。希望你在这儿住得愉快。把门一关，你就在自己的小皇宫里了。别太吵了哦。

在住宿办公室

工作人员：你好。我能为你做点儿什么？

玛吉：我听说，除了学校宿舍以外，你们还有一些私人住宿的信息。我想要找合租公寓，离学校近的。

工作人员：好的。你大概找什么价位的？

玛吉：嗯，大约一周最多 100 英镑吧。

工作人员：好的，让我看看都有什么……查珀尔顿的色比路有一个 4 居室的房子，有 3 个女孩儿已经入住了，3 个学生。嗯，一个英国的，一个土耳其的，还有一个尼日利亚的。她们想再找个人合租。那儿有双人床、课桌、抽屉和立柜等等。客厅是大家共用的，带电视，还有公共厨房和浴室，带浴缸和淋浴。房子刚刚装修过。房租是 100 英镑一周外加账单。账单你们几个平摊，所以你自己跟她们决定如何分担吧。想让我给房东打个电话吗？

玛吉：好的。

实用短语

◆ Hello there, mate. 你好,哥们儿。
◆ I'm calling about the flat. 我打电话是为询问公寓的事。
◆ I'm looking for a flatshare. 我想要找合租公寓。
◆ Where did you see it advertised? 你在哪儿看见的广告?
◆ How much were you looking to pay? 你大概找什么价位?
◆ Well, this is it. 到了,这就是。
◆ The bathroom is through there. 卫生间在那边。
◆ The kitchenelle is over here. 厨房在这儿。
◆ Hmm… it's smaller than I thought. 嗯,它比我想象的小。
◆ How much is the rent again? 房租是多少来着?
◆ It said £160 in the ad. 广告上说的是 160 英镑。
◆ Well, £200 is a bit too much for me. 200 英镑对我来说太贵了。
◆ Look… I can stretch to £180. 我能勉强接受 180 英镑。
◆ I can't afford £200. 我负担不起 200 英镑。
◆ It's a good place for the price. 这地方物超所值。
◆ You're not going to find anywhere cheaper. 你再也找不到比这个更便宜的了。
◆ Take it or leave it, mate. 哥们儿,要就要,不要拉倒。
◆ Know what I mean? 明白吗?
◆ So you'd be responsible for bills. 所以,你得自己付账单。

词汇表

ad 广告(缩写)
bills 账单
box shower unit 淋浴房
broadband Internet 宽带网
cable TV 有线电视
chest of drawers 抽屉柜
council tax 地税(留学生通常不用付)
crap 粪便,多表示糟糕的地方
Earl's Court 厄尔斯考特(地名)
flatshare 合租公寓
form 表
fridge 冰箱
fully-fitted 设施齐全的

gas 煤气
in good nick 在完好无损的状态
in advance 提前
kettle 烧水壶
kitchenette 简易厨房
laptop 手提电脑
location 地点
mate 哥们儿
microwave 微波炉
mod-cons (modern conveniences) 现代家用电器
Nigerian 尼日利亚人
notice board 通知板
plug in 接入

renovate 装修
residents 住户
responsible 负责任的
see sth. … advertised 看到…的广告
stretch 伸展
toaster 烤面包机
transfer 转移
tube 地铁
Turkish 土耳其人
utilities 水、电、煤气等生活设施
view 风景
wardrobe 立柜

第7章
新生周
Freshers' Week

背景常识

中国大学用一周的军训来欢迎新生。英国高校的开胃菜相比之下要嫩得多。在英国,新生的大学生活开始于"新生周"。新生周是在学年正式开始前的一周。在这一周中,学校和学生会要组织一系列的活动来帮助新生熟悉学校机构并适应(adapt)英国的学术和社会生活。基本内容包括讲座(talks)、讨论会(workshop)、社交活动(socialising)、商业宣传(advertising)、小吃(refreshment)和免费纪念品(freebies)。有些学校管这段时间叫 Pre-sessional induction 或者 orientation。叫法不同,内容相似。

新生周的第一天,学校、学生会和院系的官员、秘书们都会出来介绍自己。大多数学生会里有国际学生官(International Student Officer)。他应当是你在需要帮助时的第一联络人(first point of contact)。

然后就是听讲座、学会如何使用图书馆和校园里的电脑、如何注册课程和交学费(tuition fee)、如何申请资金援助(financial aid)、如何找业余工作或实习单位、如何做课堂笔记、如何参与讨论课(seminar)、如何写论文(essay)和考试,等等。如果你没法记住或理解所有这些,学期开始以后你自然会慢慢掌握的。

到时还会有很多学生社团(society)和俱乐部(club)要招募你。许多本地的商家会利用这个机会来宣传自己。有时他们会给你免费的 T 恤衫、笔或 U 盘。新生周也是交友的好时机。别不好意思跟其他新生交谈,也不要只找华人和亚洲人模样的学生。新生周最大的好处还是它的免费小吃,可以尽情享受。你付了几千英镑的学费,吃几顿免费午餐还是不过分的。

In the Departmental Reception for New Students

Dean: Erm, good evening everyone. May I extend a very warm welcome to the new students in the Department of Economics. [to the assistant dean] How many new students have been admitted to the department this year?

Assistant Dean: A hundred and twenty this year.

Dean: Well, that's a very good rise in numbers; and I see we have a large intake from China and Korea this year... so a special welcome to you too. Could I just ask you to get yourselves a drink and mingle as much as possible. Make most of the free food, this is probably the only occasion where you can get something from the Department for free, so enjoy....

Zhao: Hello there, you aren't Chinese, are you?

Jung: No, I'm Korean actually... are you Chinese?

Zhao: Yes... whereabouts are you from?

Jung: Korea. I said.

Zhao: I know that... I mean where in Korea are you from?

Jung: Oh... sorry... Busan... it's in the far Southeast. What about you?

Zhao: Erm... I'm from Haikou, in Hainan....

Jung: Oh... where's that?

Zhao: It is a big island in the South China Sea, between Taiwan and Vietnam. Remember a few years ago—that American reconnaissance plane that clashed with a Chinese fighter and was forced to land in China? Hainan was where it landed.

Jung: Oh... I do remember, Hainan....

Dr. Haynes: Hello... are you two Chinese?

Jung: No. He's Chinese. I'm Korean.

Dr. Haynes: Oh... What do you think of Newcastle so far? Are you settling in all right?

Zhao: Well, it's very nice ... I've already found a flatshare ... and I'm quite comfortable, thanks.

Dr. Haynes: That's good. Why did you decide to come to this part of the country to study?

Jung: Well... everyone goes to London... don't you think? It's full of foreign students! We'll never get to know the real England there, and we'll end up speaking our own languages as well.

Dr. Haynes: Well you could be right there. What do you think of the local accent here? Has it been causing you any problems?

在院系新生欢迎仪式上

系主任： 嗯，大家晚上好。请允许我向经济系的新生们致以热烈的欢迎。[*对助理系主任说*] 今年录取了多少新生？

助理系主任： 今年有120个。

系主任： 嗯，增长了不少；而且我看见我们今年从中国和韩国录取的学生很多，对你们表示特别的欢迎。你们都拿杯喝的吧，尽情地聊。多吃点儿，都是免费的。这可能是你们唯一一次可以从系里拿到免费东西的机会，尽情享用吧。

赵： 你好，你不是中国人吧？

俊： 不是，我是韩国人。你是中国人吗？

赵： 对。那你具体从哪儿来？

俊： 韩国，我说过了。

赵： 我知道，我是说你从韩国的什么地方来？

俊： 噢，不好意思。釜山，在最东南面。你呢？

赵： 嗯，我是从海口来的，在海南。

俊： 噢，那是哪儿？

赵： 那是中国南海上的一个大岛，在台湾地区和越南之间。还记得几年前一架美国侦察机与中国战斗机相撞并在中国迫降吗？海南就是它降落的地方。

俊： 噢，我确实记得，海南。

海因斯博士： 你们好。你们俩都是中国人吗？

俊： 不。他是中国人，我是韩国人。

海因斯博士： 噢，你们现在觉得纽卡斯尔怎么样？都安顿好了吗？

赵： 很好。我已经找到了一个合租公寓，非常舒适，谢谢。

海因斯博士： 那很好。你们为什么来英国的这个地方学习呢？

俊： 人人都想去伦敦，你不觉得吗？那儿全是外国学生！我们在那儿根本了解不到真正的英国，而且大家到头来都说自己国家的语言。

海因斯博士： 你这么说也是有道理的。你们怎么看这里的口音？对你们有影响吗？

Zhao: Well, I think it's just a matter of getting used to it, isn't it? I am quite surprised how different the accents are in a small country like England, but I have learnt to like them. Just like in Chinese, the northern accents are humorous, and the southern accents are, well, gentle.

Jung: Do you have problems with our accents?

Dr. Haynes: Not really... well sometimes, actually, yes... haha. Look... let me introduce you to some local students here... this is Tony Barry... he's from Sunderland, which is about twelve miles from here... and Melanie Johnson... she's from Washington, which is about ten miles away.

Zhao: Washington?!

Melanie: Yes... haha... that always confuses foreigners. It's the original Washington... George Washington's ancestors came from there.

Jung: Oh!

Tony: So, are you both Japanese, then?

Zhao: No. I'm Chinese and he's Korean.

Tony: Oh... sorry... I haven't met many people from your part of the world before. Do you lads like football?

Jung: I do! I love Chelsea!

Zhao: Yes... and I like Manchester United.

Melanie: Why is it that foreigners always like those teams?

Zhao: They are famous and they always win.

Tony: Yes, but don't you think that anyone can support a winner? I mean, here in England we think you should support your home team... that's why when people say they support Manchester United we know they are not actually from Manchester! The real Mancunians support Manchester City!

Jung: Well, we are foreigners. We don't have a home team in the premier league. But I think you are right. From now on, we should support Newcastle. Which team do you support, then?

Tony: Sunderland!

Zhao: I've never heard of them.

Tony: Well, everyone in Britain has! They have a long and proud history, even though they weren't in the Premiership last season. That's the point, if you are from Sunderland, you love Sunderland whether they are up or down... and not Newcastle... [*looking at Dr. Haynes*]... they're our local rivals.

Dr. Haynes: What was that you were saying, Tony?

赵：我想只要我们习惯了就好了，不是吗？像英格兰这么小的地方竟有这么多不同的口音，我很惊讶，不过我已经逐渐喜欢上它们了。就像在汉语里，北方口音幽默，南方口音，怎么说呢，温柔。

俊：你听我们的口音有问题吗？

海因斯博士：其实没有。可能有时候，实际上，有，哈哈。这样吧，我给你们介绍几个当地学生。这是托尼·巴里，他是从桑德兰来的，离这儿大概有12英里。还有梅拉妮·约翰逊，她是从华盛顿来的，离这儿10英里左右。

赵：华盛顿?!

梅拉妮：是的，哈哈。许多外国人都搞不明白，那是最早的华盛顿，乔治·华盛顿的祖先就是从那儿来的。

俊：噢。

托尼：那么，你们俩都是日本人？

赵：不。我是中国人，他是韩国人。

托尼：哦，抱歉，我没见过多少从你们那个地方来的人。你们两个喜欢足球吗？

俊：我喜欢！我特别喜欢切尔西！

赵：是啊，我喜欢曼联。

梅拉妮：为什么外国人总是喜欢这些队呢？

赵：他们有名而且他们总赢。

托尼：也对，但你难道不觉得一个赢家谁都可以去追捧吗？在英国我们认为应当支持自己的家乡队。所以，当人们说他们支持曼联，我们就知道他们不是真来自曼彻斯特！真正的曼彻斯特人支持曼城队！

俊：我们是外国人。英超联赛里没有我们的家乡队。但是我认为你是对的。从现在开始，我们应该支持纽卡斯尔队。那你支持哪个球队呢？

托尼：桑德兰！

赵：我从来没听说过这个队。

托尼：英国人都知道！他们有悠久而令人骄傲的历史，虽然他们目前不在英超联赛里。关键是，只要你是桑德兰人，你就会爱桑德兰队，无论他们表现好与坏，而不是纽卡斯尔队。[向海因斯博士的方向看去] 他们跟我们是同室操戈的敌人。

海因斯博士：托尼，你说什么呢？

实用短语

- Good evening everyone.　大家晚上好。
- May I extend a very warm welcome?　请允许我致以热烈的欢迎。
- You aren't Chinese, are you?　你不是中国人吧?
- I know that. I mean…　我知道,我是说……
- Oh… where's that?　噢,那是在哪儿?
- Whereabouts are you from?　你从哪儿来?
- Where in… are you from?　你从……的什么地方来?
- What about you?　你呢?
- Are you two…?　你们两个是……吗?
- What do you think of… so far?　你们到现在为止觉得……怎么样?
- Are you doing… all right?　你们做……顺利吗?
- Why did you decide to come to… to study?　你为什么决定要来……学习?
- Has it been causing you any problems?　它对你们有影响吗?
- Do you have problems with…?　你……有问题吗?
- Why is it that…?　……是为什么?
- Don't you think…?　你难道不认为……?
- Which team do you support, then?　那你支持哪个队?
- What was that you were saying?　你在说什么呢?

词汇表

accent 口音
ancestor 祖先
Chelsea 切尔西/切尔西队
clash with 与…发生冲撞
George Washington 乔治·华盛顿
lad 小伙子
local rivals 同室操戈的敌人

local 本地的
Manchester City 曼彻斯特城队
Manchester United 曼彻斯特联队
Mancunian 曼彻斯特人
mile 英里
Newcastle 纽卡斯尔
Premiership (the) (英国)超级联赛

proud 骄傲的
reconnaissance plane 侦察机
Sunderland 桑德兰
the real England 真实的英国
up or down 好与坏/顺境与逆境
whereabouts 具体哪个地方

第8章
校方官员
University Bureaucracy

背景常识

在英国大学里,你可能会与很多的学校职能部门打交道(deal with)。第一是你所在的院系(Department)。如果你有学习上的问题,比如选课和请病假,你应该联系你的院系秘书(departmental secretary)和导师(personal tutor)。第二个部门是学生服务部(Student Services)。学生服务部是大学里一个庞大的机构。他们负责的内容包括学生的在校住宿和身心健康、食堂伙食、商店零售,以及校园安全等等。总而言之,所有非学术的校园生活都归它管。第三个部门是教务办公室(Academic Office),也叫学籍办公室(Registrar's Office)或学籍处(Registry)。他们负责你的学习纪录(academic record)和个人档案(personal file)。如果你要改变自己的学位(degree),或者要把成绩单(transcript)发给未来的用人单位,教务办公室就是你要找的地方。第四是财务办公室(Finance Office)。他们负责处理钱的问题,比如交学费和申请资助。在不同的大学这些部门可能有不同的名称。

跟中国大学的官方机构一样,这些英国高校的办公室服务有时是非常死板和迟缓的。如果你想见他们,最好是通过电子邮件预约(make an appointment)。许多办公室不接待非预约来访(walk-in)。这里还有一个文化差异:中国人觉得早到是有礼貌的表现;在英国,如果你的预约时间是11点整而你10点50就到门口等着了,反而会让你要见的人感到厌烦。

与中国大学里的团支部书记不同,英国大学的官员一般是不会训斥你的。你反倒应该显得固执(persistent)和缺乏耐心(inpatient),要催促他们工作。所以,这里语言上的技巧在于如何显得坚定(firm)而强硬(offensive)。

In the Finance Office

Zhang: Hello, I got an e-mail yesterday saying that I still owe £100. Do you know who I should speak to?

Secretary: Oh, you need to see the cashier's office, third door down the hallway on your right.

Zhang: Good morning, I got an e-mail saying that I still owe £100. I thought I'd paid my tuition in full.

Cashier: OK. What is your name?

Zhang: Zhang Fan, Zhang is my surname, Z-H-A-N-G.

Cashier: OK, Miss Zhang, the computer shows that you haven't made the payment for your accommodation deposit, which is £100.

Zhang: Really? I remember I paid £100 extra when I paid my accommodation fee.

Cashier: Well, in that case there should be a record on the system. Have you got your receipt with you?

Zhang: Oh, no, but I am sure I paid it when I picked up my room key at the accommodation office. Is there any way you can check with them? Maybe they have a record.

Cashier: It is possible that they still haven't processed the payment. You may want to① check with them first.

Zhang: I'm sorry, I don't want to be a pest②, but I have got a very busy schedule in the next few days and I live a long way from the accommodation office. Could you give them a call now from here, just so that I can get this thing done quickly?

Cashier: I am not sure if there'll be anyone there to answer the phone right now. You see… it is their lunch break.

Zhang: Well, do you think you could just give it a try? I'd be so grateful.

Cashier: OK then. [picks up phone and dials]

Zhang: Thanks. You're a star③.

Cashier: Well, Miss Zhang, I am sorry for the carry on④. It seems that the accommodation office did have your record of the payment. It just hasn't gone through our system yet. I am sorry to have dragged you down here.

Zhang: No problem, I am just glad that everything is all right.

在财务办公室

小张： 你好，我收到一封电子邮件，上面说我还欠100英镑。你知道我应该找谁吗？

秘书： 噢，你得去出纳室。上3楼，沿着走廊走到底，右手边。

小张： 早上好。我收到一封电子邮件，上面说我还欠100英镑。我以为我的学费都付完了。

出纳： 好吧。你叫什么名字？

小张： 张帆，张是我的姓，Z-H-A-N-G。

出纳： 好吧，张小姐。电脑上说你还没付住宿押金，100英镑。

小张： 真的吗？我记得我付住宿费的时候，多付了100英镑。

出纳： 嗯，如果是这样的话系统上应该有记录。你有收据吗？

小张： 噢，没有，但是我敢肯定我在住宿办公室取房间钥匙的时候已经付过了。你能跟他们核对一下吗？也许他们有记录。

出纳： 有可能他们还在转账。你可以先去他们那儿查查。

小张： 对不起，我不想给你添麻烦，但是我这几天都特别忙，而且我的住处离住宿办公室很远。你能不能现在给他们打个电话，我好能更快地办完这件事？

出纳： 我不敢肯定他们那儿现在有没有人接电话。你看，已经是他们的午饭休息时间了。

小张： 那，你能试一下吗？特别感谢你。

出纳： 好吧。[拿起电话并拨号]

小张： 谢谢。你太好了。

出纳： 张小姐，很抱歉，我们搞错了。看来住宿办公室确实有你的付款记录。只是他们还没有输入到我们的系统。很抱歉让你跑了一趟。

小张： 没关系，一切弄清楚了就好。

注释

① want to 这里有"应该"的意思比should友好。
② be a pest "当一个害虫"，表示"添麻烦"。
③ star "明星"，这里是"好人"的意思。
④ carry on 英国口语，表示"愚蠢的举动，轻率的行为"。

实用短语

- I got an e-mail yesterday saying that... 我收到了一封电子邮件，上面说……
- Do you know who I should speak to? 你知道我应该找谁吗？
- The computer shows that you... 电脑上显示你……
- Well, in that case there should be a record. 如果是那样的话我们应该有记录。
- You may want to check with... 你也许应该跟……核对一下。
- I'm not sure if there'll be anyone there. 我估计那里没人。
- It seems that... 看起来……
- Really? I remember I paid... 真的吗？我记得我付过……
- Oh, no, but I am sure I paid it. 噢，不，但是我肯定我付过了。
- Is there any way you can check with them? 你能跟他们核对一下吗？
- Is it possible that...? 有没有可能是……？
- I'm sorry, I don't want to be a pest, but... 对不起，我不想给你添麻烦，可是……
- Could you give them a call now? 你能不能现在给他们打个电话？
- Well, do you think you could just give it a try? 你能试一试吗？
- I'd be so grateful. 我会很感激的。
- I am sorry for... 我对……很抱歉。
- I am sorry to have... 我为……很抱歉。

词汇表

busy schedule 紧张的日程
carry on 愚蠢的举动/轻率的行为
cashier 出纳
drag 麻烦、拖延时间的事情
get... done 完成某事
give it a try 试一试

in full 全部的/作为整体
lunch break 午间休息
on the system 在系统上
owe 欠
payment 款项
pest 害虫/讨厌的人

pick up 拣起/取
process 处理/接受/转账
receipt 收据
record 记录
tuition fees 学费

第9章
见导师
Meeting Your Personal Tutor/Adviser

背景常识

中英大学之间的一个主要区别是它们对班级(class)的概念理解不同。通常来说，一个中国大学包含几个学院(college/school)。一个学院可能再包含几个系(department)。一个系把它的学生分成年级(grade)。每个年级又有若干个班(class)。所以一个学生的身份可以被表述为"北京大学国际关系学院一年级五班的一员"。英国大学就不再把学生分成班了。你无非就是一个个体(individual)，每节课和你一起上课的同学都不一样。

这对中国学生来说可能是不适应的(shocking)。没有固定的班级，也就是没有班主任(headteacher)，没有班长(monitor)，也没有其他的学生干部，比如宣传(propaganda)委员和纪律(discipline)委员。

然而这并不表示你就无依无靠了。通常，你院系里的一位教职人员会被分配给你，作为你的导师(personal tutor/adviser)。导师的作用跟班主任差不多。不过他不带某一个特定的班。他跟你的关系是一对一的。personal tutor 和研究生导师(supervisor)还不一样。supervisor 一般只负责学术上的指导。personal tutor 既可以给你提供学习上的指导，也可以跟你讨论你的社会和个人问题。即使你的 personal tutor 不能帮助你，他或她至少可以告诉你应当向谁求助。

就像在第8章中提到的，你应该在见你的导师之前先通过电子邮件跟他预约。在学年开始的时候，跟你的导师探讨选课事宜是非常重要的。让他看你的课程表(timetable)，看他是否认为你的安排是合理的。另外，你还可以跟他讨论你的职业计划(career plan)。总的来说，学生和导师之间的关系是非正式(informal)和个人化的(personal)。

On the Phone

Neil: Hello, could I speak to Dr. Foster, please?

Dr. Foster: Speaking.

Neil: Hello there, my name's Neil Zhao. I was told that you're my personal tutor. Is that right?

Dr. Foster: Let me see… what did you say your name was, again?

Neil: Zhao, Neil Zhao. Z-H-A-O.

Dr. Foster: Ah yes, Mr. Zhao. What can I do for you?

Neil: Well, I'd like to arrange to see you so that we can discuss my dissertation.

Dr. Foster: Right. How does tomorrow morning at 9.30 sound to you?

Neil: Er… OK, then.

Dr. Foster: My office is on the third floor of the Eliot Building… room E332.

9.30

Dr. Foster: Oh, hello, Mr. Zhao… do come in… please sit down.

Neil: Thanks.

Dr. Foster: I hope you enjoyed our English weather this morning.

Neil: To be honest, sir, I am not very impressed.

Dr. Foster: Hehe… I don't blame you, Neil. It will get better soon… I hope. Now, it's the dissertation you wanted to talk about, right? So, tell me, which modules are you doing on this course… apart from the core ones?

Neil: I've actually chosen EDUC5715M, School Management and Leadership, EDUC5704M, International Educational Management: Effective Development of Policies and Plans for Change, erm… let's see… EDUC5037M, Citizenship Education: Principles and Practice, and … EDUC6666M, Public-Private Partnership in the Educational Marketplace… that's in addition to the compulsory modules… erm… Critical Approaches, Lifelong Learning, Fundamentals of Educational Management and… erm the dissertation.

Dr. Foster: Some excellent choices there. As for the dissertation, do you have anything in mind?

Neil: Well, I've been thinking about this for a while… I'm quite interested in looking at the organisational culture of Chinese middle schools compared to that of British secondary schools.

Dr. Foster: Uuuhu… and what is it in particular that interests you? I mean… it sounds quite general….

Neil: Well, I'd like to look at the culture of leadership in Chinese and British education, do a comparative study….

Dr. Foster: That sounds very interesting. Have you read Deal and Peterson on leadership cultures?

Neil: No, I haven't actually.

Dr. Foster: Well, I'd recommend it. It's very interesting. OK… I need you to prepare a short proposal for this. So, what you need to do is to write down a list of about twenty questions that spring to mind about leadership culture in Chinese education… then you can work out an overarching question that you want to use as the basis of your dissertation. Shall we meet again in two weeks' time?

在电话里

尼尔：你好，我能找一下福斯特博士吗？

福斯特博士：我就是。

尼尔：你好，我的名字叫尼尔·赵。有人告诉我您是我的导师。对吗？

福斯特博士：让我查查。你说你叫什么来着？

尼尔：我姓赵，尼尔·赵，Z-H-A-O。

福斯特博士：啊，是的，赵先生。我能为你做什么？

尼尔：我想要安排个时间跟您见面，谈谈我的论文。

福斯特博士：好的。明天早上9：30怎么样？

尼尔：哦，好吧。

福斯特博士：我的办公室在艾略特大楼的3层，E332号房。

9点30分

福斯特博士：噢，你好，赵先生。请进，请坐。

尼尔：谢谢。

福斯特博士：我希望你喜欢今天早上的英国天气。

尼尔：说实话，先生，我没什么太好的印象。

福斯特博士：呵呵，我不怪你，尼尔。天气会好起来的，我希望会好的。言归正传，你要跟我讨论你的论文，对吧？那么，告诉我，你在这个课程里都学了什么课，除了必修课以外。

尼尔：我选了EDUC5715M，学校管理和领导；EDUC5704M，国际教育管理：在变革中有效的发展政策与计划；嗯，让我想想，EDUC5037M，公民教育：原则与实践；还有……EDUC6666M，教育市场的公私合作……此外，我还学了批判性方法、终身教育、教育管理概论……那么，该说论文了。

福斯特博士：选得很好。至于结业论文，你目前有什么想法吗？

尼尔：嗯，我已经考虑一段时间了。我对研究中国的中学和英国的中学在组织文化上的差异比较感兴趣。

福斯特博士：哦，那么你具体对什么感兴趣呢？我的意思是，这个题目听起来很宽泛。

尼尔：我想研究领导文化在中英教育中的作用，做一个比较研究。

福斯特博士：很有趣。你读过迪尔和彼得森关于领导文化的书吗？

尼尔：我还没有读过。

福斯特博士：那么，我建议你读一读，非常有意思。我需要你写一份简短的策划。你需要做的是写下大约20个你能随便想起来的关于中国教育领导文化的问题，然后你可以筛选出一个具有概括性的问题作为你论文的基础。我们两个星期之后再见一面，怎么样？

实用短语

- Hello, could I speak to...?　你好,我想找……
- Speaking.　是我。
- Let me see.　让我想想。
- Do you have anything in mind?　你有什么想法吗?
- What is it in particular that interests you?　你具体对什么感兴趣呢?
- I've actually chosen...　我选了……
- That's in addition to...　在……之外,还有……
- I've been thinking about...　我在考虑……
- I'd like to look at....　我想研究……
- How about...?　……怎么样?
- Shall we meet at...?　我们在……见面怎么样?
- Then you can work out...　然后你可以筛选/决定……
- What you need to do is to...　你需要做的是……

词汇表

basis 基础
citizenship 公民(身份)
comparative study 比较研究
compulsory 必修的/必须的
core 必修的/核心的
dissertation 结业论文(dissertation 和 essay 都是 "论文" 的意思,essay 一般比较短,dissertation 一般指结业论文。)
educational marketplace 教育市场
effective development 有效发展/有效制订
floor 楼层

fundamental 基本的/概论的
general 宽泛的/普遍的
in mind 在脑海中/心里
in particular 具体的
in two weeks' time 两个星期以后
leadership 领导(的行为或艺术)
lifelong learning 终生教育
management 管理
middle school 中学
organisational culture 组织文化
overarching 概括性的
personal tutor 导师

policy 政策
practice 实践
principle 原则
proposal 策划/提议
public-private partnership 公私合作关系
recommend 推荐
secondary school 二级学校/小学以后/中学
spring to mind 闪现在脑海里/轻易地想起来
timetable 课程表/时间表

第10章
银行、诊所与警察局
Bank, Clinic and Police

○ 背景常识

你到了英国以后,除了(apart from)学习和住宿问题以外,还有几件个人行政事务(personal administrative matters)需要优先考虑。比如,开一个银行账户、到诊所建立医疗档案和到本地警察局注册签证。

在银行里,你需要运用这些词汇:账户(account)、借记卡(debit card)、支票(cheque)、信用卡(credit card)、利息(interest)、存(deposit)、取钱(withdraw)、购买(purchase)、现金(cash)、汇款(transfer)、密码(personal identification number, PIN)等等。你存款的数量和课程的长短将决定你所能申请的账户种类。一个普通的学生账户(student account)通常只配借记卡,没有信用卡和支票簿(chequebook)。英国银行家们都很懒,银行都不在星期天开门,所以,尽量挑非周末的日子(weekday)去开账户。

在诊所里,你需要了解如何用英语描述自己的生理信息(biographic information),比如年龄、性别、出生地、家族病史(family disease)或者残障情况(disability)。医生有可能会给你体检。你需要学习这些词语:医生(doctor)、护士(nurse)、医疗保险(health insurance)、药店(pharmacy)、药(medicine / medication)、血型(blood type)、血压(blood pressure)、尿样(urine sample)、对……过敏(being allergic to)、患感冒(caught a cold)、感染(infection)、内/外用(for internal/external use)等等。

英国法律要求你在抵达后7日内到当地警察局注册你的签证。像银行员工和医生一样,警察也会询问你的生理信息、学籍情况和联系地址。

At the Bank

Hu: Good morning. I'd like to open a student account.

Clerk: Right ... if you could just fill out this form ... You'll need to show the following forms of ID: your passport, your student card for this academic year or a letter from your university saying that you have registered there. Oh ... and we'll also need proof of residence for yourself ... that's like a utility bill, or a rent receipt, a contract with a landlord or something like that.

Hu: OK ... here's my passport and student card. And here's my contract for the student halls....

Clerk: That's fine, Mr. Yue... now we can....

Hu: Hu....

Clerk: Sorry?

Hu: My surname is Hu... we do it the other way round in Chinese... surname then given name.

Clerk: Oh, right, sorry, so your full name is Hu Yue, but Yue is in fact your "first name" and Hu is your "second name".

Hu: That is right, but let's call the "given name" and "surname", less confusing this way.

Clerk: Mr. Hu... all right... sorry about that. Mr. Hu, we can open the account today, but it'll take about a week for your debit card to arrive. The card and the PIN will arrive separately. Once you have both, you can use your card in any cash machine, and you can change your PIN if you like... just follow the instructions on the machine. If you want to withdraw or deposit any money in the meantime, you can do it in person with your passport at any bank, but it's best to do it here because other banks might charge a commission. If you deposit cash, it'll clear straight away, but cheques and transfers take up to four working days.

Hu: OK... thanks. What about if I want a credit card?

Clerk: I'm afraid we can't offer you a credit card yet, just a debit card. However, if you would like an overdraft facility for yourself, you can apply for that and we'll consider it. The interest rates are in this leaflet, here. Welcome to HSBC Bank.

Hu: Thanks.

At the Police Station

Hu: Good afternoon, I am a new foreign student. I've come to register.

Policeman: Right, sir. I need to see your passport and take down your details. Hmmm... Mr. Hu Yue... date of birth... 30th September, 1980... oh, today's your birthday. Many happy returns... 26, yes? My daughter's the same age as you... born Qingdao... how do you pronounce that? *Kwingdao*?

Hu: No... it's pronounced more like *Chingdao*... that Q is always a problem, isn't it?

Policeman: Well it's certainly a hard language, Chinese. Right. You've got a student visa. That means you are not allowed to take more than twenty hours employment per week during term time. If you change your address, you must notify us. Before you go, I need to take a passport size photo of you... smile....

Hu: OK.

在银行

小胡：早上好。我想要开个学生账户。

工作人员：好的。你先把这个表填一下。你还得让我看看以下这些证件：你的护照、这个学期的学生卡或者学校证明你已经注册的介绍信。噢，还有，我需要你的住址证明。比如物业费账单、房租收据、与房东的合同或者类似的东西。

小胡：好的。这是我的护照和学生卡，还有我的学校住宿合同。

工作人员：好，跃先生。我们现在就可以……

小胡：胡。

工作人员：什么？

小胡：我姓胡。在中国我们是反过来的，姓在名字前面。

工作人员：噢，对不起。那么您的全名是胡跃，跃是您的前名，胡是您的后名。

小胡：对，但还是让我们叫它们名和姓吧，这样听起来不会搞混。

工作人员：胡先生，实在抱歉。胡先生，我们今天就可以给您开户，但是您的借记卡要一个星期以后才能拿到。卡和密码会分别寄到。一旦您两样都拿到手，您就可以在任何取款机上使用您的卡。而且如果您觉得有必要，您还可以改变您的密码，只要按照提款机上的使用说明做就可以了。在您的借记卡还没有到来之前，如果您想要取款或存款，您可以亲自用护照在任何一家银行办理，但是最好是在我们银行，因为其他的银行可能会收您手续费。如果您存现金，存款马上就能入户。支票和汇款要等最多4个工作日。

小胡：行，谢谢。如果我要办信用卡呢？

工作人员：很遗憾我们不能给您办信用卡，只能是借记卡。但是，如果您想要透支功能，您可以申请，然后我们会考虑。利率在这本小册子里，给。欢迎加入汇丰银行。

小胡：谢谢。

在警察局

小胡：下午好，我是个新来的外国学生。我来这儿注册。

警察：好的，先生。我需要看你的护照并记录你的个人信息。嗯，胡跃先生，出生日期是1980年9月30号。噢，今天是你的生日，又长了一岁。26了，对吗？我女儿跟你一边儿大。出生在青岛，怎么发这个音？昆岛？

小胡：不，应该读作青岛。Q不好发音，是吧？

警察：汉语确实是个非常难学的语言。好了，你已经有学生签证了。这说明你在学期中间不能工作超过20个小时一周。如果你搬家了，一定要通知我们你的新地址。在你走之前，我还得给你拍一张护照尺寸的照片……笑一笑……

小胡：好了。

实用短语

- I'd like to open a bank account. 我想开个银行账户。
- You'll need to show… 你得让我看看……
- We'll also need to see…. 我们还得看……
- It'll take about a week for… to… 做……需要大约一周。
- You can use your card in any cash machine. 您可以在任何取款机上使用您的卡。
- You can change your PIN if you like. 你觉得有必要的话还可以改变密码。
- Just follow the instructions on the machine. 按照机器上的使用说明做。
- I've come to register. 我是来注册的。
- If you want to… you can… 如果你想要……你可以……
- If you deposit cash, it'll… 如果你存款,它会……
- What about if…? 如果……会怎么样?

词汇表

cash 现金
cash machine 取款机
cheques 支票
charge a commission 收取手续费
consider 考虑
credit card 信用卡
deposit 存款/押金
details 细节/信息
emergency 急诊/紧急情况
fill out 填
first name 名
follow the instructions 按照使用说明

forms of ID (不同种类的)身份证件
given name 名
in person 亲自
in the meantime 与此同时
many happy returns 生日快乐/又长一岁了
notify 通知
overdraft facility 透支功能
PIN (personal identification number) 密码
pronounce 发音

proof of residence 住址证明
rent receipt 房租收据
second name 姓
smile 微笑
student card 学生卡
surname 姓
take down 取消/拿下
the other way round 反过来地
up to 最多
utility bill 物业费账单
withdraw 取款/退出/撤离
working day/business day 工作日

第11章
图书馆与信息服务
Library and IT Services

背景常识

在中国上大学期间，尤其是本科阶段，你可能每天都会有8个小时的课。但是在英国大学里，你每星期上课的时间可能都不到8小时。这就要求学生有很强的自学能力。当然，有不少英国学生用这些剩余的时间喝酒睡觉，但是更加坚定和勤奋的留学生们却把时间花在图书馆里。

英国的大学会为你举行关于如何使用图书馆、校园电脑和学校电子邮件的讲座。通常，负责这些事务的部门是信息服务部。你会得到一张图书馆卡，它也是你在校园里的身份证明。记住学校给你的电子邮件地址是非常重要的，因为那将是老师联系你的主要途径。大多数学校都有24小时机房（24-hour workstation），以便学生熬夜学习或完成论文。当然，半夜网上聊天的也大有人在。

在图书馆里，你需要掌握能向图书馆馆员（librarian）寻求帮助的语言技巧。要找一本书，你需要查找关于作者（author）、标题（title）、出版商（publisher）、版本（edition）、主题（subject）或关键词（keyword）等的信息。在图书馆里有用的其它词汇包括：借（borrow/loan）、还（return）、预定（request）和索引（catalogue/index）。

说到计算机英语，那就完全是另一门外语了。连很英国人都不能完全掌握信息技术的术语（jargon）。但是，如果你使用过中文版本的Windows、Word、Power Point、Internet Explorer、Outlook等等，你应该能很快掌握相对应的英语版本软件。基本的文字处理技术是英国学生必备的能力。在当今的英国大学里，用笔的机会已经越来越少了。大部分学术研究也是在网上进行的。

Library Tour

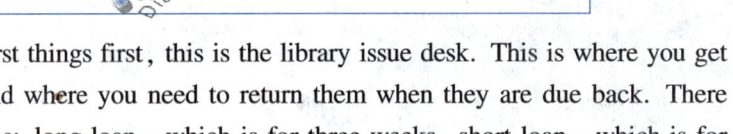

Librarian: Right. First things first, this is the library issue desk. This is where you get your books issued, and where you need to return them when they are due back. There are three types of loans: long loan—which is for three weeks, short loan—which is for three days, and overnight loan—which means exactly what it says.

Shirley: So can we borrow all of the books here?

Librarian: No... absolutely not. You can borrow a maximum of 15 books at any given time. Some of the books are on restricted access. Now, some lecturers put certain books in a special subject collection where students can access them easily, and there are usually multiple copies of certain set texts and core readings[①] there. Also, each module generally has a core reading handbook, which is a booklet containing articles from periodicals and academic journals relevant to that module.

Shirley: Oh... right

Librarian: Right. Let's go and have a look at the library catalogue. You can access this via the Intranet[②] from your own computer, but I'll just show you how to access it from the library PCs. Right... if we log onto the library site we can see the main menu: author, title, periodicals or serials title, keywords, subject headings, classmark, ISSN/ISBN and catalogue help. So, who wants to give me the name of a book?

Shirley: *Big Questions in History*.

Librarian: Ok... I'll click on title and type the name in. Right, now you can see that we have it... there's the name and there's the author's name... Harriet Swain. Actually, she's the editor, so this book is a collection of essays by other authors. Now, tell me, what is the classmark of the book?

Shirley: Erm... the classmark? Ah... you mean the number, A902/995643?

Librarian: Good... now click on the classmark and it'll take you back to the page for that book. Here is the page... where is the book held? From here you can see its full bibliographic details as well as its location in the library and status.

Shirley: I see... so it is the 2005 edition, held in the Art and Humanity Library, Floor E and it is available.

Librarian: Once you have located the book and made sure it is available, you can go to that floor to get the book. Remember to note down the classmark, because there are thousands of books on each floor and they are all arranged according to their classmarks.

Shirley: Got it.

Librarian: One more thing, if the book you are looking for is not available, in other words, already borrowed, you may reserve it, so that you will receive a notice from us once it is returned. To reserve a book, just click the "reserve" button on the top right of the page for that book and then enter your surname and student number.

图书馆参观团

馆员：好。首先，这里就是图书馆的出借柜台。这里就是你把书借走的地方，也是你在借期快到的时候还书的地方。借期一共有3种：长期的是3周，短期的是1至3天，还有通宵的，显而易见就是过了一晚上就还。

雪莉：那么，我们能借这里所有的书吗？

馆员：不，绝对不行。你一次最多只能借15本书。有些书是限制使用的。有些老师会把一些书放在特殊的专题收藏中，这样学生们就可以方便查找。一些必读的和常用的书籍，我们都不止收一本。还有，每门课都有一本核心阅读手册，那是一本包含与那门课相关的期刊杂志文章的小册子。

雪莉：哦，好的。

馆员：好了。让我们去看看图书馆的书目索引。你可以使用自己的电脑通过本地网登录书目索引，但是我先向你们展示一下如何从图书馆的电脑上登录。好，如果我们进入图书馆的网页，我们可以看到这个主目录：作者、书名、期刊名称、关键词、主题、分类号、国际标准书号和索引帮助。那么，谁想给我一个书名？

雪莉：《历史的大问题》。

馆员：好的，我会点击"书名"然后输入这个名字。现在你可以看到，我们确实有这本书。这儿是书名，那儿是作者的名字，哈丽雅特·斯温。实际上，她是这本书的编辑，所以这是一本由其他作者合写的集子。现在，告诉我，这本书的分类号是什么？

雪莉：分类号？噢，你是指这个号码吗，A902/995643？

馆员：对，现在点击这个分类号，你会到这本书的网页上去。这就是它的网页了。从这个页面上你可以看到这本书的详细出版情况以及它在图书馆里的位置和状态。

雪莉：我明白了。那么它是2005年版的，存放在人文与艺术类，E楼，而且可以借阅。

馆员：一旦你找到那本书的位置并确定它可以借阅，你就可以到那一层上去取这本书了。记住把分类号写下来，因为每层楼上都有上千本书，它们都是按分类号排列的。

雪莉：明白了。

馆员：还有一件事，如果你要找的书不能被借阅，也就是说，已经被借走了，你可以预订它。那样的话，当它被还回来的时候，我们就会通知你。要预订一本书，只需要点击那本书的网页的右上角的"预订"，然后输入你的姓和学生号。

注释

① readings 这里有"书籍"的意思。
② Intranet 本地网。

实用短语

- ◆ Right. First things first, … 好。首先,……
- ◆ So can we borrow all of the books here? 我们能借这里所有的书吗?
- ◆ No… absolutely not. 不,绝对不行。
- ◆ You can borrow, maximum, 15 books at any given time. 你一次最多只能借15本书。
- ◆ Let's go and have a look at … 让我们去看看……
- ◆ You can access this via… 你可以通过……进去。
- ◆ I'll just show you how to… 我先向你们展示一下如何……
- ◆ I'll click on title and type the name in. 我会点击"书名"然后输入这个名字。
- ◆ Right, now you can see… 现在你可以看到……
- ◆ It'll take you back to… 这将带你到……
- ◆ Where is the book held? 书存放在哪里?
- ◆ From here you can see… 从这里你可以看到……
- ◆ It is available. 可以借阅。
- ◆ It is the 2005 edition. 它是2005年版的。
- ◆ Remember to note down the classmark. 记住把分类号写下来。
- ◆ One more thing, … 还有一件事,……
- ◆ You may reserve it. 你可以预订它。

词汇表

absolutely not 绝对不行
academic journal 学术杂志
access 使用权
article 文章
be due back on… 到…(日期)归还
booklet 册子
borrow 借
catalogue 书目索引
classmark 分类号
collection 合集
core readings 必读书
editor 编辑
enter 进入
handbook 手册
hold 存放
in other words 也就是说
ISSN/ISBN 国际标准序列号/国际标准书号
issue 出借/发,签署
keyword 关键词
library issue desk 图书馆的借书台
loan 借/借期
locate 确认地点/找到
log onto/log in 登录
main menu 主目录
multiple copies 多本(指拥有不止一本同样的书)
note down 记下来
on loan 被借走的
overnight 通宵的/隔夜的
periodical 期刊
reserve 预订
restricted access 限制使用
serials 序列号
sign up 加入
status 状态
subject heading 标题
tour 参观/参观团
via 通过/于(介词)

第12章
实验室和工作室
Laboratory and Studio

背景常识

英国大学通常按学科把学生分为3类：science、social science 和 fine art。这里有不少模糊的概念。science 虽然是"科学"的意思，通常只表示自然科学（natural sciences），而不包括社会科学（social sciences）。art 通常指"文科"。所以社会科学有时也叫人文科学（humanities and arts）。文科学士也因此被称为 Bachelor of Art/BA。"艺术科"，比如美术和雕刻，叫 fine art。英语中的 art 实际上比汉语里"艺术"这个词的意思要广泛。比如，人们有时会争论天气预报到底是 science 还是 art。这里的 art 实际上是指那些不以逻辑和理性为基础，而强调感性、辩证和经验的学科。许多学科具有 art 和 science 的双重性，比如政府学、战略学、经济学和管理学。

如今绝大多数来英的中国学生都想学经济学和商学。殊不知，要想在英国大学里学好这些兼具文理双重性的科目，学生必须有在纯艺术和纯科学领域里的基本修养。亚当·斯密（Adam Smith）、卡尔·马克思（Karl Marx）、约翰·纳什（John Nash），这些人在作为经济学家的同时也是哲学或数学领域里的一代宗师。而且，物以稀为贵，中国市场虽大，但能容下多少随波逐流的"海龟"工商管理学学生呢？

因此，这一章，我们就介绍一些在实验室和工作室里的趣味实用英语，献给那些有志自费出国学习数学、哲学、政治、历史和艺术的中国学生们。虽然科学家和艺术家的典型形象（stereotype）都是不善言谈的，但实际上在实验室和工作室里还是有很多趣闻逸事的。不习惯使用第三人称被动句（third-person passive）的留学生经常把试验报告写得像食谱（recipe）和女巫配方（brew）一般。各色与实验室安全条例打擦边球的恶作剧，更令人在毕业后久久难忘。

In the Uni Bar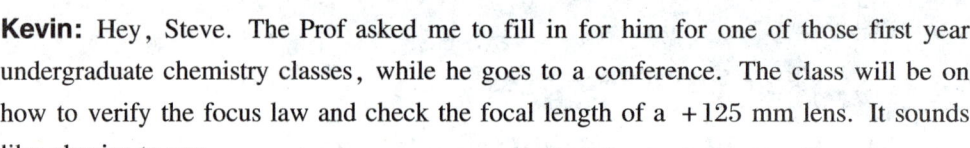

Kevin: Hey, Steve. The Prof asked me to fill in for him for one of those first year undergraduate chemistry classes, while he goes to a conference. The class will be on how to verify the focus law and check the focal length of a +125 mm lens. It sounds like physics to me.

Steven: Yes, I know... it does seem a bit weird, doesn't it? The thing is, though, that chemistry also deals with optics. It is a prerequisite for some areas.

Kevin: So, how does it go? I mean, how do you do the experiment?

Steven: Well, first, you need to put a 125 mm lens, in its mounting, into a rod holder so the lens is parallel to the long axis of the rectangular base. Second, you have to put a screen card in a bulldog clip and mount it at the right-hand end of a ruler. Third, you turn the lamp on and position it at the same distance from the ruler as the lens. You need to stand the lamp on a lamp stand to bring the image on the screen to a convenient height.

Kevin: Wait a minute... let me write it down.

Steven: After you've done this, you need to adjust the height of the lens until you have, like, a fuzzy image. The next step is to record the positions at which you get sharp images on the screen card.

Kevin: Right, then...?

Steven: Now, when the readings have been taken and recorded—this is your sixth step—you need to work out the image distances from the lens—that's the screen position on the ruler minus the lens position—and plot 1000/v versus 1000/u on regular graph paper. Finally, you write down your best result for the actual focal length of the "125 mm" lens. And that's it, more-or-less, pretty straightforward, really.

Kevin: Well, it all sounds like double Dutch[①] to me, mate. What's the point of it?

Steven: Well, it's all about optics... how the focal length of an optical system is a measure of how strongly it focuses or diverges light.

Kevin: Uh... English please![②]

Steven: Look... you wear glasses, don't you?

Kevin: Erm... yes.

Steven: Well, there you go!

Kevin: I think it's your round, mate. Mine's a pint of lager... Maybe you should fill in for the Prof, not me.

Steven: Don't worry. They are only undergrads.

在学校酒吧里

凯文： 嘿，史蒂文。教授要去参加一个会议，他让我替他上一节本科一年级的化学课。这节课要讲如何测量聚焦法则并检验一个125毫米凸透镜的焦距。这听起来像是物理啊。

史蒂文： 是，我知道。好像是有点儿奇怪，对吗？可问题是，化学也要处理很多光学问题啊。在有些领域里它可是入门课。

凯文： 那么，它怎么进行？我是说，你怎么做这个试验？

史蒂文： 第一步，你需要把125毫米凸透镜支起来，放在一个支架上，这样这个透镜就与长方形底座的长轴平行了。第二，你需要把一个屏幕片夹在一个大钢夹上，并立在一把尺子的右端。第三，你把灯点亮并放置在与尺子到透镜相同的距离上。你需要把灯立在灯架上并把屏幕上的映像调整到合适的高度。

凯文： 等等，让我把它记下来。

史蒂文： 在你做了这些以后，你需要调整透镜的高度，直到屏幕上出现一个模糊的映像。下一步是要记录下映像在屏幕上聚焦时透镜的位置。

凯文： 好，然后呢？

史蒂文： 现在，当读数已经取到并记录下来，这就是你的第六步。你需要算出映像到透镜的距离，那就是屏幕在尺子上的位置减去透镜的位置，然后按 $1000/v$ 比 $1000/u$ 在标准作图纸上画图。最后，你要记下125毫米透镜的焦距的最佳结果。就是这样，差不多，简单极了。

凯文： 哥们儿，我跟听天书似的。这有什么意义呢？

史蒂文： 这都是光学。一个光学系统的焦距如何可作为它聚光或散光的强度的测量方式。

凯文： 哦，你能说得明白点儿吗？

史蒂文： 你想想，你不是戴眼镜吗？

凯文： 嗯，对呀。

史蒂文： 那不就结了吗？

凯文： 我记得应该是你买单了，哥们儿。我只要了一杯淡啤酒。也许你应该给教授代课，不是我。

史蒂文： 别担心，他们不过是本科生罢了。

注释

① double Dutch "双重荷兰语"，表示令人费解的语言。
② English please! 并不是要对方说英语，而是请求对方说明白点儿。

实用短语

- It does seem a bit weird, doesn't it?　好像是有点儿奇怪,对吗?
- The thing is… that…　事情是/问题是……
- So, how does it go?　它怎么进行?
- Wait a minute.　稍等。
- Let me write it down.　让我把它记下来。
- After you've done this, you need to…　你做完这个之后,你需要……
- The next step is to…　下一步是……
- Now, when… have been taken/done/completed…　当你完成了……
- Finally…　最后……
- And that's it, more-or-less.　就是这样,差不多。
- Well, it all sounds like double Dutch/Greek to me.　听起来像天书。
- What's the point of it?　这有什么意义呢?
- Well, there you go!　这不就结了吗?
- Mine's a…　我要了……

词汇表

axis 坐标轴
bulldog clip 大钢夹
chemistry 化学
conference 会议
diverge 分散/散开
double Dutch 听不懂的话
experiment 试验
fill in for 替某人当值
focal length 焦距
focus law 聚焦法则

fuzzy 模糊的
graph paper 作图纸
laboratory 实验室
lens 透镜/镜头
long axis (长方形的)长轴/长边
mount… 把…立起来
mounting 立起的状态
optics 光学
parallel 平行
physics 物理

prerequisite 前提要求
rectangular base 长方形底座
ruler 尺子/统治者
screen card 屏幕片
sharp 聚焦的/清晰的
straightforward 直截了当的
studio 工作室
take place 某事发生/存在
undergraduate 本科

第13章
签手机合同
Signing a Mobile Phone Contract

● 背景常识

中英青年对科技产品的态度非常不同。这最明显地体现在(reflected by)手机的消费行为(consumer behaviour)上。中国青年对追随手机的最新科技有强烈的欲望,照相机(camera)、蓝牙(Bluetooth)、MP3、视频短信(video messaging)多多益善。而在英国,许多学生还是钟情于他们的古董诺基亚3310。当然,追求科技进步不是什么坏事,不过这些术语却为用英语买手机和选择话费套餐(service plan)增添了不少障碍。

首先,你需要区分合同(contract)和即打即付(pay-as-you-go)的区别。你可能听说过英国手机运营商(mobile phone service provider)送免费手机的事,但这只限于合同用户。如果你即打即付,你还是得自己花钱买手机。

一份典型的手机合同内含固定数额(set amount)的月租费(monthly service fee/monthly payment)。根据月租费的多少,运营商会给你一定的免费通话时间(free time)。如果你打电话的时间(call time)超过了免费时间,你就得按分钟付费了(be charged with a per-minute rate)。在英国,接电话一般都不要钱(即单向收费)。然后,还有短信(text messaging)、手机上网(mobile internet access)、彩铃(caller tone)和语音信箱(voice mail)的费用。即使你签了一份合同,也并不是所有的手机都免费。如果要买最新款的手机,你可能还得付一小笔钱配置诸如高像素照相机(mega pixel camera)、三代(3G)、Java Gaming、无线上网(wireless connection)、e-mail、三频(tri-band)或四频(quad-band)——总之,手机越高级,你要花的银子就越多。反过来,如果你选择一款老式的手机,运营商可能还会给你免费的信贷取款(cash back)或现金返还(rebate)。

In the Street *Dialogue*

James: All right① Ting? What have you been up to?

Ting: Oh… just window-shopping②… can't be bothered to study in a nice Saturday afternoon like this. I am thinking of buying a mobile phone, but I don't know how the mobile phone companies charge in Britain.

James: Well, you are talking to the right guy here. I used to work in a phone shop. It can be quite a headache, you know, choosing phones and plans and all that. Maybe I can help you.

In the Phone Shop *Dialogue*

Salesman: Hello, miss, welcome to O2, can I borrow a few minutes of your time to show you our latest contract plans and free phones?

Ting: OK, I am thinking of signing up to a contract phone anyway.

Salesman: Wonderful! We have a special offer this month. All the customers who sign a contract this month will have the first two months of their monthly payments waived.

Ting: Sounds good.

Salesman: So, how much free call time are you looking for, miss?

Ting: I don't really call that much. So, what is the lowest limit?

Salesman: Well, our cheapest contract plan gives you 100 minutes of free calls each month, and that will cost you just 20 pounds a month. However, if you choose the second cheapest, it will be 28 pounds a month with 200 minutes—£8 difference, twice as much the time.

Ting: I doubt if I can use all the 200 minutes. I text a lot, but I don't call that much.

Salesman: If that is the case, with our 200 minute plan, you can get 100 free text messages and unlimited Internet access for an extra £6 a month.

Ting: So, that'd add up to £34 a month.

Salesman: Wow, you worked that out quick! You must be brainy. How about this Sony-Ericsson? Small, light and it looks good too, it is very popular among our female customers.

Ting: I don't know. I prefer that one.

Salesman: Another great choice! Motorola's latest razor, it's the thinnest mobile phone in the world. And, thin as it is,③ it still comes with a high definition 3-mega pixel digital camera, prolonged Bluetooth range, colour screen, MP3 music player, FM radio, 60 mb built-in memory with expandable memory card slot and it comes in pink as well.

Ting: That seems to have everything I need.

Salesman: The only thing is, this one is not totally free with the plan you picked. You need to pay £20 for the phone. Still, given its original price, this is a bargain.

在街上

詹姆斯： 婷，你好吗？你干什么呢？

婷： 哦，不过就是逛逛街，懒得在这么好的星期六下午学习。我在考虑买一个手机，但是不知道手机商在英国如何收费。

詹姆斯： 好啊，你算是问对人了。我就在一个手机店里工作过。这事儿有时挺烦人的，你知道，选择手机和计费方式之类的事情。也许我能帮你。

在手机店里

推销员： 您好，小姐，欢迎到 O2 来。我能占用您几分钟时间来展示一下我们最新的合同计费方式和免费手机吗？

婷： 好的，我正想签一部手机呢。

推销员： 太好了！我们这个月有一个优惠活动。所有签合同的用户将免头两个月的话费。

婷： 听起来不错。

推销员： 那么，小姐，您想要多少免费电话时间呢？

婷： 我不打那么多电话。所以，你们的最低限额是多少？

推销员： 那，我们最便宜的合同计费方式给你每月 100 分钟的免费时间，而价钱是 20 英镑一个月。但是，如果你选择我们第二便宜的计费方式，那将以 28 英镑一个月的价钱给您 200 分钟的免费时间——8 镑钱的区别，两倍的时间。

婷： 我怀疑我用不完所有的 200 分钟。我发很多短信，但不怎么打电话。

推销员： 如果是那样的话，在我们 200 分钟计费方式的基础上，只要你每月再付 6 英镑，就能得到 100 个免费短信和无限手机上网。

婷： 那么，一共就是 34 英镑一个月。

推销员： 哇，你账算得真快！你肯定很精明。这款索尼-爱立信怎么样？小巧、轻便而且美观，在我们的女顾客中非常流行。

婷： 我不知道。我更喜欢那个。

推销员： 也是一个很好的选择！摩托罗拉最新的超薄手机，目前世界上最薄的手机。而且，虽然如此之薄，它仍然配备了高清晰 300 万像素数码摄像头、加长的蓝牙范围、彩屏、MP3、调频收音机、60 兆内置内存，还有外置内存卡插槽，而且这一款还有粉红色的。

婷： 看来这有我需要的一切。

推销员： 只不过，在您选择的计费方式下，这款手机并不是免费的。您还得再为这手机付 20 英镑。但是与它的原价相比，这还是很便宜的。

注释

① All right　英语的寒暄问候越来越简化，Are you all right? 比 How are you? 简单，All right? 就更简单。
② window-shopping　橱窗购物，表示只看不买。
③ as it is　表示让步性转折。

实用短语

- ◆ All right Ting?　婷,你好吗?
- ◆ What have you been up to?　你干什么呢?
- ◆ I can't be bothered to...　我懒得……
- ◆ I am thinking of...　我在考虑……
- ◆ Well, you are talking to the right guy here.　好啊,你算是问对人了。
- ◆ Hello, miss, welcome to...　您好,欢迎到……来。
- ◆ Can I borrow a few minutes of your time to show you...?　我能占用您几分钟时间来为您展示……吗?
- ◆ We have a special offer this month.　我们这个月有一个优惠活动。
- ◆ Sounds good.　听起来不错。
- ◆ Well, our cheapest plan gives you....　我们最便宜的计费方式给你……
- ◆ I doubt if I can...　我怀疑我能否……
- ◆ If that is the case, ...　如果是那样的话,……
- ◆ That'd add up to...　那一共就是……
- ◆ Another great choice!　也是一个很好的选择!
- ◆ ... as it is, it still...　虽然它……,它仍然……
- ◆ The only thing is, ...　只不过,……

词汇表

3G, third generation 第三代(手机技术)
3-mega pixel camera 300万像素照相机
bargain 让买方占便宜的商品(名词)/好价钱(名词)/讨价还价(动词)
bluetooth 蓝牙技术
brainy 精明的/聪明的
built-in 内置的
cash back 免费信贷取款

contract 合同
expandable memory card slot 外置内存卡插槽
free calling time 免费电话时间
headache 头疼/麻烦事
high definition 高清晰
monthly service fee 月租费
pay-as-you-go 即打即付
plan 计费方式(这里不是"计划"的意思)

prolong 延长
rebate 回扣
free calls 免费电话
set amount 固定数额
SIM card 手机卡
text message 短信
top up 充值
use up 用完
window-shopping 橱窗购物/只看不买

第14章
点 菜
Ordering a Meal

背景常识

说到英国菜,大部分人会马上联想到炸鱼薯条(fish and chips)。其实 fish and chips 通常是见不了大场面的快餐。真正经典和传统的英国食品还得数 steak and kidney pie(肉排腰子饼)、lamb chop(羊排)、roast beef(烤牛肉)、Yorkshire pudding(约克郡布丁)、apple crumble(苹果酥)、custard(奶油甜羹)和 spotted Dick(麻子迪克——葡萄干布丁)。

中国和欧洲饮食文化的主要区别体现在空间和时间这两个概念上。典型的中国用餐方式是空间性的。食物被分为主食(main dish)和菜(side dish)。所有饭菜都同时呈上来,而且不同的饭菜摆在桌子不同的位置上。而典型的欧洲用餐方式则是时间性的。食物被分为开胃菜(starter)、主菜(main course)和甜点(desert)。每一段时间只上一类菜,而且菜跟着时间转换。饭菜的摆放没有什么讲究,因为一个人面前只有一个盘子。

传统的英国主菜通常包括:肉食——牛肉(beef)、羊肉(lamb)和猪肉(pork);土豆——烤的(baked)、做成泥的(mashed)或炸的(fried),和青菜的组合搭配。开胃菜通常是沙拉(salad)或面包抹黄油(bread with butter)。甜点通常是蛋糕(cake)、水果拼盘(fruit cocktail)和冰淇淋。点菜的步骤一般是先点喝的,然后服务员会给你时间看整个菜谱,然后再点开胃菜和主菜。在你吃完这些以后,服务员会再给你甜点菜谱。

如果你没有时间来应付这些繁文缛节,那就尝试一下快捷的外卖(take away)。比如,土耳其肉串(kebab)、法国夹菜长面包(baguette)、美式双层奶酪汉堡(double cheeseburger)以及中国的炒饭(fried rice)和炒面(Chow Mien)。关于吃的词汇实在太多了,你只能寓教于"饿"了。

At the "Indian"

Waiter: Good evening, gentlemen, would you like to see the menu?
Dave: Yes please.
Waiter: Would you like to order something to drink while you look at the menu?
Dave: Yes please. We'll have four bottles of beer, please.
Waiter: Kingfisher or Cobra?
Dave: Cobra please.
Waiter: Thank you, sir.
Dave: And can we have some poppadoms please?
Waiter: Are you ready to order, sir?
Dave: Yes, please.
Waiter: Starters, sir?
Dave: Yes… we'll have one chicken tikka, a shami kebab, a sheek kebab and a prawn cocktail.
Waiter: Thank you, sir. And for the main course…?
Dave: Can we have one chicken tikka massala, a prawn vindaloo, lamb madras and a chicken korma?
Waiter: Yes sir. What kind of rice or bread?
Dave: Erm… We'll have a plain naan, and a peshwari naan… and we'll have a plain rice and a pilau rice.
Waiter: Thank you, sir.

In the Chip Shop

Woman: Next please.
Ben: Can I have a large cod and chips, please?
Woman: One large cod and chips… is that all?
Ben: No… we'll have a plaice and chips… and can we have extra batter with that? Erm… and a portion of mushy peas… oh and a steak and kidney pie.
Woman: One large cod'n'chips, a plaice'n'chips, one mushy peas and a steak'n'kidney pie. Anything to drink?
Ben: A can of Irn Bru and a Sprite.
Woman: That's £3.25… plaice'n'… £7.00… mushy… pie… erm… Irn… sprite… that's £14.60 altogether please, love. You'll need to wait five minutes for the plaice, all right, dear?
Ben: That's alright… here you are….
Woman: £50… I dunno… you students… have you got anything smaller?
Ben: Sorry… here's £20… is that better?

在印度餐馆里

服务员：晚上好，先生们。您要看看菜单吗？
戴夫：是的。
服务员：你们愿意在看菜单的时候先点些酒水吗？
戴夫：好的。我们就来4瓶啤酒吧。
服务员：翠鸟牌还是眼镜蛇牌？
戴夫：眼镜蛇。
服务员：好的，谢谢。
戴夫：还有，我们能不能先来点儿印度锅巴？
服务员：先生，您可以点菜了吗？
戴夫：是的。
服务员：您要开胃菜吗？
戴夫：是的，我们要一个酸奶腌鸡块、一个叙利亚肉串、一个葱香羊肉串和一份鸡尾虾。
服务员：好的，先生。那主菜呢？
戴夫：我们能不能要一个辣鸡肉汁饭、一个红酒蒜虾饭、辣油羊肉饭和椰香辣鸡饭？
服务员：好的，先生。你是要什么样的米饭或面包呢？
戴夫：嗯，我们要一个原味馕，和一个干果葡萄干馕……还有白米饭和肉油饭。
服务员：谢谢，先生。

在炸薯条店里

女人：下一位。
本：我能来一个大号鳕鱼和薯条吗？
女人：一个大鳕鱼和薯条。不要别的吗？
本：要，我们要一份欧鲽和薯条，能多放些面糊吗？嗯，还要一份豌豆酱。噢，再来一个肉排腰子饼。
女人：一个大鳕鱼配薯条、一个欧鲽配薯条，一个豌豆酱和一个肉排腰子饼。要喝的吗？
本：一罐儿艾恩布鲁和一罐儿雪碧。
女人：那是3镑25便士……欧鲽和……7镑……酱……饼……嗯……艾恩……雪碧……一共是14镑60便士，亲爱的。要欧鲽你得等5分钟，行吗，亲爱的？
本：好的，给你钱。
女人：50英镑。我不知道，你们这些学生，你没有零钱吗？
本：对不起，给您20。这回可以了吧？

Woman: Thank you, love... here you are... 5 pounds and 40p change. Do you want salt and vinegar on your chips?

In the Kebab Shop

Man: Yes mate?

Jeff: I'll have a large chicken donner please.

Man: One large chicken donner... You mate?

Jerry: Erm... small shish kebab please.

Man: One small shish... are you together?

Jeff and Jerry: Yeah, but could you make it separate?

Man: That's £4.20 for the donner, £4.00 for the kebab.

Jeff and Jerry: Here you go, mate.

Man: Do you want salad on these? Everything?

Jerry: No onions on the donner.

Man: OK... chilli sauce, garlic sauce, mate?

Jerry: Not on mine.

Jeff: I'll have both, please, mate.

Man: There you go... have a nice evening... see you.

女人：谢谢，亲爱的。给你，找你5镑40便士。你要往薯条上撒盐和醋吗？

在肉串店里

男人：要点儿什么，哥们儿？

杰夫：请给我一个大号鸡肉卷。

男人：一个大号鸡肉卷。你呢，哥们儿？

杰里：嗯，一个小号什锦肉串。

男人：一个小号什锦肉串。你们是一起的吗？

杰夫和杰里：是，但你能给我们分开算账吗？

男人：肉卷4镑20便士，肉串4镑。

杰夫和杰里：给，哥们儿。

男人：要往里放沙拉吗？全套？

杰里：肉卷里不要洋葱。

男人：好的。辣椒酱、蒜酱，哥们儿？

杰里：我不要。

杰夫：我两样都要，哥们儿。

男人：给。晚上愉快，再见。

实用短语

- Would you like to see the menu?　你要看看菜单吗?
- Would you like a drink?/Would you like to order something to drink?
  你要喝点儿什么吗?
- Are you ready to order, sir?　您准备好点菜了吗,先生?
- Yes, mate?　要点儿什么,哥们儿?
- You, mate?　你呢,哥们儿?
- What about you?　你呢?
- Next please.　下一个。
- Are you together?　你们是一起的吗?/要一块付账吗?
- Could you make it separate?　你能分开算账吗?
- Is that all?　还要别的吗?
- Chilli sauce, mate?　要辣椒酱吗,哥们儿?
- Do you want salt and vinegar on that?　你要往里放盐和醋吗?
- You'll need to wait five minutes for the plaice, alright, dear?
  要欧鲽你得等5分钟,行吗,亲爱的?
- Have you got anything smaller?
  你没有更小面值的货币吗?/你没有零钱吗?
- That's £14.60 altogether please, love.　一共是14镑60便士,亲爱的。
- We'll have… please.　我们要……
- And can we have some… please?　还有,我们能不能来点儿……?
- Could we have… and…?　我们能不能点……和……?
- Here you go, mate.　哥们儿,给。
- There you go.　给你,好了。

词汇表

can 罐
chicken 鸡肉
chilli sauce 辣椒酱
chips 薯条
Cobra 眼镜蛇牌啤酒
cod 鳕鱼
garlic sauce 蒜酱
Kingfisher 翠鸟牌啤酒

lamb 羊肉
menu 菜单
mushy peas 豌豆酱
naan 馕饼
onion 洋葱
order 点(菜)
plaice 欧鲽
plain 纯的/没有别的味道的

poppadoms 印度锅巴
portion 份
prawn cocktail 鸡尾虾
salad 沙拉
separate 分开的
starters 头盘/开胃菜
steak and kidney pie 肉排腰子饼
together 一起

第15章
超市购物
Shopping in the Supermarket

背景常识

在英国买东西,人们很少讨价还价(bargain)。这并不表示英国的物价总是公平合理,这不过是不同的商业文化罢了。对留学生来说,这倒让用英语购物简单了不少。

大型超市是在英国经常被讨论的社会话题。Tesco,ASDA,Morrisons 和 Sainsbury's,统称为"四大天王"(the Big 4),占据了英国 74% 的食品日用品零售市场。大型超市里提供从食物、衣服到电器的各种商品。

如果只选一个你必须记住的关于购物的词,那就是 Sale(特价销售)。在英国,特价销售活动都是实实在在的。特价销售前后的价格可以让你目瞪口呆。大部分商店都有规律地进行特价销售。如果你住在一个附近有不止一家超市的地方,你可能每天都能买到你需要的打折(discount)商品。有些商店有专门的学生折扣(student discount),但是你需要把你的国家学生会统发的学生卡(NUS Card)带在身上。从今年起,NUS 还将发行 NUS Extra Card 专门鼓励商家为学生提供折扣。

用英语购物有两大挑战。第一,当然是数字了。即使是英国人有时也分不清 40 和 14。如果你不敢肯定,你可以说这句话来确认:Is that four zero or one four? (你说的是 4-0 还是 1-4?)

另一个挑战是名词,各种水果、蔬菜、干调料(herbs)、酱料(sauces)、服装和洗漱用品(toiletries)的名字。

从以下的对话中你可以学到一部分。剩下的你就得慢慢积累了。超市也是一个课堂。而这个课堂里的知识往往比校园里那个课堂的知识更关乎生计。

At the Supermarket

Jie: Right. Here we are. Have you got the shopping list? Let's see. Pasta, rice, mince, mixed seafood, milk, salad stuff, fish, eggs, tea bags①, coffee, sugar, ketchup... oh, and pasta sauce.

Jun: Well, the fruits and vegetables are usually kept in the first aisle, near the entrance, so let's get the salad stuff first. Shall I get a trolley or a basket?

Jie: A trolley, I think.

Jun: OK... we need tomato, cucumber, coriander, lettuce... oh, look, they've got pak choi as well... shall we get some? And we'll② get some apples and pears... oh and these plums look nice.

Jie: Woah... hold on... we don't want to get so much that we can't eat it all... and don't get too many polythene bags... they're bad for the environment. In fact, I think we can probably get the fruit and veg down at the farmer's market... it'll be cheaper and fresher. Let's get the easy stuff first... pasta and rice; they are in the second aisle. Right... do we want spaghetti or pasta shells?

Jun: Pasta shells, I think... they're easier, aren't they?

Jie: OK... pasta shells it is. Now... rice... basmati rice? patna rice? Indian? Thai?

Jun: Thai rice, I think... I like the jasmine flavour it's got.

Jie: Mmm... scented. Right... let's look for the meat and the seafood... They'll③ be in the chiller cabinets.... Right... prime Irish minced beef... buy two packs, get one free. Is that OK?

Jun: Yes, fine.

Jie: Now for the seafood... we're making seafood pasta, right? So we need, like, a mixture... shrimps, mussels, oyster, cockles and stuff.... How about this... seafood mix? Two-for-one... £2.99. That's a good deal. Now... let's see, milk, coffee, tea bags... they're all round there. Are you ticking these off as we go?

Jun: Yes... don't worry.

Jie: Right, we need some tins of pasta sauce... where are they... excuse me [to shop assistant], where do you keep the pasta sauce?

Assistant: Aisle three, under condiments.

Jie: Thanks... oh look [to Jun], shall we have a look at the cooked-meat counter. Hello [to counter assistant], what are those things?

Assistant: They're Scotch eggs... like hard-boiled eggs wrapped in mincemeat. Do you want to try a bit?

Jie: Scotch? What? With whisky in them? Sure.

Assistant: No... there's no whisky in them. Scotch just means Scottish. Why don't you try something else... we've got pork pie, pork pie with egg in it, black pudding, sausages, haggis....

Jie: What's haggis?

Assistant: It's a traditional Scottish dish... minced lamb cooked with oatmeal and spices in a sheep's stomach... only, we use plastic, not sheeps' stomachs, these days.

在超市里

洁：好了，开始吧。你带购物单了吗？好的，让我们看看。空心面、大米、肉馅、混合海鲜、牛奶、沙拉配料、鱼、鸡蛋、袋泡茶、咖啡、糖、番茄酱……噢，对了，空心面酱。

军：水果和蔬菜一般放在第一排，靠近入口，所以先去买做沙拉用的东西吧。咱们是拿个手推车还是筐？

洁：手推车，我估计。

军：咱们需要西红柿、黄瓜、香菜、生菜……噢，看，他们这儿还有中国白菜，我们买点儿吧？我们还应该买点儿苹果和梨。噢，那些李子看起来不错。

洁：唔，等会儿。我们不能买太多了，到时候吃不完，而且也别拿那么多塑料袋，对环境不好。实际上，我觉得我们也许可以从农贸市场买到这些水果和蔬菜，更便宜也更新鲜。我们先去买容易的东西，空心面和大米，它们在第二排。哦，我们到底是要面条还是面片儿？

军：面片儿，我觉得。它们更容易做，不是吗？

洁：好，那就面片儿吧。现在，大米，是要巴斯马蒂米？巴特那米？印度米？还是泰国米？

军：泰国米，我觉得，我喜欢它的茉莉香味。

洁：嗯，加香的。好了，咱们去找肉和海鲜吧，它们应该在那些冰柜里。嗯，上等爱尔兰牛肉馅，买两包赠一包，怎么样？

军：好吧。

洁：该到海鲜了。我们是要做海鲜空心面，对吧？那么我们需要，比如虾、贻贝、牡蛎、乌蚌之类的混合包装。那包怎么样，海鲜大杂烩？买一赠一，2.99英镑，好价钱。现在，让我们看看，牛奶、咖啡、袋茶，它们都在这附近。你把我们买过的都划掉了吗？

军：是的，别担心。

洁：哦，我们还需要几听空心面酱，它们摆在哪儿？打扰一下 [对店员]，你们的空心面酱在哪儿？

店员：第3排，在调味品下面。

洁：谢谢。噢，看呐 [对军]，我们去看看熟肉柜台怎么样？你好 [对售货员]，那些东西是什么？

店员：那些是苏格兰蛋，煮熟的鸡蛋裹在肉馅里。你要试试吗？

洁：苏格兰？什么？那里面一定是有威士忌了？一定的。

店员：没有，里面没有威士忌。这只是说它是苏格兰产的。你要不要试试别的？我们还有猪肉饼、带鸡蛋的猪肉饼、黑布丁、香肠、肚包羊杂碎……

洁：什么是肚包羊杂碎？

店员：一道传统的苏格兰菜，用燕麦和辣味调料做的羊肉末，塞进羊胃里烹制，不过我们现在用塑料而不是羊胃。

注释
① tea bag 英国人很喜欢喝茶,但是大部分茶都是袋装的。
② 在口语中,will 和 want to 都可以有 should 的意思,表示提议。
③ will 这里表示推测,没有将来时的意思。

实用短语

- Right. Here we are. 我们到了/咱们开始吧。
- So let's get… 咱们买点儿……
- Shall I get a…? 我买一个……怎么样。
- And we'll get some… 我们应该买点儿……
- You don't want to buy too much… 你不应该买太多……
- And these plums look nice. 还有那些李子看起来也不错。
- Now for the… 现在轮到……
- Let's look for… 咱们找找……
- They'll be in… 它们在……
- OK… pasta shells it is. 好吧……就要面片儿。
- That's a good deal. 好交易/好价钱/好买卖。
- Excuse me, where do you keep…? 对不起,你们把……放在哪儿?
- Are you ticking these off as we go? 你把我们买过的都划掉了吗?
- Shall we have a look at… 我们去看看……吧。
- Do you want to try a bit? 你要试试……吗?
- Why don't you try…? 你要不要试试……?

词汇表

aisle 行/排
basket 篮子
buy-two-get-one-free 买二赠一
chiller cabinet 冰柜
condiments 调味品
cooked-meat 熟肉
coriander 芫荽(通称香菜)
cucumber 黄瓜
discount 折扣
environment 环境
haggis 肚包羊杂碎
jasmine flavour 茉莉花香味

ketchup 番茄酱
lettuce 莴苣/生菜
mince 馅/做成馅的
mixed seafood 混合装海鲜
oatmeal 燕麦
pack 包
pak choi 白菜(也叫 chinese lettuce)
pasta sauce 空心面酱
pasta shells 面片儿
pasta 空心面
polythene 聚乙烯/塑料

sausage 香肠
Scotch egg 苏格兰蛋
seafood mix 海鲜大杂烩
sheep's stomach 羊的胃
shopping list 购物单
spaghetti 面条/意大利面
spices 辣味调料
tomato 西红柿
trolley 手推车
two-for-one/buy-one-get-one-free 买一赠一

第16章
买衣服
Buying Clothes

背景常识

在英语中指内衣(underwear)的词包括：三角短裤(briefs)、平脚短裤(boxers)、睡裙(女)(slip)、胸罩(女)(bra)、睡衣(pyjamas)、睡袍(dressing gown)和衬裤(long johns)等等。这里有些词只在复数情况下才有衣服的意思。比如boxers,单数boxer是拳击手的意思。另外,它们中有些衣物是女性专用的。至于上衣(top),你可以穿衬衫(shirt)、T恤衫(T-shirt)、马甲(vest)、运动衫(sweater)、毛衣(jumper)、夹克衫(jacket)、羽绒服(parka)、大衣/风衣(coat)等等。下身衣服(bottom)中,中国学生知道trousers(裤子)、skirt(裙子)和shorts(短裤),这些都是统称。它们还可以被细分为牛仔裤(jeans)、散腿裤(baggies)、运动裤(sweatpants)、休闲裤(chinos/slacks)和七分裤(three-quarters)。西服(suit)、运动服(tracksuit)、男晚礼服(tuxedo)和女晚礼服(dress)是指上下身成套的衣服。大部分中国学生认为shoes是鞋的统称,但其实它也特指皮鞋。其他种类的鞋包括：靴子(boots)、凉鞋(sandals)、跑鞋(trainers)、运动鞋(sneakers)、拖鞋(flip-flops/slippers)。

布料包括：棉(cotton)、牛仔布(denim)、亚麻(linen)、尼龙(nylon)、皮革(leather)、羊毛(wool)、法兰绒(flannel)、帆布(canvas)、聚酯纤维(polyester)。

另外,买衣服鞋帽还要留心尺码。常用的尺码标准主要有英式、大陆式和美式3种。中国主要使用大陆尺码。一双在欧洲大陆43号的男鞋在英国就是9号,在美国就是9.5号。另外,别忽略英寸和厘米的区别。

In the Clothes Shop

Assistant: Hi there, are you looking for anything in particular?

Lisa: Yes, I'm looking for a woollen cardigan, and my boyfriend's looking for a pair of trousers.

Assistant: Well, we've got these lambswool cardigans. They've just come in... have a feel... they're really soft.

Lisa: Oooh, yes... that feels lovely. How much are they?

Assistant: Erm... let's see... £39.99. That's a pretty good price for real lambswool... and you can see that the quality is really good. Look... double stitching around the neck and under the arms... look here and here....

Lisa: Could I try one on?

Assistant: Sure... here, let me take your coat. The fitting room is over there. [*turning to Sam*] Maybe I can show you some of the trousers we've got.

Assistant: Here, we've got these chinos on sale... there's two styles... flat front and pleated front... and they look pretty cool and relaxed whatever your age.

Sam: Oh... these are like slacks... that's just what I was looking for. Could I try some of them on?

Assistant: Of course... what size are you?

Sam: 32 waist, 34 inside leg.

Assistant: [*turning to Lisa*] What do you think of the cardigan?

Lisa: It's really nice... I'll take it. Can I have a look around for some other stuff, though, while I'm waiting?

Assistant: Of course. Take your time.

Sam: [*comes out of the fitting room*] Hey, Lisa, what do you think?

Lisa: Erm... do you really want to know?

Sam: What do you mean?

Lisa: Well they're not really "you", are they? I mean, red's not really your colour, is it? Maybe beige would be better... or brown.

Sam: OK... but what about the fit?

Lisa: Well they look a bit tight on you... if you lost a bit of weight they might be OK... why don't you get the next size up?

Sam: Yes, but then they'll be too baggy, won't they?

Assistant: Could I suggest something? Maybe you could try these ones... they're the same style, but "slim fit"... the legs are narrower... then get a size 34 instead.

Sam: OK... let me try a couple of pairs on.... [*goes into fitting room*]

Assistant: Well, we've got a whole selection of them over here. Look, these are cotton... they're quite nice.

Lisa: Oooh, yes... I like this yellow one... can I just try it on?

Assistant: Sure….

Lisa: [*comes out of the fitting room*] Let's see… hmmm… I'm not sure now… maybe the colour's not quite right. What do you think?

Assistant: I think it looks nice… it probably won't go with the cardigan though.

Sam: OK, well, why don't I pay for this stuff and I'll meet you in the pub across the road when you've finished?

在服装店里

售货员：你好，你有什么具体要找的吗？

莉萨：是的，我想买一件羊毛衫，我男朋友要买条裤子。

售货员：我们有这种小羊毛的羊毛衫，刚刚到货。你摸摸，非常软。

莉萨：唔，真的，摸起来很舒服。多少钱？

售货员：嗯，我看看。39镑99便士，对小羊毛来说这可是很好的价钱。而且你也能看出来它质量有多好。看看，领子和胳膊后面都是双线的。看看这儿，还有这儿。

莉萨：我能试试吗？

售货员：当然，来，让我帮你拿大衣。试衣间在那边。[对萨姆说] 也许我能带你去看看我们卖的裤子。

售货员：这个，我们这儿有打折的休闲裤，一共两个款式，前面平整的和前面压裤线的。不管多大尺码，它们穿起来都又酷又舒适。

萨姆：哦，这些看起来像便裤，我要的正是这样的。我能试试吗？

售货员：当然，你穿多大号的？

萨姆：腰围是32，腿长34。

售货员：[对莉萨说] 你觉得那羊毛衫怎么样？

莉萨：非常好，我要了。我随便逛逛，再看看其他的东西，顺便等我的男朋友。

售货员：当然了，慢慢看。

萨姆：[从试衣间里出来] 嘿，莉萨，怎么样？

莉萨：嗯，你真想知道吗？

萨姆：你什么意思？

莉萨：这条裤子不适合你，不是吗？我是说，你不适合穿红色，对吧？米黄或棕色可能会好一些。

萨姆：好吧，但是大小合适吗？

莉萨：你穿起来有点儿紧，如果减减肥就可以了。你怎么不选大一号的呢？

萨姆：也行，但那就有点儿太拖拉了，不会吗？

售货员：我能提个建议吗？也许你可以试试这些款式。这两条是一个款式的，不过这个是紧身的，腿比较瘦，你可以穿34号。

萨姆：好，让我再试几条。[走进试衣间]

售货员：好的，我们有很多不同款式的裤子，在这边。这些是棉的，它们很不错。

莉萨：噢，对，我喜欢这个黄的，我能试试吗？

售货员：没问题。

莉萨：[从试衣间里出来] 让我看看。嗯，我不是很肯定，也许是颜色不太对。你觉得呢？

售货员：我觉得不错，但是跟那件羊毛衫可能不是很配。

萨姆：好吧，那要不然我先把这些买了，然后在路对面的酒馆里等你逛完怎么样？

实用短语

- Are you looking for anything in particular? 你有什么具体要找的吗?
- I'm looking for… 我想买……
- That feels lovely. 很舒服。
- Could I try one on? 我能试试吗?
- Maybe I can show you… 也许我能带你去看看……
- We've got… on sale. 我们有这些打折的……
- There's two styles. 一共两个款式。
- What size are you? 你穿多大号?
- What do you think of…? 你觉得……怎么样?
- Can I have a look around for…? 我能随便看看……吗?
- Take your time. 不着急慢慢看。
- They're not really "you". 这条裤子不适合你。
- Red's not really your colour. 你不适合穿红色。
- But what about the fit? 大小合适吗?
- They look a bit tight on you. 你穿起来有点儿紧。
- Why don't you get the next size up? 你怎么不选大一号的呢?
- They'll be too baggy, won't they? 但那就有点儿太拖拉了,不会吗?
- Maybe you could try these ones. 也许你可以试试这些款式。
- Let me try… on… 让我试试……
- I think it looks nice. 看上去不错。
- It probably won't go with the cardigan though. 它跟那件羊毛衫可能不是很配。

词汇表

baggy 拖拖拉拉(像个袋子似的)
beige 米黄
cardigan 羊毛衫
chinos 休闲裤
double stitching 双层的/双线的
fit 合适的
fitting room 试衣间
flat front 正面没有裤线的
go with… 为…相配

lambswool 小羊毛
leg 裤长
lose weight 减肥
lovely 好看的/舒服的
next size up/down (the) 大/小一号
pleated front 前面压裤线的
relaxed 舒适的

section 部分
slacks 便裤
slim fit 紧身的
style 款式
try… on 试某衣物
under the arms 胳膊下面(衣袖胳膊肘的部分)
waist 腰围

第17章
购　书
Buying Books

背景常识

　　跟在中国相比,在英国上大学需要买更多的书,而且书在英国要比在中国贵得多。学期开始前,老师都会开列读书单(reading list)。然后你就得按图索骥地去买书了。了解一些关于书的英语对你买书和将来课堂讨论都有好处。一本典型的学术书刊通常会由这些部分组成:封面(front cover)、扉页(title page)、版权页(publication information page)、前言(preface)、目录(contents)、图数目录(table of graphics or figures)、鸣谢(acknowledgements)、序(foreword)、编者按(editor's note)、内容简介(introduction)、正文章节(chapters)、结论(conclusion)、脚注(footnotes)、尾注(endnotes)、索引(index)、词汇表(glossary)、参考书目(bibliography)和封底(back cover)。

　　在中国,每门课可能都只有一本标准教科书(textbook)。这本书一般由权威的专家编写、国家级出版社出版,内容全面(comprehensive)且深入浅出(introductory)。全班所有的学生都读同样的内容。这一本书会在整个学期内使用。在很多情况下,只要从头到尾把这一本书背诵下来,就可以应付期末考试了。在英国,很少有老师会用仅仅一本权威的书来作为课程的基础。老师们倾向于为班级注入更多的出版物(publications)和观点(views),并在学期的不同阶段使用不同的书。有时他们甚至要求不同的学生读不同的资料,以便鼓励学生进行辩论和批判。

　　应该说,这两种教育方式各有千秋。中国的方式保证标准的教育成果。所有的学生都所"见"略同。英国的方法则更强调学术上的制衡和多样性。

At the Bookstore

Shop Assistant: Good morning. How can I help you?

Gang: Oh, hello. I was looking for Richard Dawkins' *The Selfish Gene*. Have you got it?

Shop Assistant: I'll just run a check on the computer. How do you spell the author's name?

Gang: Dawkins. D-A-W-K-I-N-S, Richard. The title of the book is *The Selfish Gene*.

Shop Assistant: Is it fiction or non-fiction?

Gang: Non-fiction. It's kind of science, but not academic.

Shop Assistant: Do you know who it's published by?

Gang: Sorry?

Shop Assistant: Who is the publisher?

Gang: Oh, I'm not sure… I know that it's quite well known.

Shop Assistant: Right, let's see① what we've got … Dawkins … Raymond, Dawkins… Rebecca, Dawkins… Richard… *The Ancestors' Tale*, Dawkins *A Devil's Chaplain*, Dawkins *The Selfish Gene*, first published 1976… Oxford University Press, 30th anniversary edition, 2006. Is that what you're after?

Gang: Yes, that's it.

Shop Assistant: It's downstairs in the basement, under Popular Science.

Gang: Thanks. I'm also looking for this….

Shop Assistant: Wang Shuo, *Please Don't Call me Human*. What is it?

Gang: It's a Chinese thriller.

Shop Assistant: Oh, sorry, we don't stock foreign language titles here. You'll need to go to a specialist bookshop. Have you tried Grant & Cutler in Soho②?

Gang: No… no… this is the English translation that I'm looking for.

Shop Assistant: Oh, right. Let's see… Wang Shuo… I'll try it with the title because sometimes we stock foreign authors under the first and sometimes under the second name, so it'll be quicker like this… *Please Don't Call Me Human*… Wang Shuo, 2002… right, used to have it in stock, but it's been remaindered.

Gang: Sorry?③

Shop Assistant: It's no longer in print. Chinese thrillers aren't really mass-market, you know….

Gang: I know… I just wanted to try something I've already read in Chinese in order to practise my English.

Shop Assistant: Well, you could try a bookshop called Crime In Store… that's opposite The British Museum. Failing that, you could try the second-hand bookshops in Charing Cross Rd.

Gang: Thanks.

在书店

售货员： 早上好。我能帮您做些什么？

刚： 噢，你好。我在找理查德·道金斯的《自私的基因》。你们这儿有吗？

售货员： 我用电脑查一下。作者的名字怎么拼？

刚： 道金斯。D-A-W-K-I-N-S，理查德。书的名字是《自私的基因》。

售货员： 是文学还是非文学？

刚： 非文学。类似科学读物，不过不是学术性的。

售货员： 你知道是哪里出版的吗？

刚： 什么？

售货员： 出版商是谁？

刚： 哦，我不敢肯定，比较有名的出版商就是了。

售货员： 好吧，看看我们都有什么，道金斯……雷蒙德，道金斯……丽贝卡，道金斯……理查德……《祖先的故事》，道金斯《魔鬼的传教士》，道金斯《自私的基因》，首版于1976年，牛津大学出版社，2006年30周年纪念版。你要找的是这个吗？

刚： 对，就是它。

售货员： 这本书在地下，在科普读物区。

刚： 谢谢。另外，我还要找这个。

售货员： 王朔，《千万别拿我当人》。这是什么？

刚： 中国悬疑小说。

售货员： 哦，对不起，我们不进外文书。你需要找一家专项书店。你去了索荷区的格兰特和卡特勒书店了吗？

刚： 不，不，我要找的是它的英文译本。

售货员： 哦，明白了。咱们看看，王朔。我拿书名来查，因为我们在给外国作家归类的时候，有时用名字，有时用姓，这样会快一些。《千万别拿我当人》，王朔，2002年版。我们原来是有的，不过已经被清货了。

刚： 什么？

售货员： 这本书已经不再印刷了。你也知道，买中国悬疑小说的人不那么多。

刚： 我猜也是。我只想读一本我看过中文版本的书，通过这样来练习英语。

售货员： 那么，你也许可以试试一家叫作犯罪商店的书店，就在大英博物馆的对面。如果那里也没有，你可以去查令十字街的那些二手书店看看。

刚： 谢谢。

注释

① Let's see　表示"我正在找"或"给我一些时间想想"。
② Soho　是伦敦市中心的一个区，也是中国城的所在。
③ Sorry?　表示没听清。

实用短语

- Have you tried…? 你试过/去过……吗?
- Well, you could try… 那,你可以到……试试。
- Failing that, you could try… 如果还不行,你可以试试……
- Let's see… 咱们看看……
- Right, let's see what we've got. 好的,来看看我们都有什么。
- I'll just run a check on… 我在……先查一下。
- I'll try it with the title. 我拿书名来查。
- Is that what you're after? 你要找的是这个吗?
- Who is the publisher? 出版商是谁?
- Do you know who it's published by? 你知道是谁出版的吗?
- Is it fiction or non-fiction? 是文学还是非文学。
- Sorry? 什么?

词汇表

anniversary 周年纪念
basement 地下室
be after… 要某物/寻找某物
British Museum 大英博物馆
chaplain 传教士
devil 魔鬼
fiction 文学(许多字典把 fiction 翻译成"小说",其实是不对的;诗歌和戏剧也都可以是 fictional;所以在书的分类上,fiction 应该是文学的统称)
in stock/out of stock 有货/卖完了
kind of 某种/类似…的
mass-market 大市场/买的人多
non-fiction 现实文学
Oxford University Press(OUP)牛津大学出版社(英国最大的出版社之一,许多学术用书都是它出版的)
please don't… 千万别…
popular science 科普读物
publish 出版
remaindered 清货/被廉价销售的(尤指书)
specialist bookshop 专项书店
stock 库存/囤积(尤指商店)
tale 故事/传说
thriller 悬疑小说或电影
title 书/书名/书目
well-known 出名的/众所周知的

第18章
课程和学分体制
Modules and the Credit System

背景常识

与中国的大学相比，英国大学给学生更多的自由。在大多数英国大学的本科学位课程中，必修（compulsory）课可能只有两三门。大量的选修（optional）课使你能自由设计自己的教育结构。虽然这一自由听起来很好，但是它也会给你带来不少负担（burdens）。对新生来说，选择适合自己兴趣和思维方式的课程是很复杂的。因此，在你做决定之前应该仔细参考课程手册（module handbook）并与导师交谈。在你把一门课选入你的课程表之前，你应该问自己四个问题：

首先，你对这门课的内容（subject-matter）是否感兴趣？仅仅因为某门课有一个令人眩目的（striking）标题，并不表示你真的对其有热情（be genuinely passionate）。第二，你是否喜欢这个老师？在选这个老师的课之前，读一些他写的东西或者旁听（audit）他的课。儒家文化把老师放在一个神圣的地位上，而在西方，学生对老师挑三拣四很正常。第三，你是否喜欢这门课的设计？大部分课程都是由讲座（lecture）和讨论课（seminar）组成的。如果你喜欢发言并从同学身上学习，那你就应该选择讨论课多于讲座的课程。第四，你对这门课的考核手段是否擅长？英国大学通常通过论文（essay）、考试（exam）和演讲（presentation）来综合考核学生。不过各种考核在总成绩中占的比重不一样。如果你在限时写作方面比较擅长，那么你就应该选择考试成绩比论文成绩占比重大的课。

你的课程选择也受学分体制的限制。中国家长经常听说某些神奇留学生在国外一年学完三年课程的传闻。这从学校管理制度上讲就是不可能的，更不要说欲速则不达的道理了。扎扎实实按规则出牌才是上策。

Walking on Campus

Adam: Hi Ann, I hear you're doing the MSc in Economics. Have you decided which modules you're going to take yet, then?

Ann: Well, in the first term I have to take "Microeconomics", "Macroeconomics", and "Econometric Theory and Methods". These are the compulsory modules, and they are all examined as well. Then in the second term I can choose four optional modules from two sets of modules... look... List A is "Game Theory", "Advanced Macroeconomic Theory", "Microeconometrics" and "Time Series Econometrics", and list B is "Topics in Money and Finance", "Economics of Development", "Economics of Government Regulation" and "Economics of Migration"... they're all very topical and I'm really interested in all of them. It's just a pity I don't have two years instead of one.

Adam: Poor you! Do you want me to help you choose your options?

Ann: OK. What do you think?

Adam: Well you spent a year working in a government department, didn't you? And you're interested in how the government is involved in economic development, so why don't you do "Economics of Development" and "Economics of Government Regulation", and then do "Game Theory" as well... that looks kind of cool and cutting-edge.

Ann: I know, but I've heard that the lecturers on those first two are not very inspiring ... it's often the case that the boring lecturers teach the exciting-looking courses and *vice versa*①, isn't it?

Adam: Yeah... I know what you mean. But at least your course looks, you know, practical and robust. Mine looks a bit airy-fairy, compared to yours.

Ann: Which course are you taking again? MA in "Comparative Literature"?

Adam: Yes, that's right. I'm doing a dissertation too. I'm not too worried about that because I did a foundation course at another university, and I had to write an 8000 word mini-dissertation there, plus about six long essays. Here, though, I've got to do two out of these three... "Modern Literary Theory", "Translation Studies", and the "Practice and Methodology of Comparative Literature". Then I have to choose three options from "Modern African literature and the West", "East Asian Literature and Modernity: China and Japan", "Literatures of South East Asia", "Chinese Literature in Translation", "Marxist and Postmodern Literary Criticism", and "Poetic Voices—Cross-cultural Interpretations".

Ann: Mmm, I see what you mean about it being airy-fairy. "Poetic Voices—Cross-cultural Interpretations"! What on earth does that mean?

走在校园里

亚当：嗨,安,我听说你学的是经济学硕士。你决定选什么课了吗?

安：第一学期,我必须选"微观经济学"、"宏观经济学"和"计量经济学的理论和研究方法"。这些都是必修课,而且都得考试。然后第二个学期我可以从两组课程中选4门课。你看,A表上有"博弈理论"、"高等宏观经济学理论"、"微观计量经济学"和"时间序列计量经济学"。B表上有"货币与金融简介"、"发展经济学"、"政府调控经济学"和"移民经济学"……这些都是很热门的课程,而且我对它们都感兴趣。我只有一年而不是两年的时间,真是太可惜了。

亚当：真可怜!你想要我帮你做选择吗?

安：好啊!你怎么想?

亚当：你不是在政府部门工作过一年吗?而且你又对政府如何涉足经济发展感兴趣,那你为什么不学"发展经济学"和"政府调控经济学"呢?然后学"博弈理论"。这看起来比较酷而且前沿。

安：我知道,但是我听说前面这两门课的老师都不是很吸引人。总是没意思的老师教有意思的课,有意思的老师教没意思的课,不是吗?

亚当：对,我明白你的意思。但是最起码你的课看起来,怎么说呢,实用而且富有生气。而我的课呢,跟你的比起来,都是空中楼阁。

安：你学什么来着?比较文学硕士?

亚当：对。我也得写毕业论文。但我不是非常担心,因为我在别的学校上过预科。在那儿我必须写8000字的小型结业论文,再加上6个长的普通论文。而在这里,我得在以下3个题目中写2个:"现代文学理论"、"翻译学"和"比较主义文学的实践与方法论"。然后我得在以下几门课里选3个:"现代非洲文学与西方"、"东亚文学与现代性:中国和日本"、"东南亚文学"、"翻译中的中国文学"、"马克思主义的和后现代的文学批判主义"、"诗歌的声音——跨文化解析"。

安：嗯,我明白你说空中楼阁是什么意思了。"诗歌的声音——跨文化解析",那到底是什么意思?

Adam: Well it's about, you know, how to identify and compare the different ways that poetry speaks to us across different cultures. It's a bit difficult to pin down precisely, but look—it's taught by James Beaney… he won a Nobel Prize ten years ago! I'm thinking of taking it.

Ann: What? So it's just reading poems and talking about them? That sounds like a doddle! I suppose it'll be interesting though….

Adam: Come on!② You know it's not like that! You're just trying to wind me up! Look, some of this stuff is vital in the understanding of the human condition and in bridging cultural perspectives between East and West. Look… Translation Studies and Modern Literary Theory are really important issues. Also, comparing the literatures of East and West can give much deeper insights into why we act as we do than just doing some shallow Business-type study of cross-cultural differences!

Ann: I know… I'm just kidding. But I'm pretty sure my course is going to give me more chance of a high-flying job! You'll probably end up working in a university… haha….

Adam: Well that may be true, but money and prestige aren't everything, are they? There's also beauty and truth… huh?

注释
① vice versa 是拉丁语，表示某观点反过来也成立；在学术英语中，简练的拉丁语是经常被使用的。
② come on 英语中最常用的一句口头禅。

亚当：那是关于，嗯，如何辨别和比较诗歌在不同文化中的表达方式。准确地定义是不容易的。但是，看呐，这门课是詹姆斯·比尼教的。他 10 年前得过诺贝尔奖！我在考虑选它。

安：什么？也就是说光是念诗和讨论诗？听起来有点儿弱智！但是我估计应该比较有意思。

亚当：别逗了！你知道我们的课不是那样的！你不过是拿我开玩笑罢了！有些东西对理解人类社会现状和促进东西方文化观点的交流是至关重要的。你想想，翻译学和现代文学理论就是很关键的课题。而且比较东西方文学可以使我们更深刻地认识我们当今的行为，比浅显的商学式的跨文化研究要深刻得多。

安：我知道，我跟你开玩笑的。但是我估计我的课程更有可能给我一个好工作！而你最后也许只能在大学里谋个职位，哈哈。

亚当：也许是吧，但是金钱和名望不能换来一切，不是吗？生活中还有美和真理。

实用短语

- ◆ Have you decided... yet? 你决定……了吗?
- ◆ These are the compulsory modules. 这些是必修课。
- ◆ Which courses are you taking again? 你又选了哪些课呢?
- ◆ What on earth does that mean? 那到底是什么意思?
- ◆ I have to take... 我必须学……
- ◆ I can choose... 我可以选……
- ◆ I'm really interested in... 我对……很感兴趣。
- ◆ It's a bit diffcult to pin down... 准确地定义……是不容易的。
- ◆ I'm thinking of taking... 我在考虑选……
- ◆ I've got to do... 我必须学……
- ◆ What on earch does that mean? 那到底是什么意思?
- ◆ I know what you mean./I see what you mean. 我明白你的意思。
- ◆ Well that may be true, but... 那也许是真的,但是……
- ◆ Come on! 算了吧/别逗了/正经点!
- ◆ You're just trying to wind me up! 你不过是拿我开玩笑罢了!
- ◆ I'm just kidding! 我跟你开玩笑的!

词汇表

a doddle (slang) 简单的事/白痴也可以做的事(俚语)
airy-fairy 空中楼阁
comparative 比较的/比较主义的
cool 冷/酷
cross-cultural 跨文化的
deep 深/深刻的
end up 最终成为/以……告终
foundation course 预科课程
Game Theory 博弈理论
government regulation 政府调控
high-flying 令人骄傲的
human condition 社会状态
insight 认识/深刻的认识
inspiring 吸引人的(话或个性)/发人深省的

interpretation 理解/解释/解析
kid 开玩笑
literary criticism 文学批判主义
literary theory 文学理论
Macroeconomics 宏观经济学
Marxist 马克思主义的
Microeconomics 微观经济学
migration 移民
modernity 现代(一个饱含争议的概念,可被粗略地定义为启蒙运动以后的,以科学和理性为核心的思想、社会和时代)
Nobel Prize 诺贝尔奖
on earth 到底/究竟

option 选项
perspective 观点/角度
pin down 定义/把握/确定/找到
pity 可惜的
poetic 诗歌的/有诗意的
Postmodern 后现代的
precisely 准确地
prestige 声望
Time Series Econometrics 时间序列计量经济学
vital 重要的
voice 言论/发言权(也有"声音/嗓音"的意思)
wind sb. up 拿某人开玩笑

第 19 章
安排课程表
Arranging Your Timetable

● 背景常识

在中国,学生们在开学的时候都会得到课程表(class schedule/timetable)。而在英国,因为每个学生选的课都不一样,你必须制作你自己的课程表。在最终敲定选课结果之前,你最好先确定你的课程表安排是否可行(viable)。与你的导师讨论这个问题。总的来说,在制订课程表时,你需要问以下5个问题:

第一,你课程表上的哪些项目在时间上是灵活的(flexible)?比如,在一门主要的课程里,一个老师可能在一周内不止一次地讲同一堂课。这样的话,你可以选择与其它课程不冲突的(clash)时段。第二,时间上不灵活的项目有没有冲突?如果你最喜欢的两节课都在星期一下午3点,而且每个星期都只上一次,那你就只能放弃(drop)其中一个了。第三,在空间上有没有冲突(conflict)?比如,如果你有两节课,一节在9点,一节在10点,而它们的教室却在校园的两个对角上。那么,在10分钟的课间休息内你很可能没有足够的时间赶到第二节课的教室。第四,你的时间表是否符合你的生活方式(lifestyle)?如果你的社交活动很多而且在凌晨3点才能睡觉,那你绝对不希望有很多早上9点的课。第五,你的安排是否给你足够的时间做作业、锻炼身体、打工或从事其他的事情?有些人喜欢把课程集中在星期二到星期四,这样就可以有四天的周末。不过周二到周四那几天过于疲劳,可能会影响学习效率。

安排自己的时间表是十分有挑战性的,尤其是对于习惯了学校包办一切的中国学生来说。在选课时有更多的自由是好事,但是正如西方人所说:没有责任就没有自由。正是这些责任使得在英国的留学经历如此有趣并发人深省。

Tutor's Office

Tutor: Oh, hello Jim. Come in. How are you finding your first week?

Jim: Not too bad... apart from my timetable this term. I can't get my head round it. In China we don't have so much choice and I'm finding it all very confusing.

Tutor: OK... let's see what we can do. Have you got your term one lecture and tutorial schedule with you?

Jim: Yes... here you are. The problem is with my Business Studies classes... I've got my Academic Writing class on Tuesday at nine, and it clashes with my Business Studies seminar.

Tutor: OK... let me have a look. The first thing we need to look at is which items here are moveable... which ones you have some flexibility on. Because there are so many Chinese students doing Business Studies, you've got some flexibility on when you do the seminars. If you can't do it on Tuesday at nine, then you can do it on Thursday at eleven o'clock. All right?

Jim: Yes, but I have a Development Studies lecture on Thursday at eleven.

Tutor: Ah... yes... that looks like a bit of a problem, doesn't it? It looks as though you're going to have to drop one of these options because of the clash. Let's have a look at the module handbook and see what other options there are... look... there's International Relations... are you interested in that? Some of the issues that are in that course will be broadly comparable to what you look at in Development Studies anyway... you know... theories of colonialism, politics, aid issues as well... why don't you do Business Studies and International Relations instead?

Jim: I suppose I could, but the problem is that I don't really know anything about politics and colonialism.

Tutor: Yes, but you've put down on your preferences form that you don't know anything about Business either, but that you want to do it anyway... why's that?

Jim: Well, it's important for my future.

Tutor: Well I think you'll find that studying International Relations will probably make you better at Business Studies... it'll give you a different, more academic, perspective on things.

Jim: OK then... if I do the Academic Writing class on Tuesday at nine, I can do the Business Studies lecture on Wednesday, and the seminar on Thursday at eleven. Right, when are the International Relations classes?

Tutor: Tuesday afternoon at three is the lecture, and Friday afternoon at one is the seminar time. Can you do that?

Jim: Let's see... hmmm... how long is the lecture? One hour?

Tutor: Yes.

Jim: OK... but it's going to be a tight squeeze... I have a Research Methods class at four o'clock on Tuesday.

Tutor: I'm sure the Research Methods teacher won't mind you being five minutes late… all classes actually begin at five minutes past the hour, and end at five minutes to the hour anyway. That's to give people time to switch between rooms.

Jim: OK then… it looks as if I've got Wednesday afternoons free… that's good. I do *kung fu*, and I've just joined the martial arts club… they have a practice session every Wednesday afternoon.

老师办公室

老师：噢，吉姆，你好。进来。你开学第一周怎么样？

吉姆：除了我这个学期的时间表以外，不算太坏。我对它有点儿搞不明白。在中国我们没有这么多选择，我对这一切都很糊涂。

老师：好吧，看看咱们能做些什么。你带你的第一学期讲座与讨论课课程表了吗？

吉姆：带了，在这儿。有问题的是我的商学课程。我的学术写作课是星期二9点，这跟我的商学讨论课相冲突。

老师：嗯，让我看看。首先我们需要考虑的是哪些课可以变动，哪些可以灵活对待。由于学商学的中国学生很多，你上讨论课的时间是可以灵活处理的。如果你星期二9点没有时间，那可以上星期四11点的那一节。怎么样？

吉姆：可以，但是我星期四11点有发展学的讲座。

老师：啊，是的，看起来是有点儿问题。因为课程冲突，你可能不得不放弃其中一门。来看看课程手册上有没有其他选择。看，国际关系，你对这个感兴趣吗？这门课的内容和你在发展学里要学的差不多。比如，关于殖民主义、政治、国际援助等问题的理论。你为什么不改成商学和国际关系学呢？

吉姆：我估计可以，但问题是我对政治和殖民主义一点儿也不了解。

老师：但是在你的学习倾向表上你也说对商学一无所知，可你却仍然想学它。这是为什么呢？

吉姆：哦，它对我的将来很重要。

老师：我认为你会发现学习国际关系对你的商学学习有帮助。它将给你一个不同的学术性更强的世界观。

吉姆：那好吧。如果我星期二9点上学术写作，就可以在星期三上商学讲座，星期四11点上商学讨论课。对了，国际关系的课都在什么时候？

老师：讲座星期二下午3点，讨论课是星期五下午1点。你能在这些时间上课吗？

吉姆：让我想想。嗯，一节讲座多长时间？一小时？

老师：对。

吉姆：好吧，但是我得马不停蹄才行。我星期二4点有研究方法课。

老师：我肯定研究方法课的老师不会介意你迟到5分钟的。实际上所有课都是在整点过5分的时候才开始，整点前5分钟就结束。那就是为了给人时间从一个教室赶到另一个教室。

吉姆：那好。这样看起来我星期三下午比较空闲，这很好。我练习中国功夫，而且我已经加入了武术俱乐部。他们的练习时段是每个星期三下午。

实用短语

- How are you finding…?   你觉得……怎么样?
- Not too bad… apart from…   不算太坏……除了……
- I can't get my head round it.   我对它有点儿搞不明白。
- I'm finding it all very confusing.   我对这一切都很糊涂。
- Let's see what we can do.   让我们看看能做些什么。
- The first thing we need to look at is…   我们首先要考虑的是……
- If you can't do it on… then you can do it on…
  如果你不能在……(时间)做这件事,那你还可以在……(时间)做它。
- That looks like a bit of a problem, doesn't it?   看起来是有点儿问题,不是吗?
- It looks as though you're going to have to…   这样看起来你似乎不得不……
- I suppose I could, but the problem is that…   我估计可以,但问题是……
- OK then… it looks as if I…   那好吧……看起来我……
- All classes actually begin at five minutes past the hour, and end at five minutes to the hour.   实际上所有课都是在整点过5分时才开始,整点前5分就结束。

词汇表

Academic Writing 学术写作
aid 援助(在政治学中通常作 international aid)
broadly comparable 大致上差不多
clash 冲突/碰撞
colonialism 殖民主义
drop 放弃
flexible/flexibility 灵活的/灵活性
instead 取而代之地
International Relations 国际关系学

kung fu 中国功夫
martial arts 武术
moveable 可以变动的
practice session 练习时段
preferences form 学习倾向表
put down 写下/明确表示
Research Methods 研究方法
schedule
switch 变/换成

tight squeeze 时间紧的状态/马不停蹄
timetable 时间表(在大部分情况下,schedule 和 timetable 是可以互换的;但 timetable 尤指那些循环的、有规律的事项,比如每周的课程;schedule 有时有"日程安排"的意思)
viable 可行的

第20章
上课第一天
First Day in Class

背景常识

现在,你已经到了英国,找到了住宿,付了各种账单,在警察局和医院完成了注册,开了银行账户,学会了如何使用学校硬件设施,购买了日常用品,加入了社团,选了课而且解决了时间的问题,是该从事你的主要使命——上课了。在你第一次走进英国的教室之前,你应该闭上眼睛并深吸一口气(take a deep breath),深刻回味一下你到今天为止克服(overcome)的所有困难。你唯一应该说的一个词就是wow(哇塞)。

第一印象(first impression)总是非常关键的。而且,作为留学生,你应当在你的老师和同学们面前展示(present)一个有自信(confidence)、富有个性(personality)和独特魅力(charm)的自己。对英国学生来说,中国是遥远(distant)而神秘(mysterious)的。你应当让他们的好奇心为你服务。学术上,你要敢于表达与公认常识(received wisdom)不同的观点(alternative)。在英国,与那些正确但墨守成规的学生相比(clichéd),老师更喜欢那些错误但敢于创新的学生。

一般来说,学生们在第一堂课里往往要介绍自己。所以,应当构思一段简短而令人印象深刻的自我介绍,包括你是谁、从哪来、为什么选这门课和你今后几年的计划。

英国的课堂气氛通常比中国课堂要轻松很多(more relaxed)。你甚至可以在教室里吃喝,只要不影响别人。当然,对你来说,第一堂课可能是既令人兴奋也令人沮丧和恐惧的。适应新的学习环境需要时间。留学跟谈恋爱其实差不多,一开始都会有些紧张。

In a Foundation Course Class

Convenor: Good morning. My name is Tom and I'm the convenor for this course. You'll be seeing a lot of me during the next nine months because I am responsible for organizing your timetables and the teaching schedules, as well as the assignments deadlines and exams. I just need to get a bit of admin out of the way, and then I'll be asking you to introduce yourselves to each other. Right. First of all, I just need to check that everyone is here… can you say "yes" or "here" or something when I call your name out…? Right… Al Khalifa, Fatima… Bourgas, Kamel… Chen Xue… Du Yue….

Later

Convenor: Right… I'm going to ask you to get into pairs. That means, speak to the person next to you and find out as much about them as possible. You want to know about how to spell their names, where they are from, their educational background, why they are studying on this course and their plans for the future. Also try to find out about their hobbies and interests, and what they want to do in their spare time here. OK… I'll give you about fifteen minutes, then you can feed back to the group. Remember to take notes.
Yue: Hello… I'm Du Yue, from Shandong in China. What's your name and where are you from?
Fatima: Fatima Al Khalifa… I'm from Bahrain.
Yue: Oh… erm… sorry… where?
Fatima: Bahrain… it's a small island in the Gulf near Saudi Arabia….
Yue: Oh… I'm no good at geography… ha ha. How do you spell your name?
Fatima: F-A-T-I-M-A, A-L, K-H-A-L-I-F-A

15 Minutes Later

Convenor: All right, could you all listen please? I'm going to ask you all to take turns introducing your partner. Fatima… could you introduce Yue please?
Fatima: OK… this is Elizabeth Du… Elizabeth is her English name, but her Chinese given name is Yue. I think it's a bit weird having an English name as well as your own, but there you go… she's from Shandong and she is 22 years old. She graduated in Economics from Qingdao Ocean University, and she is doing Development Studies here because she wants to know about the main issues to do with economic development in China… in particular, population and development. I think this is quite interesting. She's an only child. Her parents are teachers….
Yue: No. My mother is a teacher. My father is a civil servant.
Fatima: Oh, sorry… right, and her hobbies are reading and surfing the Internet. She likes nightlife and is very sociable and she wants to get to know a lot of British students.

Later

Convenor: OK… any questions?

Yue: I have a question. What if I want to complain about a lecture or a lecturer?
Convenor: Right… that's good… protocol… we hope that you will be satisfied with the teaching provision on this course. However, if you have any problems you should have a word with your lecturer first of all. It's only polite to tell the person involved directly. So, please, if you are unhappy with what a teacher or a lecturer is doing, try to talk to them… you'll find them very understanding.

在预科班里

组织老师：早上好。我的名字叫汤姆，我是这门课的组织老师。今后 9 个月里你们会经常见到我，因为我负责安排你们的教学日程，还有作业的上交日期和考试。我需要先解决一些行政问题，然后我会让你们互相介绍一下。好了，首先，我查查是不是所有人都到齐了。当你听到自己的名字的时候，请说"是"或者"到"或者别的什么。奥·卡立伐，法蒂玛……保加斯，坎莫尔……陈雪……杜月……

稍后

组织老师：好了，我要让你们组成对儿。也就是说，跟你身边的那个人说话并尽量了解他们。你需要知道他们的名字怎么拼写，他们从哪里来，他们的教育背景，他们为什么学这门课和他们的未来计划。同时，再问问他们的爱好和兴趣，他们平时没事的时候干什么。好了，我给你们 15 分钟，然后你们再向全班反馈。记住做笔记。
月：你好。我的名字叫杜月，来自中国北京。你叫什么名字？从哪儿来？
法蒂玛：法蒂玛·奥·卡立伐，我是从巴林来的。
月：哦，嗯，对不起，哪儿？
法蒂玛：巴林，海湾地区的一个靠近沙特阿拉伯的小岛。
月：噢，我的地理不是很好，哈哈。怎么拼你的名字？
法蒂玛：F-A-T-I-M-A, A-L, K-H-A-L-I-F-A。

15 分钟以后

组织老师：好了，安静下来吧。我要你们轮流介绍你们的搭档。法蒂玛，你能给我们介绍一下月吗？
法蒂玛：好的。这是伊丽莎白·杜，伊丽莎白是她的英文名字，她的中文名字是月。我觉得有自己的名字又再起一个英文名字很奇怪。不过下面就是她。她来自山东，22 岁，从青岛海洋大学毕业，学习经济学。她在这儿学发展学是因为她希望了解中国经济发展的问题，具体地说，是人口和发展的问题。我觉得这很有意思。她是独生女。她的父母是老师……
月：不，我妈妈是老师，我爸爸是公务员。
法蒂玛：哦，对不起，好的。她的爱好是读书和上网，她喜欢夜生活，非常善于交际，而且她想认识很多的英国学生。

稍后

组织老师：好了，有什么问题吗？
月：我有一个问题。我如果要投诉一堂课或一个老师该怎么办？
组织老师：好，问得好。按规矩……我希望你们对这门课里的教学和服务感到满意。但是，如果你有任何问题，你应该首先与你的老师谈谈。直接告诉当事人是起码的礼貌。所以，如果你对哪个老师的做法不满意，请你跟他们交流。你会发现他们非常善解人意。

实用短语

- Where's that, exactly?　到底在哪儿？
- How do you spell your name?　怎么拼你的名字？
- Tell me something about your family.　跟我说说你的家庭。
- Why are you doing this course?　你为什么学这门课？
- What do you want to do afterwards?　你以后想干什么？
- I mean, after you graduate?　我是说你毕业以后？
- What do you do in your spare time?　你没事的时候干什么？
- Turn… to your advantage. /Use… to your advantage.　让……为你服务/使……变成你的优势。
- To have a word with…　跟……交谈。
- It's only polite to…　……是起码的礼貌。
- What if…?　如果……怎么办？

词汇表

Bahrain 巴林
complain 抱怨/投诉
convenor 组织老师
deadline 上交时间/截止日期
feed back 反馈
find out 发现/搞清楚
get into pairs 组成对儿
get to know 了解
gulf 海湾（gulf 表示"海湾"，可以是任何海湾；the Gulf 是指"海湾地区"，也就是波斯湾沿岸的国家）
hobbies and interests 爱好和兴趣
island 岛
nightlife 夜生活
only child 独生子女
protocol 规范/条例
Saudi Arabia 沙特阿拉伯
see a lot of sb. 经常见某人
sociable 可交往的/善于社交的
spare time 空闲时间
student handbook 学生手册
surf 冲浪
take notes 做笔记
the person involved 当事人
there you go 给/看吧/怎么样/我说了吧
weird 奇怪

第21章
提问题
Asking Questions

背景常识

我们都知道在英语中关于提问的基本语法。一个问句的开头通常是：what（什么）、where（哪里）、when（什么时候）、who（谁）、which（哪个）、why（为什么）、how（怎么样），或者助动词 be（是不是）、do（做没做）、have（有没有/是否已经）、can（能不能）、should（应不应该）、will（会不会）或 must（是否必须）——没什么大不了的（no big deal）。不过，一个好问句需要的不仅仅是正确的语法。

比如，你可以用"究竟（exactly/precisely）"或"到底（on earth）"之类的词来强调你提问的语气。比较 When will Blair stand down?（布莱尔什么时候才下台？）和 When exactly/on earth will Blair stand down?（布莱尔究竟/到底什么时候下台？）这两句话，后者明显语气更强。

有时，一个问题并不需要回答，因为它自己就包含着答案。这一类问句叫作修辞性问句（rhetorical question），其实就是汉语里的反问句。一个设计修辞性问句的简单方法，就是用肯定结构表否定，否定结构表肯定。比较 Don't you love me? 你难道不爱我吗？（其实是爱的）和 Do you love me? 你爱我吗？（不见得爱）提问的人心中早已有了设想的答案。

还有，当中国学生用英语问问题的时候，他们经常对词序感到困惑。在英语中，人们说 What is your name? 但是在中文里，正确的问法应该是"你的名字是什么？""什么"和"你的名字"的位置在英汉互译的时候是相互对调的。

然而，不要把我们上面说的当作语法规则来记忆。语法有它存在的道理，你必须理解它。你从来不背汉语语法，却可以听出别扭的句子。英语语法也一样。如同打太极拳，无招胜有招。

In an Introductory Seminar about Britain

Tutor: Tell me then, what's the difference between England, Britain, Great Britain and the UK?

Leon: Isn't England part of Britain, along with Scotland, Wales and Northern Ireland?

Tutor: Almost correct. Strictly speaking, Britain only refers to the island, which is made of England, Wales and Scotland. If you count Northern Ireland in, then it becomes the UK.

Fang: But people sometimes use England, Britain or Great Britain to mean the entire UK, right?

Tutor: That is right. The UK is in fact a quite young and dynamic political entity. Who knows when the UK was first formed?

Tahira: Was it 1707?

Tutor: Excellent! 1707 was the year when England, Wales and Scotland first formed the United Kingdom of Great Britain. From 1801 to 1921, the UK also included the whole of Ireland. Since then, Ireland has been divided into two and the northern part remains in the UK, hence the United Kingdom of Great Britain and Northern Ireland.

Leon: How does Britain differ from Great Britain then?

Tutor: Anyone want to take this one?①

Fang: I am not sure, but I guess it has something to do with the small islands around Britain.

Tutor: Good guess... Great Britain refers to the island of Britain and the small islands around it.

Tahira: Could you also explain a little about the British Commonwealth?

Tutor: Of course, the Commonwealth of Nations, as it is formally known, is a loose association of countries and overseas territories that used to be British colonies. Members of the Commonwealth share similar cultures and values, have similar political and legal systems, and cooperate in areas such as trade and education.

Leon: How many members are there?

Tutor: There are about 50 independent countries and 25 overseas territories.

Tahira: Which countries and territories are in the Commonwealth, for instance?

Tutor: The independent countries include the UK, Australia, New Zealand, Canada, Bangladesh, Cyprus, Fiji, Cameroon and so forth. Overseas territories include Bermuda, Gibraltar and the British Virgin Islands....

Fang: Why would the former colonies want to remain associated with the UK, after becoming independent?

在英国简介讨论课上

老师： 下面告诉我，英格兰、不列颠、大不列颠和联合王国之间有什么区别？

利昂： 英格兰不是跟苏格兰、威尔士和北爱尔兰一样是不列颠的一部分吗？

老师： 基本正确。严格地说，不列颠仅指由英格兰、威尔士和苏格兰组成的这个岛。如果你算上北爱尔兰，那就是联合王国了。

芳： 但是人们有时用英格兰、不列颠或大不列颠来表示联合王国，对吗？

老师： 对。联合王国实际上是一个很年轻而富有活力的政治实体。谁知道联合王国最早成立的时间？

塔希拉： 是1707年吗？

老师： 很好！英格兰、威尔士和苏格兰在1707年最早成立大不列颠联合王国。从1801年到1921年，这个联合王国还包括了整个爱尔兰。从那以后，爱尔兰就被一分为二，北方的部分依然保留在联合王国，也就是现在的大不列颠和北爱尔兰联合王国。

利昂： 那，不列颠和大不列颠有什么区别呢？

老师： 谁愿意回答这个问题？

芳： 我不敢肯定，但我猜它跟不列颠周边的小岛有关。

老师： 猜得好，大不列颠指不列颠岛和它周边的小岛。

塔希拉： 您能不能再稍微解释一下英联邦？

老师： 当然可以，英联邦，作为它正式的称谓，是一个松散的由国家和海外领地组成的联合会，这些国家和海外领地都是英国以前的殖民地。英联邦的成员国家拥有相似的文化和价值观。他们的政治和法律体制也相似。在贸易和教育领域他们互相合作。

利昂： 那它共有多少成员呢？

老师： 一共有将近50个独立国家和25个海外领地。

塔希拉： 哪些国家和领地在这个联邦中？举几个例子。

老师： 独立国家包括英国、澳大利亚、新西兰、加拿大、孟加拉、塞浦路斯、斐济和喀麦隆等等。海外领地包括百慕大、直布罗陀和英属维京岛等。

芳： 为什么那些前殖民地在得到独立以后，仍然想与英国保持关系？

Tutor: Well actually, there are two major reasons. First, the Commonwealth is a voluntary association. It is not an empire. Members can withdraw freely, and they are not bound to comply with the Commonwealth's decisions. So there must be some benefits, if they choose to cooperate. Second, for some countries and territories, because they have been British colonies for so long, they have been deprived of a self-sustaining economic and political system. So, if Britain suddenly gave them independence and left them alone, they could fall into chaos and civil war.

Tahira: I heard that the Queen of the UK is the head of state of all Commonwealth countries. Is that true?

Tutor: No, the Queen is the head of the Commonwealth. There are 15 countries that recognise the British Monarch as their head of state. A few others have their own monarchs. Half of the Commonwealth countries are not monarchies at all; they are republics. The head of state is only a symbolic position; she has no actual power.

注释 ① 口语中省略了 does;原句应当是 Does anyone want...。

老师：事实上，有两个原因。第一，它是一个自愿联合体而不是一个帝国。成员可以自由退出，而且它们也不必服从联邦的决定。所以，既然它们选择合作，那说明这里是有利可图的。第二，对于某些国家和领地来说，它们作为英国殖民地这么长时间，已经被剥夺了可独立生存的经济和政治体系。所以，如果英国突然让他们独立并对其置之不理，它们可能会陷入混乱和内战。

塔希拉：我听说英国女王也是所有英联邦国家的国家元首。这是真的吗？

老师：不，女王是整个英联邦的元首。其中有15个国家认可英国君主为它们的国家元首。还有几个国家有自己的君主。英联邦里有一半的国家都不是君主制，他们是共和制。国家元首是一个标志性的职位，没有实际权力。

实用短语

- ◆ What's the difference between... and...? ……和……之间的区别是什么？
- ◆ Shall we begin with...? 让我们以……来开始怎么样？
- ◆ What do you know about...? 你们对……都知道什么？
- ◆ Who knows when the UK was first formed? 谁知道联合王国是什么时候成立的？
- ◆ How does Britain differ from Great Britain? 不列颠和大不列颠之间的区别是什么？
- ◆ Which countries and territories are in the Commonwealth? 这个联邦包括哪些国家和领土？
- ◆ Why would the former colonies want to...? 这些前殖民地为什么要……？
- ◆ Can someone give me some examples of...? 谁能给我几个……的例子？
- ◆ Anyone want to take this one? 谁愿意回答这个问题？
- ◆ I guess it has something to do with...? 我猜它跟……有关。
- ◆ Could you also explain...? 你能不能也解释一下……？
- ◆ Isn't England part of Britain? 英格兰不是不列颠的一部分吗？
- ◆ Was it 1707? 是1707年吗？
- ◆ People sometimes use Britain to mean the entire UK, right? 人们有时用不列颠来表示整个英国，对吗？

词汇表

and so forth 等等（与and so on 是一个意思）
association 联合/集会/协会
be bound to 被约束于…
be made of… 由…组成
Commonwealth 联邦（federation 也是联邦的意思，不过federation 有一个中央政府；commonwealth 要更松散）
comply with 服从

cooperate 合作
dynamic 富于变化的
former 前/以前的/前者
has something to do with… 与…有关
head of state 国家元首
hence 基于此，从此
monarch 君主
monarchy 君主制
overseas territories 海外领地

remain 仍然是/保持某状态
republic 共和制/共和国
self-sustaining 可依靠自己独立生存的
such as 比如
symbolic position 标志性的职务
the Queen 英国女王
the United Kingdom of Great Britain and Northern Ireland 大不列颠及北爱尔兰联合王国

第22章
敷衍搪塞
Hedging Answers

背景常识

对于任何一个问题来说，通常都有3种答案——正确答案、错误答案和"我不知道"。在中国教育中，因为考试总有标准答案(standard answer)，一个好学生是一个能够回答出正确答案的人。但是，在英国教育中，一个好学生有时需要能够使错误答案听起来正确，或者使"我不知道"听起来内容丰富(informative)、博大精深(knowledgeable)。因此，能做到"不知为知之"也是一门艺术。

比如，面对这样一个问题：What do you think is the reason behind the failure of America's second war on Iraq?（你觉得美国在第二次伊拉克战争中失败的原因是什么？）这个问题很难说，不过你不必直接回答。I don't think America failed. I can't say what the reason behind the failure is, because there is no failure to begin with.（我不认为美国失败了。我没法告诉你它失败的原因，因为这个失败本身就是不存在的。）这样一来，通过质疑这个问题的前提(premise)，你就可以从一个难缠的问题中解脱出来。

另外，当你对某个答案没有完全把握的时候，不要使用太肯定的语气。比如，不要说 A is B 而说 A is likely to be（可能是）B，或者 A appears to be（看起来是）B。你可以说这是投机取巧，也可以说是治学严谨、实事求是。即使是书本上得来的知识，没有通过验证就不能轻易确定。

你会发现你们班里善辩的(eloquent)同学经常使用这些伎俩。他们这样做的能力也往往受到老师的赞赏(praise)。但是，你也不应该总依靠这些伎俩。在大多数时间里，实际上，你还是应该阅读规定的书目并直接而诚实地回答问题。毕竟，口才和知识都是教育的目的。

During Dr. Robinson's Office Hours

Dr. Robinson: Hello Alan, I've called you in to see me because I'm a bit concerned about the way you've written this essay... look... you've written this... "Everyone knows that companies need missions. Mission statements are statements of a company's overall purpose. They are succinct, distinctive and broad in scope. They have to be lacking in statistics and full of rhetoric. All mission statements aim to answer the question, 'what business are we in?'..." Can you see anything wrong with it?

Alan: No.

Dr. Robinson: OK, let me ask you. You've written, "Everyone knows,"... well, my question is, "Do they, indeed? My mother doesn't! Neither do my friends in my local pub!" You can't go making wild claims and blanket statements like that.

Alan: Well, I guess what I meant is, everybody in Business Studies knows....

Dr. Robinson: Really? Are you telling me① that no one in the entire academic world disputes the importance of mission statements?

Alan: Oh... but our textbook said it is important. I just generalised a little to sound more convincing.

Dr. Robinson: Ah... now② that's the problem. If you borrow an idea from a book, you have to remian true to the author's meaning. You can't bend the text to fit your argument. Also, books are not always right. You can't just lift an idea from a textbook without thinking about whether it is valid or not. In other words, you are being uncritical here.

Alan: But, why would I criticise a book that supports my argument? Wouldn't that make my argument sound weak?

Dr. Robinson: Maybe to you it indicates confidence and conviction in the writer. However, in British academic culture the strength of an argument comes from analysis and evidence. People do not believe you just because you are absolutely sure; they do so because you are rigorous.

Alan: Then, how would you suggest I should write it instead?

Dr. Robinson: For instance, "More and more companies seem to feel that they need to publish a mission statement." This way, no one would be able to challenge you, because vague words like "more and more" and "seem to" leave you a lot of space to manuovre. So, instead of saying "something is true", you could say "something might be true, if...", "something appears to be true", "it is arguable whether something is true" or "it is reasonable to say something is true". Now... can you make the second sentence sound more hedged too?

Alan: Right, let's see... "Mission statements can be said to be statements of a company's overall purpose."

罗宾逊博士的办公时间

罗宾逊博士：你好,艾伦。我叫你来是因为我对你写论文的方式有点儿担忧。看,你写的"人人都知道,公司需要使命。使命声明是关于公司总体目的的陈述文件。它们简练、有特色并且范围广泛。要省略统计数据而富于修辞。所有的使命陈述的目的是回答这个问题:我们是做什么生意的?"你看出有什么不妥吗?

艾伦：没有。

罗宾逊博士：好,那我来问你。你写了"人人都知道,"我的问题是:真的人人都知道吗?我妈就不知道!我当地酒馆里的朋友们也不知道!你不能像这样无凭无据地一概而论。

艾伦：其实,我想我的意思是,商学界里人人都知道。

罗宾逊博士：真的吗?你是在告诉我,整个学术界没有一个人会质疑使命声明的重要性吗?

艾伦：哦,教科书上说它很重要。我只不过是把它概括了一下,让它听起来更有说服力。

罗宾逊博士：哈,这就是问题所在!如果你从书上借鉴一个观点,你就必须忠实于作者的原意。你不能扭曲书上的文字来为你的论证服务,而且书并不一定总是正确的。你不能只把观点从书上抄下来而不去思考它是否可靠。也就是说,你没有批判性。

艾伦：但是,我为什么要批判支持我观点的书呢?那不会使我的论证听起来没有力量吗?

罗宾逊博士：也许,对你来说,这表现出作者的自信和坚定。但是,在英国学术文化里,一个论证的说服力来自于分析和证据。别人相信你不会因为你毫无保留地肯定,而是因为你治学严谨。

艾伦：那你认为我应该怎么写呢?

罗宾逊博士：比如说:"越来越多的公司似乎感到他们需要发布他们的使命声明。"这样,没有人能对你提出异议,因为像"越来越多"、"似乎"这样模糊的词汇给你留有很大的回旋余地。所以,与其说"某事是真实的",不如说"某事应该是真实的,如果……"、"某事看起来是真的"、"某事可以被论证为是真实的"、"说某事是真实的是有道理的"。那么,你能把第二句话改得更严谨一些吗?

艾伦：好吧,让我想想。"使命声明可以说是关于公司总体目的的陈述文件。"

Dr. Robinson: Good! Now… "It is recommended that they be succinct, distinctive and broad in scope… as Hannegan (2002) says, lacking in statistics and full of rhetoric. It is commonly believed that mission statements should aim to answer the question, 'what business are we in?'" That's better, isn't it?

Alan: So do academics ever feel certain about anything?

Dr. Robinson: Well, if you have presented compelling evidence in a rigorous analysis, and feel that you are in a good position to make an assertion, of course, you can increase the confidence in your tone. However, you still have to be cautious, because anything worth studying must involve some uncertainty.

Alan: Shouldn't you have said that "anything worth studying seems to involve some uncertainty"?

Dr. Robinson: *Touché*![3]

注释
① Are you telling me…. 表示难以相信。
② now 这里不是"现在"的意思,只表示强调。
③ *Touché*! 是一个在英语里常用的法语词,是一种自我解嘲,表示对方说的话钻了自己的空子。

罗宾逊博士：好！那么，"它们应当简练、有特色并且范围广泛……如汉尼根（2002）所说，要省略统计数据而富于修辞。使命声明被普遍认为是要回答这个问题：我们是做什么生意的？"这样是不是好多了？

艾伦：那么，学者们会不会充分肯定什么事呢？

罗宾逊博士：如果你已经在严谨的分析中展示了有说服力的证据，并觉得你已经到了可以断言的地步，那么当然，你可以提高你口吻中的自信程度。但是，你仍然需要小心，因为任何值得研究的东西都肯定涉及到一些不确定性。

艾伦：是不是应该说"因为任何值得研究的东西都似乎涉及到一些不确定性"？

罗宾逊博士：以其人之道还治其人之身啊！

实用短语

◆ I've called you in to see me because…   我叫你来是因为……
◆ Can you see anything wrong with it?   你能看出什么错误吗?
◆ Ah… now that's the problem.   哈,那就是问题的所在。
◆ It also looks like…   看起来似乎也……
◆ Are you telling me that…?   你是在告诉我……?
◆ Bend the text to fit your argument.   扭曲书本来为自己的论点服务。
◆ … might be true, if…   ……应该是真的,如果……
◆ … appears to be true.   ……看上去是真实的。
◆ It is arguable whether… is true.   ……可以被论证为是真实的。
◆ It is reasonable to say… is true.   说……是真实的是有道理的。

词汇表

analysis 分析
be concerned about 对…担忧
blanket statements 一概而论的陈述(blanket 是"毯子"的意思;毯子式的申述或声明,表示高度概括的)
broad in scope 范围广泛
cautious 小心
conviction 坚定

distinctive 独到的
evidence 证据
hedge 避其锋芒
lift 照搬/抄袭(这里是比喻意;原意是"搬")
mission statement 使命声明
reasonable 有道理的
responsibility 责任

rhetoric 修辞/空话
rigorous 严谨的
succinct 简练的
touché 感叹词,表示自己说的话被对方抓住把柄了
absolutely sure 毫无保留地肯定
wild claims 狂野的断言/没有根据的言论

第23章
对比和比较
Contrast and Comparison

背景常识

所有我们可以学到的知识一定都以某种对比和比较作为基础。不知道什么是"左"、"善"或"黑",就不能了解什么是"右"、"恶"或"白"。同样的,没有仔细地学习西方文化,一个中国人就不能全面地了解什么才是中国的文化。这就是掌握对比和比较性语言的重要性。

在涉及对比的句子里,经常用到的词包括:while、whereas 和 whilst(三个词都是"而"或"但是"的意思)。它们在对比句里通常可以互换。但是,有时它们会被用在句子的开头,表示"虽然"。在这个情况下,这个句子不一定涉及比较。让我们来看两个例子:

Newton's laws apply to our day-to-day life, while Einstein's physics better explain the relations between gigantic astrophysical bodies.(牛顿定律适用于我们的日常生活,而爱因斯坦的物理学则更好地解释了巨大天体之间的关系。)While Newton and Einstein were scientists, they were both quite religious as well.(虽然牛顿和爱因斯坦都是科学家,他们却也都有相当强的宗教信仰。)这里,第一句话是比较,第二句话不是。在第二句话中,while 只表示"虽然"。

另一个可以用来做比较的词是"比较(comparison)"本身。Compared with Paris, London is more multi-cultural.(与巴黎相比,伦敦要更加文化多元化。)By comparison, London is more multi-cultural than Paris.(相比之下,伦敦比巴黎更文化多元化。)

做比较的能力表现出一个人对差异和细节的洞察力,应当多加锻炼。这是被很多老师和用人单位所欣赏的。

In the Uni Bar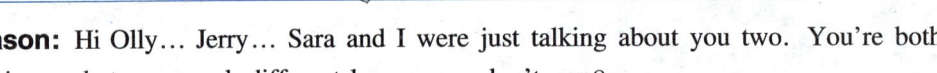

Jason: Hi Olly... Jerry... Sara and I were just talking about you two. You're both Chinese, but you speak different languages, don't you?

Olly: Well, yes and no... I mean we both speak Mandarin because that's the official language, but I also speak another dialect, Cantonese, because I'm from Hong Kong.

Jason: So... what's the difference between them?

Jerry: Mandarin just sounds nicer... haha!

Olly: Get lost, you! The thing is actually that... I mean, they're both tonal languages based on the same written characters... but whereas Mandarin has four tones, Cantonese has seven or eight.

Sarah: So, Mandarin is easier, then?

Olly: Not necessarily... there are just fewer tones.

Jason: So is the vocabulary different, then?

Jerry: Well, for example, although the number one is "*yī*" in Mandarin, "*yat*" in Cantonese and "*tsit*" in Hakka, they derive from a common ancient Chinese word and are written with the same character. Yet, when we talk to each other we say it's like the chicken talking to the duck!

Olly: So what it means is that while a Chinese person might understand only either Mandarin or Cantonese, he or she can communicate with other Chinese people—and even Japanese and Koreans sometimes—by writing because they use more-or-less the same written characters. However, the colloquial Cantonese written down in words is sometimes hard to understand for Mandarin speaking people because the Cantonese use lots of different expressions in their daily spoken Cantonese. Also, in Mainland China they use simplified characters, whereas in Hong Kong and Taiwan they use traditional characters.

Jason: So you're saying that in Taiwan they speak Cantonese, and Cantonese is written in traditional characters?

Jerry: No... in Taiwan they have Mandarin as the official language... but while in Mainland China it's called *Putonghua*, in Taiwan it's called *Guoyu*. It's essentially the same language... only the accent is different.

Sarah: So what's the difference between Beijing and Shanghai... I want to go to Beijing next summer.

Jerry: Well, compared with Beijing, Shanghai is more commercial, entrepreneurial and go-getting. Shanghai is the business capital of China, while Beijing is the political capital. Whilst Beijingers see themselves as cultured and sophisticated, Shanghainese often consider themselves to be cosmopolitan and business-minded.

Sarah: That's really interesting. I guess it's like in my country, Brazil, where there's like a rivalry between Rio de Janeiro and São Paulo... the people from Rio are considered more laid-back and easy-going... and they also think of themselves as more cultured sometimes. São Paulo, by comparison, is seen as more of a working city… a business centre. "São Paulo is for work while Rio is for play" is what they always say. The contrast is quite amazing. Jason is from Dublin in Ireland… how different from London is Dublin?

Jason: Come on! There's no comparison!

在学校酒吧

贾森：奥莉，杰里，你们好。我和萨拉刚刚还在说你们两个。你们都是中国人，但你们说不同的语言，对吗？

奥莉：对，也不对。我是说我们都说普通话，因为那是中国的官方语言。但是我还说另外一种方言，广东话，因为我来自香港。

贾森：那么，它们之间有什么区别吗？

杰里：普通话更好听一些。哈哈！

奥莉：你尽胡说！其实，我的意思是，它们都是基于相同文字的音调式语言。普通话有4个声调，而广东话则有7到8个声调。

萨拉：那么，普通话要简单一些了？

奥莉：不一定，它只是声调少而已。

贾森：那词汇上有什么不同吗？

杰里：比如说，虽然数字1在普通话中是yi，但在广东话中是yat，在客家话中是tsit，它们都发源于古汉语中的同一个词而且写起来都是一个字。可是当我们交谈时却互相都听不懂！

奥莉：所以，这表示，虽然一个中国人只能听懂普通话，或者只能听懂广东话，但是他可以通过写字跟其他中国人，甚至跟韩国人和日本人沟通，因为他们都使用大致相同的文字。但是，写出来的广东话对说普通话的人来讲可能是难以理解的，因为广东话的日常口语有很多不一样的表达方式。而且，在中国大陆，人们使用简体字，而在香港和台湾地区，人们使用繁体字。

贾森：你是说在台湾地区，人们说广东话，而且广东话是用繁体字写的？

杰里：不，在台湾地区，人们把普通话作为官方语言。但是，它在中国大陆叫普通话，在台湾叫国语。其实都是一种语言，只是在口音上不同。

萨拉：那么，北京和上海有什么区别吗？我明年夏天想去北京。

杰里：与北京相比，上海更商业化、企业化而且节奏快。上海是中国的商业之都，而北京是政治之都。上海人总觉得自己更国际化而且更有生意头脑，而北京人则觉得自己有文化而且高雅。

萨拉：真有意思。我估计这跟我的国家巴西差不多。在那儿，里约热内卢和圣保罗之间跟冤家一样。从里约来的人被认为随便、好相处，他们也觉得自己很有文化。相比，圣保罗被认为是工作的城市，是商业中心。人们常说"圣保罗是工作的地方而里约是娱乐的地方。"反差十分明显。贾森是从爱尔兰的都柏林来的。都柏林和伦敦有什么区别？

贾森：算了吧！这没法比嘛！

实用短语

- We were just talking about you. 我们刚刚还在谈论你们。
- Well, yes and no. 对,也不对。
- What's the difference between them? 它们之间有什么区别?
- Mandarin just sounds nicer. 普通话更好听。
- They are both…, but whereas… 它们都是……,但……
- The thing is, actually, that… 其实,事情是……
- So what it means is… 所以,这表示……
- While in… it's called…, in… it's called… 在……被叫做……,而在……被称作……
- Compared with…, … is more… 与……相比,……更……
- It's essentially the same. Only the… is different. 其实是一样的,只是……不同。
- … consider themselves to be… ……认为他们自己是……
- …, by comparison, is seen as a… 相比,……被认为是……
- The people of… are more… ……的人更……
- The contrast is quite amazing. 这反差是十分明显的。
- How different from… is…? ……和……之间有什么区别?
- … are considered more… ……被认为更……
- They think of themselves as more… 他们认为自己更……
- There's no comparison! 这没法比嘛!

词汇表

based on 基于
business-minded 有生意头脑的/会做买卖的
Cantonese 广东话
character 字
colloquial 大白话的
commercial 商业的
cosmopolitan 国际化的
cultured 有文化的/高雅的
derive from 发源于/从…总结出来
dialect 方言
Dublin 都柏林
easy-going 好相处的
entrepreneurial 企业的/企业家的
get lot! 别扯了(表示对方说的话是完全荒唐的)!/别胡说!
go-getting 节奏快的
hakka 客家人/客家话
mainland China 中国大陆
Mandarin 普通话
Rio de Janeiro 里约热内卢
rivalry 对头/敌人
São Paulo 圣保罗
Shanghainese 上海人/上海话
simplified 简化的
sophisticated 复杂的/讲究的
Taiwanese 台湾人/台湾话
tonal 声调式的/区分声调的
traditional characters 繁体字

第24章
引用与转述
Quoting and Paraphrasing

背景常识

英国人热爱寻章摘句。一个关于名人名言的 BBC 广播 4 台的明星猜题综艺节目,"前引号……后引号"("Quote… Unquote"),几十年来在英国听众中经久不衰。尽管英国教育提倡创造性思维,作为一个学生的重要任务仍然是用别人的理论来支持自己的。引用和转述是课堂里最为常用的语言技巧。

作为书面形式(in written form),由于引号(quotation mark)的存在,引用句的特征是很明显的。在口语中,也有一些象征引用的标志性词汇。Say 就是一个例子。可以放在说话人之后,也可以放在说话人之前。Aristotle said that… 和 …, said Aristotle 都是"亚里士多德说过……"的意思。人们为了强调引用,有时会把引号念出来。比如, the saying, quote, I came, I saw, I conquered, unquote, is attributed to Julius Caesar(前引号,我来,我见,我征服,后引号,这句话被认为是恺撒说的)。

在英语里还有一种独特的表示引用的方式——空引(air quote)。空引是一种肢体语言。说话的人抬起胳膊,使双手与肩齐高。伸出双手的食指和中指,然后反复曲伸这四个手指。看上去,说话的人似乎在用双手来模仿兔子的耳朵。实际上,这四根手指表示的是前后两个引号。当说话人一边说话一边做这个动作的时候,就表示他在引用。

Paraphrasing(转述)和 quoting 不同。to paraphrase 就是重复某人的意思而不用其原文。使用转述能够展示说话人对其引用文字的深刻而灵活的理解。而这样做的挑战在于如何准确地捕捉(capture)原文的意思,而不至于误引(misquote)。

In the Classroom

Liu: Mark, could you tell us again what the four main ways of using evidence to support an argument are? I mean… I think I know about quotations, but what are the others.

Mark: Yes … sure … the four techniques you should know how to use are the following: "illustrative incident", "examples", "statistics" and "quotations".

Liu: So, what's the difference between them? What's the first one?

Mark: OK… look… here's an argument… [*writes on whiteboard*] "The foundation programmes at the University of London are very successful in preparing international students for university study."

Pinar: Yes, well we all know that, don't we… haha! That's why we're here!

Mark: Yes, very funny, Pinar… but we need to back it up, don't we? You can't just say it if you want people to take you seriously. How can I write it to make people believe me?

Becky: "Everyone knows that the foundation programmes at the University of London are very successful in preparing international students for university study."

Mark: You're joking, of course… look, try an illustrative example… "Zhang Kaige finished the Postgraduate Preparation Programme at London in 2000. He then went on to the LSE, where he studied International Relations. He is now completing a PhD at Cambridge and hopes to return to China to lecture at Peking University next year."

Becky: Oh… that's good… will we all be able to get PhDs after this?

Mark: No. You have to be bright to get a PhD, Becky. Another way of giving support to an argument is like this: [*writes on whiteboard*] "Since 1990, thousands of students from over forty countries including China, Japan, Brazil, Kazakhstan, Turkey and Morocco have graduated from the PPP and have gone on to study at universities like Oxford, Cambridge and the LSE."

Liu: Wow… that's good….

Mark: Yes, but you still have to work hard, you know…. Here's another way you can use statistics to back up your argument… [*writes on whiteboard*] "According to the university report, 2006, there were 120 students on foundation programmes at London in 2004-2005. 98% of students who completed the PPP went on to do master's courses at UK universities."

Pinar: That's good…. [*writes*]

Mark: Now that brings me on to the one you were asking me about… the quotation. Now this can be direct or indirect… what the person actually said, or what you say he said… what you are reporting… [*writes on whiteboard*] "In his speech at the British Council Education Fair in 2006, the British Education Secretary commented that courses like the PPP provided an excellent preparation for university study. 'We are grateful to all the teachers on such courses for their hard work,' he added."

Becky: So, the last one is the best, then?

Mark: No ... not at all. You have to be very careful because writers, especially journalists, can become very adept at using quotes selectively and out of context.

在教室

刘：马克，你能再跟我说说用论据支持论点的 4 种方法吗？我是说，我知道引用，另外 3 个是什么？

马克：好，没问题。你需要掌握的 4 种方法是：个例、泛例、统计数据和引用。

刘：它们之间有什么区别？第一个是什么？

马克：这么说吧。考虑这个论点。[*在白板上写*] "伦敦大学的预科课程在为国际学生准备大学学习方面做得非常成功。"

皮娜：当然了，这我们都知道，哈哈，要不然我们就不会来这里了。

马克：你真幽默，皮娜。但是我们需要支持这个论点，不是吗？你不能空口无凭就希望别人相信你。我怎么写才能让人相信我呢？

贝姬："大家都知道，伦敦大学的预科课程在帮助学生为大学生活做好准备方面是非常成功的。"

马克：你显然是在开玩笑。想一个能说明问题的例子。"张凯歌于 2000 年结束了伦敦大学的硕士预科课程，然后他上了伦敦政治经济学院，学习国际关系。他目前在剑桥大学读博士，希望明年回国到北京大学教书。"

贝姬：哦，太好了。我们以后都能读博士吗？

马克：不行，不聪明是考不上博士的，贝姬。另外一种证明观点的方法是这样的。[*在白板上写*] "自从 1990 年以来，已经有来自中国、日本、巴西、哈萨克斯坦、土耳其和摩洛哥等四十多个国家的上万名学生从 PPP 毕业，并考取牛津、剑桥和伦敦政经这样的大学。"

刘：哇，不赖嘛！

马克：对，但是你们还得努力才行。还有一个办法就是使用数据来支持你的观点。[*在白板上写*] "根据 2006 年的大学报告，在 2004 到 2005 年期间，在伦敦上预科的学生一共有 120 名。完成了 PPP 的学生中，98% 都进入了英国大学的研究生课程。"

皮娜：好词儿。[写]

马克：现在，这就把我们带到了你问的那个问题上：引用。引用可以是直接的，也可以是间接的。可以是某人说了什么，也可以是你说某人说了什么，你报告某事。[*在白板上写*] "2006 年，英国教育部长在英国文化委员会的教育展演讲中，称 PPP 是一个出色的学前准备课程。他还说：'我们对在这些课程中辛勤工作的所有老师表示感谢。'"

贝姬：那么，最后这个办法最好了？

马克：不，一点儿也不。你必须非常小心，因为写东西的人，尤其是记者，经常在引用时断章取义。

实用短语

- Could you tell us again, what are the...? 你能再跟我们说说……是怎么回事吗？
- The four techniques you should know how to use are... 你应当学会使用的4种方法分别是……
- How can I write it to make people believe me? 我应该怎样写才能让人相信我？
- You're joking, of course. 你显然是在开玩笑。
- Another way of doing/giving/saying... is like this... 另外一个做……的办法是这样的……
- Here's another way you can use... 这是另外一个……的办法。
- Now, that brings me on to... 那么，这就把我们带到…问题上来了。
- ... are very successful in... 在……方面非常成功。
- He then went on to the..., where he studied... 他继而去了……，在那里他学习了……
- He is now completing a... at... and hopes to... 他现在正在……攻读……，并希望……
- In his speech at the... 在他……的演讲中。

词汇表

adept 擅长某事
argument 辩论
back up 支持（论点）
bring... on to... 把…带到…话题上
British Council 英国文化委员会
Cambridge 剑桥
clarify 澄清
comment 评论
direct 直接的
Education Fair 教育展
Education Secretary 教育部长

examples 例子
foundation programme 预科课程
give support to 支持
grateful 感激的
illustrative incident 典型个例
indirect 间接的
joke 开玩笑
Kazakhstan 哈萨克斯坦
LSE (London School of Economics and Political Science) 伦敦政治经济学院
Morocco 摩洛哥

of course 当然
Oxford 牛津
postgraduate preparation programme 研究生预科课程
quotations 引用
selective 有选择的/不全面的
statistics 统计数据
take someone seriously 认真严肃对待某人
technique 技术
Turkey 土耳其
whiteboard 白板

第25章
教中文
Teaching Chinese

背景常识

教英国人学中文和当中英文翻译是学习和锻炼英语的最佳方式。它们能锻炼前面提到的许多语言技巧,比如转述和改变句子顺序,也能帮助你理解某些英语词汇和语法的真正含义。

比如说,To be or not to be; that is the question.这句莎士比亚剧作中哈姆雷特的台词,通常被翻译成"生存还是毁灭;这是一个值得考虑的问题。"实际上,to be 的含义远远超过"生存",而具有哲学上的"使生命完整"的意思。如果你回忆一下 human being(人类)这个词,你就能理解 being 或 to be 的真正含义了。同样,如果你按照字面意思把苏轼的《念奴娇·赤壁怀古》翻译成英语,也有很多意思表现不出来——The big river going east, washes up all the romantic characters in history.(大江东去,浪涛尽,千古风流人物。)一个好的翻译不仅仅是一个英汉对照词典,在他的脑海中,两种语言应当可以并驾齐驱、各显神通。

只有当你将中文和英语反复对照翻译的时候,你才能完全了解(appreciate)两种语言的特点(character)和每个单词的个性(individuality)。虽然你会发现无论如何也不能把唐诗宋词的意境(sensation)完全用英语表达出来,你却会深思"东去"和"风流"这些词的喻义。同样地,在英语中,当你发现无论如何也不能把一个词准确地翻译成中文的时候,你就算是开始真正理解这个词了。

语言之间不应该有竞争关系。正是它们的共同存在(co-existence)才使得各自独一无二(unique)。

Arranging a Language Exchange

Peter: OK... so, how are we going to do this? I mean should we have an hour of English and an hour of Mandarin?

Jane: I don't really know... I mean, I've done a couple of language exchanges in China before, but we spoke mostly English... very little Mandarin.

Peter: Yes, that's what I've found... I've done loads of language exchanges with students here... but most of them just want to speak English all the time, or they can't speak in Chinese without translating into English... or they're looking for a boyfriend if they're girls.

Jane: Yes... that's a problem, isn't it? Don't worry about me, though... I already have a boyfriend, and he'll kill you if you try anything on... haha. Actually, I think we should be quite strict and use just direct method... just Mandarin when we're doing the Chinese bit, and English when we're doing the English bit.

Peter: OK... it's hard to do that, though... we'll need to have a plan... you know... about the topics we're going to talk about.

Jane: Yes. If we know what topics we want to talk about, we can plan the vocabulary in advance and use it in our conversation. Let's start off now and talk about how we've studied and what we find difficult about studying each others' languages.

Peter: Yes... gosh... what do I find hard about Mandarin... everything... the vocabulary, the new words, the tones, the grammar, the measure words, the aspect markers... I mean when I was studying it at my first university it was terrible... the teacher was a total dragon! She just chanted everything really quickly, shouted out twenty new words and expected us to memorise them... then she spoke English 90% of the time! How can you learn a foreign language if you're speaking your own language all the time in class? It's no wonder most of the students dropped out. Then I went to some classes here at this uni and the teacher just put everything up on PowerPoint—a Chinese sentence followed by an English sentence, and the English was wrong! So you see what I mean about us having to be strict about only speaking the target language? I don't think any of the teachers I've had have had any training in language teaching theory and techniques at all.

Jane: Well, that's a problem, isn't it? That's the way we learn English in China... grammar-translation method with no chance to speak. There's also this idea that if you speak a language as a native you can teach it, which is not always the case....

Peter: I know what you mean, but at the same time grammar is important, isn't it?

Jane: I always found phrasal verbs difficult in English... and tenses... especially past simple and present perfect....

Peter: Sorry? What are they?

Jane: See... that's the thing about not being a trained English teacher; you don't know the terminology in your own language, but you know it for the language you want to learn. I mean, I don't know what you mean when you say "aspect marker"….

Peter: I mean like 了，还，过, and words like that….

Jane: See how hard it is not to translate and use both languages in a language exchange? Haha!

Peter: All right, all right… but I don't want us just to slip into English when I can't understand you in Chinese, OK?

Jane: OK… and *vice versa*! Shall we say all of this in Mandarin now…?

安排语言交换活动

彼得： 我们应该如何入手？一小时英语，一小时中文普通话？

简： 我也不知道。我在中国参加过几次语言交换活动，但我们大部分时间都在说英语，中文说得很少。

彼得： 对，我也意识到了。我跟这儿的学生搞过好多次语言交换了，但是大部分人都只想说英语，或者不加英语翻译就说不了汉语。再有就是女生来物色男朋友的。

简： 这是个问题，不是吗？不过，你不用担心我，我已经有男朋友了。如果你有非分之想，他能跟你玩儿命，哈哈。实际上，我觉得我们应该有严格的规矩，方法要直接。说普通话时大家就都说中文，说英语时大家就都说英语。

彼得： 好，不过，这样做有些难度。我们得有个计划。你琢磨琢磨，我们应该谈什么话题呢？

简： 对，如果我们事先知道应该谈什么话题，我们就可以提前准备在对话中会遇到的单词。我们先聊聊咱是如何学习对方的语言和发现了哪些难点吧。

彼得： 好。天呐，我觉得学中文有哪些难点，全是难点，词汇、生词、声调、语法、量词、动态修饰……我在我第一所大学的学习经历是非常糟糕的，那个老师整个是个暴君！她念东西特别快，一口气把二十几个生词都嚷嚷出来，就指望我们能记住，而且她90%的时间都在说英语！如果你总说自己的母语，你怎么能学会外语呢？难怪大部分学生都退学了。后来我来这个大学学了几门课，这儿的老师把所有内容都放在幻灯片上。一句中文，一句英语，而且英语还是错的！现在你明白我为什么严格要求我们只能说要学的这种语言了吧？我估计我以前那些老师根本没有在语言教学的理论和技巧上受过训练。

简： 这确实是个问题。我们在中国就是这么学英语的，语法加翻译，根本没机会练口语。而且人们还觉得谁都能教自己的母语，其实不一定。

彼得： 我明白你的意思，但是语法也同样很重要。

简： 我总觉得英语的动词短语很难，还有时态，尤其是一般过去时和现在完成时。

彼得： 对不起？你说的是什么？

简： 你看，这就是未经培训的英语老师的特点。你不知道你自己母语里的术语，但是你却知道你学的外语里的术语。比如说，当你说"动态修饰"的时候，我也不知道你说的是什么意思。

彼得： 我是指"了、还、过"这类词。

简： 看吧，两种语言要是不翻译也不混着用，交流起来就很困难，哈哈！

彼得： 好吧，好吧，但是我可不想在我听不懂你的中文的时候我们就说英语，明白吗？

简： 好，彼此彼此！我们现在是不是该用中文说这些了？

实用短语

- OK, so how are we going to do this…? 我们应当如何入手？
- I don't really know. 我其实不知道。
- That's what I've found. 我也意识到了。
- Actually, I think we should… 其实,我觉得我们应该……
- If we know… we can… 如果我们知道……我们可以……
- How can you… if you…? 你怎么能……如果你……？
- So you see what I mean about…? 你现在知道我……是什么意思了吧？
- It's no wonder… 难怪……
- I know what you mean, but… 我理解你的意思,但是……
- That's the thing about… ……就是这个样子。
- See how… it is (not) to…? 你意识到做(不做)……有多……了吧？
- I don't want us just to… 我不希望我们马上就……

词汇表

aspect marker 动态修饰
at all 根本
be the case 符合上述情况
chant 念(尤指念经)
direct method 直接的方法
dragon 龙
drop out 退学

gosh! 天哪！
native-English speaker 以英语为母语的人
past simple 过去时
phrasal verb 动词短语
present perfect 现在完成时

slip into 不小心滑入
strict 严格
tense 时态
terminology 术语
topic 题目/话题
vice versa 反之亦然

第26章
讨论课
Seminars

背景常识

讨论课(seminars 或 tutorials)是一种在英国大学里非常普遍的教学方式。在中国大学里,老师主要是通过讲座的方式来教学的;学生之间和学生与老师之间有组织的讨论和辩论的机会很少。英国的教育理念提倡学生独立思考,并能挑战老师的观点。讲座上,老师发言,学生听讲;讨论课则是学生发言,老师听讲。讨论课一般都很小,有时可能只有两三个学生和一个老师。通常,一门本科课程每周有一节讲座和一节讨论课,两节课的内容相互照应。

许多中国学生对讨论课感到恐惧(terrifying)。它不仅是一个不可回避的对英语口语的考验(test),同时也要求学生能通过自学来提炼自己的观点,并有勇气在众人面前陈述(state)和捍卫(defend)自己的看法。不过,你也不必惊慌,掌握下面的几种表达方式,你还是可以活下来的(survive)。

首先,要思维独到、敢于参与(be original and engaging)。如果某个观点确实是你独立思考的结果,说话就要当仁不让:In my opinion...(在我看来……)这里要强调 my。其次,要有礼貌、有耐心(be polite and patient)。学者辩论,不能失了礼节(lose manners)。尝试去欣赏对方的论点:I totally agree with you, yet...(我完全同意你的看法,但是……)。第三,如果你走神儿了或者不知道应该如何回答,可以说:I really don't think I've got anything meaningful to add.(我没有什么要补充的了。)

除了有助学习以外,在讨论课上的表现还有一个重要意义。表现出众的学生还会得到老师的注意和青睐——到了期末打分阶段,这可是非常重要的优势。

In the Classroom

Tutor: Good morning everyone. I hope you all managed to get the course reading done. The topic of immigration controls is a controversial one, but I personally think that it is one which needs an honest and open debate. Does anyone have any comments?

Joe: Well, in my personal opinion the government has failed to deal with the issue of immigration because they are afraid of being labelled racist. It's not racist to argue that immigration needs to be controlled.

Wendy: Sorry, but I'd like to comment on that: most people who want immigration limited are talking about non-white immigration. They ignore the fact that most of the foreigners in this country are actually white! French, Italians, Americans, Australians and so on.

Hamza: I'd like to say something here, if I may… my parents are British citizens who came here from Pakistan in the '60s and they want to see immigration limited too. It's a question of numbers pure-and-simple, not….

Jack: Excuse me for interrupting, but that's just typical, isn't it? The first set of immigrants gets in and then wants to stop others getting in behind them. You see it everywhere from the States to Australia. They think they're better than the people back home!

Hamza: Well maybe, but don't you think that British Pakistanis are actually more British than the ones who are coming in now? My parents came in legally and helped to build this country, whereas the ones who are coming in now are coming in illegally….

Fatima: You're right there. My parents are from Jamaica originally, and they've worked hard here. They feel British! Now they see illegal immigrants coming in from Eastern Europe who are really racist towards black people. It's a real problem.

Tutor: Can we get back to the point please? The original reading looks at economic reasons for and against controlled immigration….

Wendy: Well, to my mind, immigration is necessary because of the falling birth rate and the ageing population. Somebody needs to work and pay taxes to pay our pensions when we retire….

Hamza: Well, I would disagree with that. If the government increased child benefit and tax credits for the families who are already here, people would have more children, they would grow up speaking English and go into the workforce, and we wouldn't have the expense of trying to integrate people who can't speak English.

Fatima: What are you on about?! Your family speaks Urdu at home!

Wendy: Could we be less emotional about this please? The fact is that whatever you say, Britain is a country which is founded on immigration. There have always been migrants from elsewhere coming here. My great-grandparents were Italian, and people said the same thing about them back in 1900… immigrants! Not everyone will agree with me, but I believe immigration is good both in terms of economic growth and social vibrancy.

在教室

老师：大家早上好。我希望你们都看了这堂课的阅读材料。移民控制是一个富有争议的话题，但是我个人认为这个话题需要一场开诚布公的辩论。有谁要发表见解吗？

乔：我个人认为，现任政府在处理移民问题上是失败的，因为他们担心被冠以种族主义之名。主张控制移民并不是种族主义。

温迪：抱歉，我想针对你的观点谈谈我的看法：大多数支持限制移民的人是要限制非白人移民。他们忽略了这个国家里大部分的外国人是白人的这个现实！法国人、意大利人、美国人、澳大利亚人等等。

哈姆扎：我也有话要说，如果可以的话。我父母是60年代从巴基斯坦来的英国公民，而他们也希望限制移民。这是一个简单的数量问题，而不是……

杰克：很抱歉打断你，但这种看法非常典型，不是吗？第一批移民入境以后就不希望后面再有移民。在澳大利亚的各个州里，这种现象非常普遍。他们认为自己比在家乡的人优越。

哈姆扎：也许吧，但是你不觉得巴基斯坦裔英国人比如今的来英移民要更加英国化吗？我父母是合法移民，而且参与了这个国家的建设，而现在的移民都是非法的。

法蒂玛：你说得对。我父母是从牙买加来的，他们在这里工作得非常辛苦。他们觉得自己就是英国人！现在，他们眼看着歧视黑人的东欧非法移民涌入这个国家。这是一个非常现实的问题。

老师：我们还是回到讨论的题目上来好吗？原本的阅读材料探讨了支持与反对控制移民的经济原因……

温迪：对我来说，由于出生率的降低和人口老龄化，吸纳移民是必须的。总得有人工作纳税来负担我们的退休金吧。

哈姆扎：我不同意。如果政府能提高子女补助和移民家庭的税务补偿，人们自然会多生孩子。他们长大后会说英语，成为英国的劳动力。这样我们就不需要费时间同化那些不会说英语的人了。

法蒂玛：你胡说什么呢？你家里人在家都说乌尔都语！

温迪：咱们能不能别这么冲动？无论如何，现实是，英国是一个以移民为本的国家。我们还有从其他地方来的移民呢。我的祖辈是意大利人，当初在1900年的时候，人们也是这样说他们的……移民！可能不是所有人都同意我的看法，但是我认为，从经济增长和社会活力两个方面来看，移民都是一件好事。

实用短语

- Does anyone have any comments? 有谁要发表看法吗?
- In my personal opinion... 我个人认为……
- Not everyone will agree with me, but... 可能不是人人都同意我的看法,但是……
- To my mind... 在我看来……
- Excuse me for interrupting, but... 抱歉打断你,但是……
- What are you on about?! 你在胡说什么呢?
- No. You're absolutely wrong there! 你在那个问题上是绝对错误的!
- Sorry, I can't agree with you there. 对不起,我不能同意你的看法。
- Well, I would disagree with that. 我认为不然。
- Yes, but... 是,但是……
- Can we get back to the point, please? 我们能不能回到原来的题目上?/不要跑题好不好?
- Could we try to be less emotional about this? 我们都不要太冲动了好吗?
- Sorry but... 对不起,但是……
- Can I add something here? 我能补充两句吗?
- I'd like to comment on that. 我想对那个问题谈谈我的看法。
- I'd like to say something here... 我想说两句……
- You're right, there. 你在那个问题上说得对。
- Well maybe, but... 也许吧,可是……

词汇表

child benefit 子女福利
controlled immigration 限制性移民
controversial 有争议的
economic 经济的
emotional 感情的/感情用事的
great-grandparents 曾祖父母
growth 增长/成长
integrate 整合/融入
pure and simple 直截了当
racist 种族主义者/种族主义的
tax credits 税收补偿
typical 典型的/俗套的
vibrancy 活力
workforce 劳动力

第27章
论文与演讲
Essays and Presentations

背景常识

在中国大学里，一学期一般只有两次测验(assess)，期中(mid-term)和期末考试(final exams)。而在英国大学中，测验的形式和次数都种类繁多。除了期末考试以外，老师每学期会留若干次作业(assignments)，其形式常为论文或演讲(essays and presentations)。这些作业的成绩是算入总成绩的。中国教育中的及格(pass)分数线是60%，但是在英国，低于40%才算不及格(fail)。中国的评分系统中，好学生可以拿到90%或100%。在英国大学里，尤其是文科科目，70%就是优秀(excellence)了。如果你的一篇文学或社会学论文能拿到80%，你就应该开一瓶香槟来庆祝一下。英国学界里的论文写作在格式上有细致的要求。比如字数限制(word limit)、上交期限(deadline)、结构(structure)、创新性(originality)、对资料的使用(use of resources)等等。一篇内容极佳的文章如果格式上不符合标准，是不能拿高分的。

剽窃(plagiarism)是所有学生都必须注意的一个问题。在英国，从你本科入学的第一天起，老师就会不断地强调如何在写作中避免剽窃。总之，你论文中的一切观点和证据，只要不是你自创的，你就必须通过脚注(footnotes)、尾注(endnotes)、括号(brackets)或参考书目(bibliography)来标注其来源。如今所有学校都有反剽窃软件，如果你从某个期刊书本上抄袭了一段文字却没有注明来源，学校十有八九是会发现的。剽窃的后果十分严重。

不过，英国大学在测验学生这个方面还是有它温柔的一面。和中国不同的是，英国大学视学生的考试成绩为个人机密。永别了，令人尴尬的全班成绩排名表！

Presentation Discussion

Wang: So in conclusion ... what I am arguing is that trade blocs themselves, involving, as they do, a number of independent sovereign states, are a twentieth century phenomenon and that is why the current spread of globalization is qualitatively different to that of the age of 19th century trade globalization, which was based more on transnational trading agreements. That concludes my presentation... now, if you have any questions I'd be happy to answer them.

Dr. Dixon: Thank you, Mr. Wang. That was fascinating. Please sit down... we do have some questions we'd like to ask. Now... first of all, I was particularly interested in your comparison of the Qing Dynasty's trade agreements with Britain, Japan and Germany and those of developing countries' agreements with the major trading blocs like the EU and NAFTA... but isn't it true that agricultural produce from developing countries today are, more-or-less, totally locked out of the EU and NAFTA because of protective tariffs, while Qing-dynasty China was not really in the business of even wanting to export agricultural produce to Europe and North America?

Wang: You are right of course, but what I was trying to point out was that these nineteenth-century transnational agreements performed the same function as modern trade blocs do. That is, they were unfair and protectionist in nature. So, what I'm saying is that globalization itself ultimately benefits the haves—not the have-nots.

Dr. Dixon: That's interesting. Yes... there was, of course great interest in Chinese cultural artefacts in Europe and North America during the Qing dynasty, wasn't there? And China did export a lot of porcelain, lacquerware and so on... and there was an enormous cultural value placed on China at that time.

Wang: With respect, Dr. Dixon, a few cultural artefacts hardly count as an equal trading regime. My aim, though, is not to bang the drum for China here... it is to point out that trade and economics are just politics and international relations under another name, and that any agreements are going to be in the political interests of the stronger nations, whatever the historical period.

Dr. Dixon: Quite. Some economists and historians might disagree with you, but certainly the critical schools would side with what you are saying... Dr. Jackson... do you have any questions?

Dr. Jackson: Yes... that was very interesting, Mr. Wang. I was just wondering about, for instance, where an individual state within a trading bloc has tariffs, which clash with those of the bloc as a whole. What happens then? I mean, say China, which is a member of APEC, has a favourable trading agreement with one APEC member which APEC as a whole doesn't have?

Wang: Yes, that's a very interesting question... I think this is an issue which....

演讲讨论

王：综上所述，我的观点是：涉及若干独立主权国家的贸易集团是20世纪的现象，也就是为什么当今全球化与19世纪全球化贸易有质的不同的原因。19世纪的全球化主要是以跨国际贸易合约为基础的。我的演讲到此结束。如果你们有什么问题的话，我会很高兴回答。

狄克逊博士：谢谢你，王先生。你的演讲很有趣。请坐。我们确实有一些问题要问你。首先，我对你关于清朝与英日德的贸易协定和当今发展中国家与诸如欧盟和北美自由贸易协议这样的贸易集团之间的贸易协定的比较很感兴趣。但是，现今由于保护主义关税，发展中国家的农产品几乎都被封锁在欧盟和北美自由贸易区之外，而清朝时的中国根本没有向欧洲和北美出口农产品的愿望，不是吗？

王：你说得对，但是我要证明的观点是：19世纪的跨国贸易条约与现代贸易集团有相同的功能。那就是：它们本质上都是不平等的和保护主义的。所以，我要说的是：全球化从根本上使富者获利，使穷人遭殃。

狄克逊博士：有意思。对，清朝时期，欧洲和北美倒是对中国的艺术品有着浓厚的兴趣，不是吗？而且中国也确实出口了不少陶器和漆器等商品。在当时，中国被加注了浓厚的文化价值。

王：不是我要冒犯您，杰克逊博士。少数艺术品很难算作一个对等的贸易势力。不过，我的目的也不是要在这里为中国击鼓鸣冤。我的目的是要点明，贸易和经济其实就是政治和国际关系的化名，而且无论是哪一个时代，任何协定都是有利于政治上的强者的。

狄克逊博士：有道理。有些经济学家和历史学家也许会不同意你的看法，不过批判主义学派应该会和你站在一个阵营里。杰克逊博士，你还有什么问题吗？

杰克逊博士：是的，你的演讲很有意思，王先生。我只是想知道，比如，当贸易集团里一个独立国家的关税与整个集团的利益相冲突的时候，那该怎么办？我是说，比如，中国作为亚太经合组织的成员，与另一个成员有优惠贸易关系，但与亚太经合组织整体却没有这样的关系？

王：是的，这是一个有趣的问题。我认为这个问题是……

实用短语

◆ That's interesting. Yes... there was, wasn't there? 很有意思。对,……不是吗?

◆ Yes... that was very interesting. 对……很有意思。

◆ I was just wondering about... 我只是想知道……

◆ I mean, say, for example... 我是说,比如……

◆ We'd like to ask... 我们想要问……

◆ Now... first of all, I was particularly interested in... 首先,我对……尤其感兴趣。

◆ But isn't it true that...? 但是……难道不是吗?

◆ We do have some questions. 我们确实有几个问题。

◆ So in conclusion... what I am arguing is that... 综上所述,我要论证的是……

◆ That concludes my presentation. 我的演讲到此结束。

◆ Now, if you have any questions, I'd be happy to answer them. 如果你们有任何问题,我会很高兴回答。

◆ Do you have any questions? 你们有什么问题吗?

◆ With respect, ... 不是要冒犯您,……

◆ Quite. Some might disagree with you, but certainly... 有道理。有些人可能不会同意你的看法,但是……

◆ You are right of course, but what I was trying to point out was that... 你当然是对的,不过我要指出的是……

词汇表

agricultural produce 农产品(produce 通常是动词,"生产"的意思,一般只在农业上作名词"产品"。其他情况下,produce 的名词形式为 product "产品" 和 production "生产劳动")
APEC 亚太经合组织
bang the drum 小题大做/为…助威
broad 宽的
claim 声称/要求
cultural artefacts 文化艺术品
developed 发达的
developing 发展中的

dynasty 朝代
European Union (EU) 欧盟
fascinating 令人好奇的/引人入胜的
favourable 受倾向的/受惠的
globalization 全球化
haves and have-nots 拥有者和非拥有者
in nature 本质上
lacquerware 漆器
be locked out 封锁在…之外
more-or-less 或多或少/多多少少
North America Free Trade

Agreement (NAFTA) 北美自由贸易协议
political forces 政治势力
porcelain 瓷器
presentation 演讲/讲座/表现
protectionist 保护主义
regime 政权/法律体制
sovereign state 主权国家
statement 陈述/言论
to sum up 总而言之/综上所述
trade barriers 贸易壁垒
transnational agreement 跨国协议
unfair 不公平的

第28章
考试与复习
Exams and Revision

背景常识

中国和英国大学之间的一大区别就是考试模式。英国大学里的考试很少使用选择填空。大部分的考试都是限时论文(timed essays)，即使数学考试有时也如此。选择题和填空题一般都用在中小学或外语课程考试中。一个典型的限时论文考试通常是2个小时。其间，你需要回答2个问题。但是，你可以从大约10个问题中任选2个你最拿手的问题来回答。通常每门课一个学期会有15堂左右的讲座。这10个问题就在这15个讲座题目中。这就表示，在考试之前，你不用把一个学期学过的所有内容都复习一遍。保险一点儿，复习4个；如果你觉得自己运气不错，那只复习3个就够了。只要你把自己锻炼成那4个问题方面的专家，10个问题里你肯定可以碰到2个你拿手的。

有时，与其让你写2篇长论文，老师更倾向于让你写5篇短文，来定义(define)5个课程里出现过的概念(concepts)。或者一篇长论文和几篇短文。无论考试模式如何，你总会有选择的余地，不必"有问必答"。英国大学这样做是为了减少记忆力在学生成绩中的重要性。高等教育的成果不是记忆力，而是理解力以及思辨的能力。

另外一个重要的问题是失语症(dyslexia)。失语症是一种影响人阅读和写字效率的先天性病症。患有失语症的人通常比一般人要聪明，只是写字和读书的速度明显比普通人慢。如果你被诊断为有失语症，你将可以在考试中得到额外加时(extra time)和辅助工具。失语症是一种非常普遍的症状——大约每20个英国学生中就有1个是有失语症的(dyslexic)。你所在学校的健康中心(health centre)会为你提供免费诊断。不要觉得有失语症是一种耻辱，它其实跟左撇子和双眼皮一样。

At the End of the Exam

Invigilator: Time's up! Put your pens down now! No talking... the invigilators will come round and collect your answer booklets. YOU MUST NOT TALK! Mr. Lin... put your pen down now, or your exam will be void. Wait until all of the papers have been collected.

Afterwards, in the SU

Wang: How did you find that, then?

Lin: It was a bit hard, I thought. I mean, I'd revised strategy and marketing, but that question on trade barriers and trading blocs just stumped me completely.

Wang: What did you do, then?

Lin: Well I think I wrote two really good essays on strategy and marketing; I just concentrated on them, but I only had about fifteen minutes left, so I just wrote a paragraph on the third one.

Wang: Oh... tut tut... that wasn't too smart. It's better to write three average essays than two good ones, I think. You should have given yourself, like, thirty five minutes per essay and stopped yourself even if you hadn't finished. If you'd done that, you'd have had time to go back and complete what was missing and you'd have done better overall... I think so, anyway. How did you revise?

Lin: Well, I revised everything... I just crammed everything wholesale... read through all of my notes, the chapters from the course books, memorized sentences and that.

Wang: What? You revised all fifteen topics? No wonder you couldn't remember everything. Nobody can remember that much information. You know, I think some Chinese students are so obsessed with rote memorization that they end up remembering nothing and panicking in these foreign exams. It's like acting... you know like when an actor forgets his lines? He forgets one line and the rest just evaporates as well.

Lin: How did you revise?

Wang: I looked through all of the past papers from the previous five years. You can get them from the library. Then I listed all the questions and looked at the ones which came up most often. The same areas come up every year but the questions are always phrased differently, so you have to be careful. Then I got rid of the areas that had come up as assignment questions this year. That left me with a set of areas that I could work with. I decided to revise four thoroughly.

Lin: You were taking a bit of a risk there, I think.

考试结束

监考官： 时间到！现在放下笔！不要交头接耳……监考官们会下去收你们的试卷。严禁交头接耳！林先生，立即把笔放下，要不然你的成绩就会被取消。等着，直到所有试卷都收齐以后。

稍后，在学生会

王： 你觉得怎么样？

林： 我觉得有点儿难。我是说，我复习了战略和市场营销，但是那个关于贸易壁垒和贸易集团的问题完全把我难住了。

王： 那你怎么做的？

林： 我觉得我关于战略和营销的 2 篇文章都不错，我把大部分的时间都用在它们 2 个上了。最后只剩下 15 分钟，所以第 3 个问题我只回答了一段话。

王： 哦，啧啧，这样可不是很明智。我认为，写 3 篇泛泛之作要比写 2 篇佳作要强。你应该让自己每 35 分钟写完一篇文章，写不完也要强迫自己停下来。如果你那样做了，你还可以回头把遗漏的部分再补上，这样你的平均成绩会高一些，最起码我是这么认为的。你是怎么复习的？

林： 我把什么都复习了，所有题目都强记了下来，读我所有的笔记和教科书里要求的章节，背诵句子什么的呗。

王： 啊？你把所有 15 个题目都复习了？难怪你记不住所有内容呢。谁也记不住那么多信息。我觉得有些中国学生太喜欢死记硬背了，结果在面对外国考试的时候一紧张全忘了。就像演戏似的，忘词儿。忘掉一句后面的也就都想不起来了。

林： 那你是怎么复习的？

王： 我先把前 5 年的考试题目看一遍。往年的考试题在图书馆里可以找到。我把所有的话题都罗列出来，看看哪些话题考得最频繁。每年出现的研究领域都差不多，只是具体问题的措词不一样。所以，你得留心。然后我再去掉那些在今年的作业里已经考过的话题。这样我就确定了一组我可以正式复习的领域了。我决定对其中 4 个仔细复习。

林： 我觉得你有点儿冒险。

Wang: Yes but look... I followed a system... first I read through all of my lecture notes, handouts, seminar materials and the chapters that I had read in the course books, expanding all my notes with new ideas as I went. Then I chose four questions out of the past papers. I took one per day and worked on it.

Lin: How did you revise for each individual question then?

Wang: I analysed the questions and picked out the key words, the question words and the instruction words... you know... discuss, evaluate, compare, who, how much? to what extent? Maslow's Hierarchy of Needs and so on... then I drew mind maps using these and my notes. Then I wrote out the mind maps in longhand, and last of all I wrote an essay against-the-clock. When time ran out, I stopped myself and checked how much I had missed out. The important thing is always to answer the question using the essay format... so you need to get to the conclusion in time... if you don't, the temptation is to eat into the time you should be spending on your next essay, and in the end you only write a little bit for your last essay in the exam. It's all down to timing in the end.

王：对,但是你看,我有一套系统。首先我把课堂笔记、讲座概括、讨论课资料和我看过的课内阅读章节都看一遍,再一边添加新想法。然后我从以前的试卷中找出4个问题,每天拿下一个。

林：你怎么复习每个单独的问题呢?

王：我分析这些问题并挑出关键词、问题词和指示词。比如,讨论、评价、比较、谁、多少、什么程度、马斯洛的需求层次等等。然后我用我笔记上的内容来规划一个思维路线图,再粗略地把这个路线图写下来。最后我给自己计时把整个答案写出来。时间一到就停下,看看还有多少没写完。重要的是坚持使用论文的格式,所以你必须及时进入结论阶段,不然你就总想占用下一篇的时间,答到最后一个问题时不得不草草收场。说到底,就是要把握时间。

实用短语

- Time's up! 时间到！
- You must not talk! 严禁交头接耳！
- How did you find that? 你感觉怎么样？
- That wasn't too smart. 这可不太明智。
- You should have… 你本应该……
- If you'd… you'd have had more time to…
  如果你……了，你就能有更多时间……
- I think so, anyway. 最起码，我这么认为。
- You were taking a bit of a risk, there. 你这么做有点儿冒险。
- The important thing is… 重要的是……
- It's all down to… 说到底/关键是……

词汇表

against-the-clock 限时地
answer booklet 答题簿
average 平均的
be down to 最终归结到
be phrased (differently) 措词
cram 塞/挤
eat into 占用
evaluate 评估
evaporate 蒸发
forget 忘记
get to 到…地步或地方
Hierarchy of Needs 需求结构

in longhand 粗略的
invigilator 监考官
look through 浏览
marketing 市场营销
memorise 记忆
mind map 思维路线图
overall 总体上的
paragraph 段落
past papers 以前的考试试卷
per 每
phrase 短语

rote memorisation 死记硬背
run out 用完
set 组
strategy 战略
take a bit of a risk 冒一定的风险
temptation 吸引
time's up! 时间到！
to what extent 到什么程度
trading bloc/trade bloc 贸易集团
void 无效的
wholesale 全面的

第29章
请一天假
Take a Day Off

背景常识

在英国大学里,不仅上课的时间比中国大学少得多,课程的出勤还是自愿的。通常,讨论课是你必须参加的(compulsory attendance),而听讲座就是自愿的了(optional attendance)。当论文的上交期限快到了的时候,有时讲座课的出勤人数可能还不到一半。中国老师在看到空空如也的教室时肯定会大发雷霆,但是英国老师通常只能苦笑一下然后照常上课。需要留心的是,英国的老师喜欢用他的课堂笔记来设计考试题,所以虽然出席讲座是自愿的,最好还是不要缺课(be absent)。

对于那些必须参加的课,旷课的后果(consequences of absence)是相当严重的。在没有正当理由(legitimate reason)的情况下,缺两节讨论课就会导致不及格。在有些英国大学里,你只有在生病(be ill/sick)的时候才能在必须出勤的课里请假。如果你真的要请病假(take a medical leave),你必须在痊愈后向院系提供医生证明(doctor's note)。

你还得知道你应该跟谁请假。通常你必须通知教那门课的老师。一般本科讨论课都是由院系里的博士生主讲,或者叫半职教学员工(Part-time Teaching Staff, PTTS)。那样的话,你可能得通知那门课的组织老师(course convenor)。有些院系有专门的教务秘书(academic secretary)来记考勤。这种情况下,你就应该通知教务秘书。

请假的时候,你的假条或口头假条应该提到以下几点:你哪节课要请假?请假的原因是什么?你对错过这堂课有多遗憾?你准备如何把落下的课赶上?不要把假条写成通知,要用疑问而不是陈述的口吻。

Beginning of Class

Dr. Manton: Oh, hello stranger! Where have you been hiding?

Wang: I'm so sorry, Dr. Manton, [*sniffling*] I've had a really bad bout of the flu.

Dr. Manton: The flu?! Gosh! Did you go to hospital?

Wang: Erm... no. I just stayed at home in bed.

Dr. Manton: Oh. So it wasn't really flu, then. You just caught a cold. You know, everyone catches colds from time to time—especially when there's a change in the weather. Did you call in sick, though?

Wang: Erm... no... sorry. It's this weather, though. It's so cold.

Dr. Manton: You don't get colds and flu from cold weather, Mr. Wang! They are viruses... you get them from other people.

Wang: Oh... erm....

Dr. Manton: You should always call in to inform the department that you cannot attend lectures or classes. I mean, attendance at seminars is not optional—it's compulsory and, apart from the fact that we have a duty of care towards you, it's only good manners to inform us, don't you agree?

Wang: Yes, I'm really sorry. I'll remember next time.

Dr. Manton: That's OK. Just remember to pick up any handouts that you are missing from the VLE. Also, you'll need to have a look at your classmates' lecture notes so that you can catch up. Er... [*to everyone*]... could I just make a point of saying that if you are sick or are going to have to miss any seminars, you must notify the department by phone beforehand, and if you are off for a significant period, or you are going to miss an assignment deadline or an exam, you need a doctor's note. If you don't, the consequences can be serious. All right?

Everyone: Yeah, OK, right.

After Class

Lucy: Dr. Block, I need to take a few days off because my parents are coming over to visit, and I need to show them around.

Dr. Block: Hmmm... it's not really a good idea to take time off, you know. You are trailing behind a bit, and you need to attend all the classes you can. Are your parents not old enough to fend for themselves?

Lucy: Well, you know, they've never been to the UK before and they don't speak English... and I need to be their guide.

Dr. Block: Hmm... you know there are thousands of tourists in London who can't speak English and they manage to get by... you'd be amazed at how little actual

║║║刚上课 ‹‹‹║║║║║║║║║║║║║║║║║║║║║

曼顿博士：嗨，陌生人！你最近藏哪儿去了？

王：对不起，曼顿博士，[抽鼻子] 我得了重流感。

曼顿博士：流感？天呐！你去医院了吗？

王：哦，没有。我在家卧床休息来着。

曼顿博士：噢，也就是说其实不是真的流感啰。你只是感冒了。人人都会感冒，尤其是天气变化的时候。不过，你请病假了吗？

王：哦，没有，对不起。天太冷了。

曼顿博士：天冷并不会引起感冒或流感，王先生！那是病毒，别人身上携带的病毒传染给你了。

王：哦。

曼顿博士：你不能来上课总应该通知院系里一声。讨论课的考勤可不是自愿的，是必须的。而且我们还有照顾你的责任，出于礼貌，你也应该通知我们吧，是不是？

王：是，真的很抱歉。我下次一定记住。

曼顿博士：好吧。不过记住从虚拟学习环境系统上下载你错过的讲座概要，而且你还得借同学的笔记看看，以便能赶上全班的进度。哦，[转向全班] 我要在此强调一下，如果你病了或者不能来上讨论课，必须打电话提前通知系里。如果你要缺很长时间的课或者要错过作业上交日期或考试，你必须有医生证明。不然的话，后果是非常严重的。明白了吗？

所有人：明白了。

║║║下课后 ‹‹‹║║║║║║║║║║║║║║║║║║║║

露西：布洛克博士，我得请几天假。我父母要来看我，我得带他们逛逛。

布洛克博士：嗯，请假可不是什么好主意。你的成绩本来就有点儿落后，每堂课都得上才行。你父母还不到自己观光的年龄吗？

露西：他们从来没来过英国，而且他们不会说英语。我得给他们当导游。

布洛克博士：嗯，你知道在伦敦有上千名游客不会说英语，但他们仍然能对付过去。一个游客所需要的语言会少得让你吃惊。你知道吗？语言学的研究显示……

language you need as a tourist. Do you know that there is linguistic research that shows....

Lucy: Yes, I know, but they really do depend on me... and they expect me to be there. It's cultural; Chinese parents expect their children to do things like this....

Dr. Block: I know, but surely if they really care about your education, they'll understand....

Lucy: Maybe... but do you think I could take maybe just two days?

Dr. Block: OK... two days, but you must catch up on all of the work and get all of the materials and handouts. All right? I don't know! Sometimes I'm such a soft touch!

In Media Studies Department

Liu: Hello, is that the Media Studies department?
Secretary: Yes.
Liu: This is Liu Yu here. I'm in Dr. Molloy's seminar group, but I'm not feeling well today so I'm going to have to miss today's sessions.
Secretary: OK, I'll let Dr. Molloy know. I think there might be a part-timer doing his seminar today, though. Dr. Molloy's off sick as well.
Liu: Thanks. Bye.

露西：是的，我知道。不过他们真的非常依赖我，而且他们希望我陪他们。这是文化差异，中国的父母认为子女应该做这样的事情。

布洛克博士：我知道，但是如果他们真的关心你的教育，他们应该能理解。

露西：也许吧。但是你觉得我能不能就请两天假？

布洛克博士：好吧，就两天。但是你必须把所有功课赶上并领取所有的资料和讲座简介。可以了吗？真搞不明白，有时候我心太软了。

在传媒学院

刘：你好，这是传媒学院吗？

秘书：对。

刘：我叫刘宇，是莫洛伊博士讨论小组的。我今天觉得不太舒服，所以我不得不缺席今天的讨论了。

秘书：好吧，我会通知莫洛伊博士的。印象中今天的课是由一个兼职老师来代上的。莫洛伊博士也请病假了。

刘：谢谢，再见。

实用短语

- Oh, hello stranger! 嗨,你好,陌生人!
- Where have you been hiding? 你躲到哪儿去了?
- I'm so sorry. 实在对不起。
- I've had a... 我得了……
- No. I just... 不,我只是……而已。
- It's this weather. 都是因为天气。
- I'll remember next time. 我下次一定记住。
- I need to take a few days off. 我得请几天假。
- But do you think I could take... 但是你认为我能……吗?
- I'm going to have to miss... 我不得不错过……
- I'm not feeling well. 我身体不舒服。

词汇表

a change in the weather 天气变化
a soft touch 心太软的人/好欺负的人
amazed 被吸引的/感到惊奇的
attend 出席,参加
be off sick 处于病假状态的
beforehand 之前
call in sick 请假
catch a cold 得感冒
classmate 同学
compulsory 必须的/义务的

consequences 后果
depend on 取决于
doctor's note 医生证明
from time to time 偶尔
get by 混过去/蒙混过关
good manners 礼貌/好的举止
handout 纲要
inform 通知
lecture notes 课堂笔记
look after oneself 照顾自己/好自为之

make a point 发表观点/强调
miss 错过
optional 非义务的/可选择的
part-timer 临时的员工
session 时段
significant period 长时间
take off 离开/请假
take time off 请假
virus 病毒
VLE (Virtual Learning Environment) 虚拟学习环境

第30章
像科学家一样说话
Sounding Like a Scientist

背景常识

你说话的方式能在很大程度上表现出你的专业和性格。要想融入一个群体当中,你也必须能说他们的内行话。科学家们在中国文化中的典型形象一般是沉默寡言(taciturn)、不善言谈的(tongue-tied)。而在英国文化中,科学家的典型形象通常是疯狂而古怪的(eccentric)。他们会抓住任何机会来说教或与人争论,而且总是使用多音节的术语和冗繁的句子。他们可能非常聪明,但是不太善于与人交流。

比如说,如果你不是科学家,你会这么说话:Our minds get used to what we often see.(我们的思维对常见的事物不敏感)。如果你是科学家,同样一句话,你可能会说:Our neural pathways become accustomed to our sensory input patterns.(摘自《星际迷航:下一代》)。mind 是外行人的话,neural pathway 是科学家的词。同样的,used to 可以被换成 accustomed to,things 换成 substance,people 换成 homo sapiens,animal 换成 creature,right 换成 logical,wrong 换成 erroneous,yes 换成 positive,no 换成 negative。科学家们还喜欢用长句子,这意味着他们喜欢用关系代词和连词,比如 where,by which 和 hence。他们还喜欢用拉丁语、法语和希腊语的虚词,比如 ergo(即),vis-à-vis(对于)和 i.e.(意即)。

当然,这些都是在大众文化中被夸张了的典型形象。专攻自然科学的学生们在现实生活中使用这些词汇往往是显示幽默或自我解嘲。在学术上,当今的英国科学家们,例如史蒂文·霍金,倾向于使用简单的语言以便为科学吸引更多的观众。

In the Biology Seminar

Dr. Sanders: Right, I'll just start by going over what we did in the last lecture... we were looking at the concept of "one gene, one polypeptide" right?

All: Right, yeah, erm....

Dr. Sanders: And we were saying that genes are expressed in the phenotype as polypeptides, in other words—proteins—is that right?

All: Yep, yes, right....

Dr. Sanders: So we looked at Beadle and Tatum's experiments with the bread mold Neurospora, which resulted in several mutant strains, each lacking a specific enzyme in a biochemical pathway, and we found that their results led to the one-gene, one-polypeptide hypothesis. Is that right?

Harry: Erm... I'm not quite clear about that, Dr. Sanders....

Dr. Sanders: Well, Beadle and Tatum wanted to find out the relationship between genes and enzymes in a biochemical pathway. So they carried out an experiment by putting the spores of each mutant strain on a minimal medium with no supplements... if you look at this diagram here you can see what I mean... the table shows that when no supplement is added to the minimal medium, the wild type grows on all media, and it can synthesise its own arginine. However, if you follow the table down to the bottom-right, you see that when ornithine, citrulline or arginine is added to the minimal medium, mutant strain 3 grows, and it can convert ornithine to citrulline and citrulline to arginine. See?

Harry: Oh, right. I remember now.

Dr. Sanders: So, can anyone tell me what the interpretation was?

Sally: Yes... if an organism cannot convert one particular compound to another, it presumably lacks an enzyme required for the conversion, and the mutation is in the gene that codes for the mutation.

Dr. Sanders: Right. Spot on... and Harry, what was the conclusion?

Harry: That the synthesis of arginine proceeds like this: Precursor to Enzyme A to ornithine to Enzyme B to Citrulline to Enzyme C to Arginine. Strain 3 is blocked at the Enzyme A step, Strain 2 is blocked at the Enzyme B step and Strain 3 is blocked at the Enzyme C step. At the same time, you have genes one, two and three, and each one specifies a specific enzyme.

Dr. Sanders: Well done. So we then went on to look at how certain hereditary diseases in humans had been found to be caused by the absence of certain enzymes. Julia, what did these observations support? Can you tell me?

Julia: These observations supported the one-gene, one-polypeptide hypothesis.

Dr. Sanders: Right, very good. Now in this lecture we'll be moving on to look at the molecular basis of gene interactions. This will be explained in terms of biochemical pathways and regulatory genes, otherwise known as pleiotropy. So what I'd like you all to do is to look at the table on the whiteboard here.

在生物讨论课上

桑德斯博士：好了，首先我要回顾一下我们上节课的内容。我们讨论了"一个基因与一个多聚氨基酸"的概念，对吗？

所有人：对。

桑德斯博士：我们说了，基因的表现型是通过多聚氨基酸体现出来的，也就是说——蛋白质。对吗？

所有人：对。

桑德斯博士：那么我们看了比德尔和塔特姆的面包霉菌链孢霉试验。那个试验最终产生若干变异菌，每一个在其生化过程中都缺少一种酶。最终我们发现这些结果引发了一个基因与一个多聚氨基酸对应的猜想。对吗？

哈里：哦，桑德斯博士，我对这个还不是很清楚。

桑德斯博士：那好，比德尔和塔特姆想要探求酶在生物化学中与基因的关系。所以，他们进行了这个试验，把具有不同变异菌的孢子放在没有补给的基本培养基中。如果你看看这个图表，你就能明白我的意思了。这个表格显示，在没有补给的基本培养基中，野生的种类在媒介上生长，能够合成自己的精氨酸。然而，如果你继续看这个表格，一直看到右下方，你就会发现，当鸟氨酸、瓜氨酸或者精氨酸加入到基本培养基中时，3号变异菌开始生长，并能将鸟氨酸转化成瓜氨酸，瓜氨酸转化成精氨酸。看到了吗？

哈里：对，我记起来了。

桑德斯博士：那么，谁能告诉我怎么解释这一现象？

萨莉：我能。如果一个有机体不能把某一化合物转换成另一个化合物，它很可能就缺少这个转换过程中所需要的酶，而变种又是记录变种信息的基因的变化。

桑德斯博士：对，完全正确。哈里，结论是什么呢？

哈里：精氨酸的产生过程是这样的：从与鸟氨酸对应的 A 酶到与瓜氨酸对应的 B 酶再到与精氨酸对应的 C 酶。3 号变异菌在产生 A 酶的时候受阻，2 号变异菌在产生 B 酶的时候受阻，而 3 号变异菌在产生 C 酶的时候受阻。与此同时，1、2、3 号基因各自对应这 3 种酶。

桑德斯博士：好。然后我们又研究了某些人类遗传疾病是如何由酶的缺乏而引起的。朱莉娅，这些观察结果证明了什么？你能告诉我吗？

朱莉娅：这些观察结果证明一个基因与一个多聚氨基酸对应的猜想。

桑德斯博士：对，很好。今天这节课我们将继续研究基因活动的分子基础。我们将通过生化过程和规范基因，又叫多效基因来讲解这个问题。我需要你们都来看看在白板上的这个表格。

实用短语

- ◆ I'll just start by going over what we did in the last lecture. 首先我要回顾一下我们上节课的内容。
- ◆ We were looking at… 我们看了／研究了／探讨了……
- ◆ And we were saying that… 而且我们提到……
- ◆ Is that right? 对吗？
- ◆ So we looked at… 那么我们看了／研究了／探讨了……
- ◆ and we found that… 而且我们发现……
- ◆ I'm not quite clear about that. 我对那个问题还不太清楚。
- ◆ If you look at this diagram here you can see what I mean. 如果你看看这个图表，你可以看到我说的。
- ◆ The table shows that… 这个图表显示……
- ◆ However, if you follow the table down to…
  然而，如果你继续看这个图，看到……
- ◆ So, can anyone tell me what the interpretation was? 那么，谁能告诉我怎么解释这个现象？
- ◆ Right. Spot on. 对。完全正确／不偏不倚／正好说到点子上。
- ◆ Well done. So we then went on to look at… 说得好。我们继续看……
- ◆ Is that clear now? 明白了吗？

词 汇 表

absence 缺席／不存在
arginine 精氨酸
biochemical pathway 生化机制
block 阻挡
citrulline 瓜氨酸
code 密码
compound 化合物
convert 转化
enzyme 酶
experiment 试验
express 表达
gene 基因

hereditary diseases 遗传疾病
hypothesis 猜想／假定
in other words 换句话说
interaction 相互作用
lead to 导致
minimal medium 基本培养基
mold 真菌
mutant strain 变异菌
mutation 变异
organism 生命体
ornithine 鸟氨酸
phenotype 表现型

pleiotropy 多效基因
polypeptide 多聚氨基酸
presumably 根据猜测地
proteins 蛋白质
regulatory gene 规范基因
spore 孢子
spot on 完全正确／恰到好处
step 步骤
supplement 支持／补助
synthesise 合成
wild type 野生品种

第31章
像哲学家一样说话
Sounding Like a Philosopher

背景常识

想要有哲学家的谈吐,首先要具备哲学家的思维方式。哲学家思考方式的一大特点是他们对细节的关注。波特兰·拉塞尔说:"哲学的意义就在于,开始于一个简单到不值一提的事实,然后得到一个矛盾到没人能相信的结论。"(The point of philosophy is to start with something so simple as not to seem worth stating, and to end with something so paradoxical that no one will believe it.) 可见,一个哲学家的谈吐常常涉及一些积极的吹毛求疵和愤世嫉俗。

社会科学的学生们经常在哲学层面上质疑、辩论的题目包括:生命(life)、死亡(death)、意识(consciousness)、现实(reality)、爱情(love)、憎恨(hatred)、知识(knowledge)、权利(power)、空间(space)、时间(time)、永恒(eternity)、年龄(age)、善(good)、恶(evil)、欲望(desire)、美(beauty)、自由(freedom)、责任(duty)、幸福(happiness)、苦难(suffering)、正义(justice)、道德(morality)、自我(self)、他人(otherness)、战争(war)和真理(truth)。

另外,社会科学学生的一个更明显的语言特征是对后缀-ology和-ism的使用。比如,世界观(ontology)、认知论(epistemology)、方法论(methodology)、女权主义(feminism)和马克思主义(Marxism)等等。对于中国留学生来说,真正重要的不是学哲学家的风趣言语,而是要锻炼自己以哲学和批判的眼光来看待世界的那份热情和勇气。

In the Coffee Bar

Amy: That philosophy lecture was really interesting, wasn't it? That Professor Le Boef is really cool... he's French, isn't he?

Jay: Erm... yes, I think. You know, I found him really fascinating.

Fred: Oh, man! I just hope it ain't all gonna be like that... existentialism... postmodernism... French rubbish.

Amy: [laughing] Shut up you! You know it isn't going to be like that.

Ally: Well I don't know what philosophy is all about... I mean, what's the point of it? Just sitting round discussing the meaning of life and not getting any answers. I think it's just a doss!

Amy: It's not like that at all, Ally. Philosophy is fundamental to everything!

Ally: No it isn't! We have to make a living first!

Fred: No way... it ain't like that at all. Look, without philosophy how would we know how to decide what is right and wrong, or when a society is just, or whether human beings really have rights?

Jay: Yes... you know business leaders and politicians always appeal to philosophical truths in the end.

Ally: Yes... but they never agree and look at the mess they've made of the world!

Fred: Well maybe that just shows that they should have studied philosophy in the first place.

Ally: OK... look... give me one good reason why philosophy is useful.

Jay: Well, look, the questions that it asks are the most fundamental questions there are. To study philosophy is to grapple with these questions in a systematic way and to explore what the tradition of philosophy has to say about them.

Fred: Yeah... and the skills philosophy teaches us are applicable to everything. It requires you to think clearly and deeply, to distinguish good arguments from bad ones, to use your imagination, and above all to think critically and for yourself.

Ally: That just sounds like you're mouthing what your Professor Le Boef told you this morning. I think it's just a way for rich students to waste their parents' money for three years and sit around getting drunk and drinking coffee. I mean, it isn't rigorous, is it?

Amy: What?! That's rich coming from someone who's doing Business Studies! You know, Ally, maybe if you did a bit more philosophy you would be better at Business Studies, your English would improve and you'd understand why Chinese and Westerners think differently!

Fred: Come on girls... let's not fall out over this. Remember, philosophers are supposed to be detached and objective... not emotional!

Jay: You know... I think that's the problem with us East-Asian students... most of us are doing Business Studies and Media Studies and the lecturers think we're all shallow and money-obsessed. That's a pity, because it was only about 10 years ago that they thought we were all deep and meaningful! They used to think we knew all about Confucius and Mencius and the Tao!

在咖啡屋

埃米：那个哲学讲座非常有趣，不是吗？那个勒伯夫教授太酷了。他是法国人，对吧？

杰伊：哦，是，我估计。我觉得他非常有魅力。

弗雷德：哦，天呐！我只希望那讲座不会是那套存在主义和后现代主义的法式胡言乱语。

埃米：[笑] 别胡扯了！你明知道不会是那一套的。

艾丽：我不知道哲学到底有什么用。我是说，有什么意义呢？光是坐在那儿讨论生命的意义，却怎么也讨论不出结果。我觉得哲学就是白日做梦！

埃米：才不是呢，艾丽。哲学是一切的基础。

艾丽：错！我们得首先保证生活！

弗雷德：没门儿，不是这么回事。没有哲学，我们怎么能知道什么是对与错，社会是否有正义，或者人类是否真的拥有人权。

杰伊：是啊，你要知道商人和政治家最终都要诉诸于哲学。

艾丽：也是，不过他们总是意见不一，也不看看他们捣的乱！

弗雷德：也许这就证明他们应该从一开始就学哲学。

艾丽：好吧，给我一个哲学有用的理由。

杰伊：哲学问题是最根本的问题。学习哲学就是系统性地求解这些问题并探索哲学传统中对这些问题的解释。

弗雷德：对，而且哲学教给我们的技巧能用在所有事情上。它使你能够清晰深入地思考、辨别论证的好坏、使用想像力，更重要的是批判地思考并分析自己。

艾丽：听起来你就像是在练习那个勒伯夫教授今天早上教你说的话。我觉得这无非就是富家子弟在浪费父母的钱，喝着酒和咖啡打发了3年时间。我是说，它一点儿也不严谨，对吗？

埃米：什么？一个学商学的居然说出这种话！艾丽，如果你多学学哲学，你在商学上可能还会更进一步，你的英语也能提高，而且你就能明白中西方人们想法不同的原因。

弗雷德：算了，姑娘们。不要为这件事伤了和气。记住，哲学家应该置身事外，就事论事，而不是感情用事！

杰伊：你知道吗，我认为这是我们东亚学生的一个问题。我们大多数人都学商学和传媒，老师们都觉得我们非常肤浅而且崇尚金钱。这非常遗憾，因为就在10年前，他们还认为我们都熟知孔子、孟子、道教什么的呢！

实用短语

- You know, I found him... 你别说，我觉得他……
- Oh man! I just hope it ain't all gonna be... 天哪！我希望它不会是……
- I mean, what's the point of it? 我是说，这有什么意义呢？
- Yes, but they never agree... 是，不过他们总是意见不一……
- OK look... give me a good reason why... 好吧，给我一个……的理由。
- That just sounds like... 听起来就像……
- I think it's just a way for... 我觉得这无非就是……
- I mean, it isn't... is it? 我是说它不是……吧？
- Shut up, you! 别胡说了/闭嘴！
- You know it isn't going to... 你知道它不会是……
- It's not like that at all. 才不是这样呢。
- No way, it ain't like that at all! 没门儿，事实不是这样的！
- Look! Without... how would we know...? 你想想！没有……我们怎么能知道……？
- Well maybe that just means that... 也许那只表示……
- Well look... the questions it asks are... 这么说吧……它问的问题是……
- What?! That's rich coming from... 什么？……居然说出这种话！
- Come on... let's not fall out. 算了，我们不要伤了和气。

词汇表

address 涉及/处理
ain't gonna 不会（美语，表示"be not going to"）
appeal to 求助于…
applicable 能适用的
be detached 置身事外
Confucius 孔子
conscious 有意识的
doss 白日做梦
Existentialism 存在主义
fall out 翻脸

find (someone to be...) 觉得(某人是…)
grapple with 努力解决
hey 嘿
in the first place 本来/首先
make a living 应付生活开销
Mencius 孟子
mess 混乱
money-obsessed 拜金主义的
mouth 嘴
no way 没门儿

objective 客观的
Postmodernism 后现代主义
rich 了不起的/比一般情况好的（表讽刺）
shallow 肤浅的
sit around 闲坐着
systematic 系统化的
Tao (Dao) 道教
the way things are 表面现象/正常状态
ultimate truths 最终的真理

第32章
像艺术家一样说话
Sounding Like an Artist

背景常识

一个典型的西方艺术家,除了敏感(sensitive)、散漫(liberal)和言辞考究(stylish)以外,最明显的特征是喜欢评头论足(judgmental)。这些区别也体现在东西方之间艺术欣赏手段的不同。中国过去的艺术收藏家们总在私下里欣赏艺术,国画都是被当作传家宝在家族内流传,音乐作品也只在师门之内传授。而西方艺术欣赏往往更公开化,有更成体系的画廊文化和大学艺术教育传统。

主流欧洲艺术史通常以中世纪(the Middle Ages)为开端,其起止时间大约是从5世纪到15世纪。中世纪以后是文艺复兴(the Renaissance),一般被认为是15、16世纪。16至18世纪是巴洛克和洛可可时期(Baroque and Rococo)。从18到19世纪,主要艺术流派是新古典主义(Neo-classicism)和浪漫主义(Romanticism)。从19世纪晚期到现在,在西方艺术中盛行的是现代主义和后现代主义。西方艺术家中,达·芬奇(Da Vinci)、拉斐尔(Raphael)和米开朗基罗(Michelangelo)是文艺复兴时期的代表人物。伦勃朗(Rembrandt)、巴赫(Bach)和伏尔泰(Voltaire)通常被认为是巴洛克和洛可可时期的艺术家。海顿(Haydn)、莫扎特(Mozart)、贝多芬(Beethoven)和雨果(Hugo)代表着新古典主义、浪漫主义和现实主义。毕加索(Picasso)、凡高(Van Gogh)、马奈(Manet)、莫奈(Monet)和沃荷(Warhol)都是现代派艺术家。

不过,艺术欣赏毕竟是直观感受,没有标准答案,更不用死记硬背。以上提到的诸多定义都有争辩的余地。

In the Coffee Bar

Maggie: Hi Lucy, what's that book you've got there?

Lucy: This? Oh, it's just a booklet from the National Gallery on how to appreciate art... it's quite interesting, but I don't know... it's so complicated... all this stuff about representation, personification, symbolism and allegory... I think you'd have to do a whole degree to really understand everything fully.

Maggie: Oh, I don't know... I think a lot of that stuff is just people posing and showing off. I think a lot of people fake an interest in Art just to look, you know, cultured.

Charles: I'm not so sure about that, you know. I think it's useful to have some art appreciation techniques handy so that you can, you know, get more out of a painting or a sculpture, or something.

Lucy: What do you mean?

Charles: Well, I mean, it's useful to know some basic facts like the artist's name, the medium, the title, the probable date of the work, its location now, its condition, and provenance—you know—where it came from... it's also good to know about the subject matter—Greek Mythology and Christianity, for example, had an enormous effect on Western Art, so you need at least to know about the Greek Myths, the Bible and the saints and so on. I don't think you can really appreciate European Art if you don't have that background.

Chen: What? So you're saying that someone from China like me can't appreciate European Art?

Charles: Well, what I mean is that a painting can certainly have an aesthetic effect on you... you can appreciate its beauty... it might even affect you emotionally, but, in order to really understand it you need to understand who painted it, why he—it was usually men—painted it, the style, the historical context... who commissioned it and why... it's only after that that you can exercise critical judgment and interpretation.

Chen: I still can't get you.

Charles: Well, although there's no point debating whether Michelangelo was a "greater" painter than Van Gogh, since they lived at such different times and places, we can still "read" paintings. You can do this through the same methods as you use to appreciate music or literature—you examine the historical, political, social, religious, psychological and technological context of the artwork as completely as possible in order to understand what the art "meant". There are no right or wrong interpretations, only poorly expressed or uninteresting ones.

Lucy: Well I think that's totally unscientific, and it's elitist too. Most people don't have the time or the access to education to appreciate art like that. They appreciate things that speak to them on a personal, gut level... that's why pop art and stuff related to real life is so important....

Charles: What? You mean stuff like Soviet Realism and political propaganda posters and stuff?

Lucy: No… I mean modern art… Britart—Damien Hirst, Banksy and Tracy Emin.

Charles: Well that's all elitist in the end because it's rich people like Charles Saatchi who buy up all of that. Haha….

Maggie: Calm down, calm down… let's not fall out over this. It's only art! Anyway, there's a public lecture on Picasso's Blue Period at the Slade tonight. Shall we go?

在咖啡屋

玛吉：嗨，露西，你看什么书呢？

露西：这个？哦，这是国家画廊教人如何欣赏艺术的小册子，挺有意思。但是，我不知道，这太复杂了，这些表现、拟人化、象征主义、寓意之类的东西。我觉得要学个艺术学位才能把这些东西弄懂。

玛吉：哦，不一定。我认为很多这些玩意儿都是装腔作势。我觉得很多人假装对艺术感兴趣，其实是为了显得有文化。

查尔斯：我不敢苟同。我认为，具备一定的艺术鉴赏力还是有用的。这样你能从绘画、雕塑和其它作品里看出更多的东西来。

露西：你的意思是？

查尔斯：我是说，了解一些基本常识。比如艺术家的名字、作品材质、作品名、创作年代、如今的所在地、保存状况和出处，就是说，从哪儿来。知道它的主题也很好。比如希腊神话和基督教都对西方艺术有深远的影响，所以你起码需要知道希腊神话故事、圣经和圣徒故事等等。不了解这些，我想你没法真正欣赏西方艺术。

陈：什么？那么你是说，一个像我这样的中国人不能欣赏西方艺术啰？

查尔斯：我的意思是，一幅画当然有它的美学效果。你可以欣赏它的美，它甚至可以影响你的情绪。但是，要想真正了解它，你得知道它是谁画的。画家，一般是男的，为什么要画它，画的风格、历史背景、委托人、委托原因……只有这样你才能进行批判和评价。

陈：我还是听不懂你的意思。

查尔斯：这么说吧，虽然争论米开朗基罗和凡·高哪个画术更精湛没有意义，因为他们生活在不同的时代和地域，可我们还是可以解读他们的画。你可以运用欣赏音乐和文学的方法来解读它们——尽可能全面地分析这部作品的历史、政治、社会、宗教、心理和技术背景以便能了解作品的"底蕴"。解析是没有对错之分的，只不过有的表达苍白乏味。

露西：我觉得这根本不科学，而且太精英主义。大部分人没有时间或条件去接受那样的艺术欣赏教育。他们欣赏那些能在个人和感性层面上与他们产生共鸣的作品。这就是为什么流行艺术和与生活息息相关的东西如此重要的原因。

查尔斯：什么？你是说类似苏联现实主义和大字报之类的东西？

露西：不，我是说现代艺术，英国当代艺术——戴曼·赫斯特、班克西和特里西·恩敏。

查尔斯：其实这些也是精英主义，因为到头来都是有钱人在买断所有这些作品。比如查尔斯·萨奇。

玛吉：冷静，冷静，大家不要伤了和气。不过就是艺术而已！对了，今天晚上在斯莱德有一堂关于毕加索蓝色时期的讲座。咱们一块儿去吧。

实用短语

- What's that… you've got there? 你在读什么?
- It's just… 就是……而已。
- I think you'd have to… 我觉得你必须……
- I'm not so sure about that, you know. 我不敢苟同/我不那么肯定。
- Well, I mean, it's useful to know… 我是说,了解……是有用的。
- It's also good to know about… 知道……也有好处。
- I don't think you can really… 我想你没法真正……
- What? So you're saying that…? 什么? 那么你是说……?
- Well, what I mean is… 其实,我想要说的是……
- In order to really understand it you need to… 要真正理解它,你必须……
- Well, although it is… we can still… 尽管……我们仍然可以……
- There are no right or wrong interpretations, only… 解析没有对错之分,只不过……
- Well I think that's just… 我觉得他不过是……罢了。

词汇表

aesthetic 审美观
allegory 寓意
appreciate 欣赏
artwork 艺术作品
Bible 圣经
Britart 英国当代艺术
calm down 冷静
commission 委托
context 背景/大环境
critical judgement 批判
elitist 精英主义的/上流社会的
fake 假的
get… out of… 从…总结出…/从…受益
Greek Mythology 希腊神话理论

Greek Myths 希腊神话故事
gut level 感性的/直觉上的
handy 方便的/称手的
historical 跟历史有关的(注意与 historic 区别,后者表示"有历史意义的")
medium 媒介
Michelangelo 米开朗基罗
National Gallery 国家画廊
nonsense 无理取闹/没道理的(既是名词也是形容词)
personification 个人化
Picasso 毕加索
please 令人高兴

poorly expressed 表达不清楚的
pop art 流行艺术
pose 摆出…姿态/装腔作势
propaganda posters 宣传画报/大字报
provenance 出处
psychological 心理上的
representation 代表/表现
saints 圣人/圣徒
show off 卖弄
Soviet realism 苏维埃现实主义
subject matter 主题
symbolism 象征主义
Van Gogh 凡·高

第33章
学生会与政治
The Student Union and Student Politics

背景常识

在中国,大多数学生会的职责是帮助学校管理学生。在英国,学生会和大学之间的关系要更加独立。学生会非但不帮助学校管理学生,反而代表和维护学生的利益。有时这意味着跟学校针锋相对,讨价还价。

英国学生会主要有三种职能——政治主张(campaign)、生活服务(services)和文化娱乐(entertainment)。一个典型的学生会设有一个主席(president)、一个福利官(welfare officer)、一个政治主张官(campaign officer)、一个多元文化官(diversity officer)和一个体育娱乐官(sport and activity officer)。这5个就是所谓的离校官员(sabbatical officers),全职为学生会工作并领取薪金。当选的学生要停学一年,或者在毕业那年就任。除此之外,还有30个左右的非离校官员(non-sabbatical officers)。Non-sabbs 必须在为学生会工作的同时正常从事学业,没有工资。他们通常代表某一个特殊的学生群体或学生事务,比如,国际学生官(international student officer)主要代表留学生的声音。

学生会的官员选举每年进行一次。竞选方式主要包括:海报(poster)、候选人辩论(hustings)和现场拉票(canvassing)。每个学生都有一票。你也可以自己参选。具体方法参看你们的学生会章程(constitution)。

除了投票和参选以外,你还可以通过出席学生会的常务会(General Meeting)和公决(referendum)来行使你的政治权利。General Meeting 是一个学生会的最高立法机关(legislature)所举行的例会,一般每月举行一次,只要携带学生证件就能出席并投票。在学生会的工作经历是一个英国学生个人简历上的主要卖点。

At the Hustings

Chairman: Good evening everyone… welcome to the Union's elections for non-sabbatical officers for the coming year. Remember that you've all got a vote, so please use it. The polling day will be next Friday. The ballot boxes will be in 15 different locations around the campus. Today's hustings begin with the post of international student officer. Each candidate will have two minutes for speech followed by question time. So, if you have any questions for the candidates, please raise your hand at the end and we'll pass you the mic. So, without further ado, let me introduce the candidates for international student officer. We've got six international student candidates, the first candidate, Mushtaq Sadiq.

Mushtaq: Well brothers and sisters… fellow students. As you all know, I am supported by Student Respect, and I am keen to promote….

Chairman: Our next candidate for ISO is Tom Zhang, third year Accounting and Finance student.

Tom: Thanks everyone. Look. I don't have any grand plans. I don't want to mount any political campaigns… other areas of the union are already dealing with those things. My aim is to ensure that we get all of the international students fully involved in our union. We have hundreds of students from East Asia on foundation courses here and they are completely cut-off from the student social and political life of the University for cultural and linguistic reasons. If you were to vote me in, I would do my best to bring these students into the fold and integrate them fully into campus life here. So, no gimmicks and no false-promises.

Crowd: Hooray! … [*whistling*]… boo! They don't want to integrate!

Tom: How do you know? Have you talked to any of them?

Chairman: Thanks Tom. Let's move on to our fourth candidate….

Maria: Good evening everyone. Well, I am actually a mature overseas student. I'm in my final year of a Law degree, and I know the difficulties that we all face as overseas students, and I am the only candidate….

Chairman: Right, now that you've heard all of the speeches, please raise your hand if you would like to question any of the speakers….

Joe: Yes… question for Tom Zhang… do you see any beneficial outcomes in terms of your future career if you get elected to this post.

Tom: Well, I'd be lying if I said "no", wouldn't I? The thing is….

Wang: What do you think, then? Who are you going to vote for?

Jessie: Ha! They're all the same. Careerists and self-promoters!

▎▎▎ 竞选演说中 ◀◀◀▎▎▎▎▎▎▎▎▎▎▎▎▎▎▎

主持人： 大家晚上好。欢迎来到明年非离校学生会官员的选举。请记住，你们每人都有一票，请务必行使你的选举权。选举日是在下个星期五。到时全校会有15处地方设置选票箱。今天的竞选演说从国际学生官职位开始。在进入问答时间之前，每个候选人将有2分钟的陈述时间。所以，如果你有任何问题要问候选人，请在陈述时间之后举手，我们会把麦克风传给你。好了，闲话少说，让我来介绍国际学生官的候选人吧。我们一共有6位候选人，第一个上台的是穆斯达克·萨迪克。

穆斯达克： 好的，兄弟姐妹们，同学们，正如你们所知，我是受学生尊严组织赞助的，我热中于宣传……

主持人： 我们下一个国际学生官候选人是汤姆·张，来自财会与金融系3年级。

汤姆： 谢谢大家。这么说吧，我没有什么宏伟蓝图，也不想掀起什么政治斗争，学生会的其他机构已经有这些职能了。我的目标是要让所有留学生都参与到学生会中来。我们有几百名从东亚地区来的预科学生，而由于文化和语言的关系，他们与我们大学里的社会和政治生活完全隔离。如果你们选我，我将尽我所能把这些学生吸引到学生会中来，并让他们完全融入到校园生活中。总之，我没有花言巧语，不做不能兑现的承诺。

人群： 好！［吹口哨］ 下去吧！他们才不想融入呢！

汤姆： 你怎么知道？你跟他们接触过吗？

主持人： 谢谢你，汤姆。接下来有请第4位候选人。

玛丽亚： 大家晚上好。我实际上是一个成人留学生。法学最后一年。我了解我们留学生共同面对的困难，而且我是候选人中唯一的……

主持人： 好了，现在我们已经听完所有演讲了。如果你要向哪位演讲者提问，请举手。

乔： 好的。我要问汤姆·张。如果你被选中，你是否看重这对你未来职业生涯的好处？

汤姆： 如果我说不在乎，那就是撒谎，不是吗？问题是……

王： 你怎么看？你会投谁的票？

杰茜： 他们一个样，一心向上爬的人和自我炒作专家！

Fernando: That's unfair, Jessie. I mean, maybe, they seem overtly politicised, but I liked that woman who said that she was interested in helping people with day-to-day problems. Some people are genuinely altruistic, you know.

Jessie: Do-gooders, more like! I think we should just get on with our studies. Student politics are just a diversion….

Fernando: Well, I can understand students from certain countries being frightened of getting involved in student politics. Remember though, that in Britain it's different. Did you know that the Foreign Secretary used to be president of the NUS in his younger days?

Jessie: Well maybe… but there's a case in point… he's no radical firebrand now, is he? He'll probably send the police in against the student demo tomorrow.

Jeff: Perhaps, but we do have a lot of issues that we need to deal with through the Union, you know. Like, this creeping privatisation of student services, it is having a negative effect on student life and facilities here… more expensive accommodation, poor quality cleaning and low pay and conditions for contract staff. Did you know, they don't get any sick pay or holiday pay?

Jessie: I didn't know that. No. But it's not my business.

Jeff: Did you also know that most of our teachers and lecturers are on forced part-time, hourly-paid contracts, and that they don't get sick pay, holiday pay or pensions? And did you know that some universities want to use agencies to employ lecturers so that they can cut costs further, and that all of this is going to have a negative impact on our education? It's outrageous!

Jessie: How can they do that? We pay a fortune in fees. Where does the money go?

Jeff: Not to the lecturers and teaching staff—clearly. Most of them earn less than schoolteachers, policemen and train drivers. At the same time, the vice-chancellors have given themselves massive pay increases and spent millions on consultants' fees. It's a scandal! You know, the lecturers went on strike last year, but they gave up in the end because they were worried about the students.

Fernando: [*clenches fist*] The students united will never be defeated! Haha!

Jessie: That's disgraceful! When is the demo?

费尔南多： 这么说可不公平，杰茜。我是说，他们可能看起来都明显在打官腔，但是我挺喜欢那个说要帮助人们解决日常问题的女候选人。世上还是有真心实意、大公无私的人。

杰茜： 务虚的空想家，更恰当一些！我觉得我们还是用心学习的好。学生政治完全是一种干扰。

费尔南多： 我能理解为什么有些国家的学生对参与学生政治感到恐惧。不过，记住，在英国可不一样。你知道吗，英国现在的内政大臣当年就是英国国家学生会的主席？

杰茜： 也许吧。不过他可是个典型的例子，他现如今可不是当年那个激进先锋了，对不对？他随时都可能命令警察对抗示威学生。

杰夫： 可能吧。但是我们确实有很多问题必须通过学生会来处理。比如这可怕的学生服务私有化，它对这里的学生生活和设施的影响很坏。住宿越来越贵，卫生质量差，而且给合同工的工资和福利又低。你知道吗，他们生病和节假日都没有补助了。

杰茜： 不，我不清楚。但这不关我的事。

杰夫： 另外，你知道吗，我们的老师和讲师们现在签的都是强制性的半职钟点合同，他们没有病假补助、节假补助和退休金？还有，你可知道，有些学校还想通过中介来雇用讲师，以便进一步节省开支？这些最终都会殃及我们的教育。是可忍孰不可忍！

杰茜： 他们怎么能那样做呢？我们付了一大笔学费。这些钱都去哪儿了？

杰夫： 明显没到老师和教员腰包里。他们中大部分挣得比中小学老师、警察和火车司机还少呢。与此同时，校长们给自己狂涨工资，并花掉上百万的咨询费。这是一桩丑闻！去年老师们都罢工了，但最后他们还是放弃了，因为他们担心自己的学生。

费尔南多： [握紧拳头] 团结起来的学生不可战胜！哈哈！

杰茜： 太可耻了！什么时候示威？

实用短语

◆ If you have any questions for the candidates, please raise your hand. 如果你有问题要问候选人,请举手。
◆ So, without further ado... 好了,闲话少说……
◆ If you were to vote me in, I would do my best... 如果你们选我,我将尽全力……
◆ Raise your hand if you would like to question... 要提问请举手。
◆ I'd be lying if I said "no", wouldn't I? 如果我说不,那就是撒谎,不是吗?
◆ That's unfair... 那样不公平/这么说话不讲道理。
◆ I think we should just... 我觉得我们应该老老实实地……
◆ Well, I can understand... 其实,我能理解……
◆ I didn't know that. No. But... 不,我不清楚。但是……
◆ Did you also know that...? 你还知道……吗?
◆ It's outrageous! 太过分了/是可忍孰不可忍!
◆ How can they do that...? 他们怎么能那样做呢?
◆ It's a scandal! 这是一场丑闻!
◆ That's disgraceful! 可耻!
◆ The students united will never be defeated! 团结起来的学生不可战胜!

词汇表

agency 中介机构
altruistic 大公无私的
ballot box 选票箱
be involved in/with 参与到
beneficial 有益的/受益的
candidate 候选人
careerist 只为自己晋升考虑的人
case in point 正好适用的例子
clench 握紧
contract staff 合同工
creeping privatisation 可怕的私有化
cut-off 与…隔绝
day-to-day 日常的
demo (demonstration) 示威/演示
disgraceful 可耻人/野蛮的
diversion 分散精力的事

do-gooder 务虚的空想家
down-to-earth 脚踏实地的
elections 选举
fist 拳头
fold (bring into the fold) 归宿(使结束)
Foreign Secretary 外交部长
fortune 财富
genuine 真的
gimmick 花样
give up 放弃
grand plans 远大计划
hourly-paid contracts 以小时计算的合同
hustings 竞选演说
impact 效果
International Student Officer ISO 国际学生官

mic 麦克风
not my business 不关我的事
outrageous 令人出奇愤怒的
overtly politicised 公开政治化了的
pensions 养老金
polling day 选举日
put one's case 申辩
radical firebrand 激进的组织
sabbatical 离校的/非学生的
scandal 丑闻
self-promoters 自己鼓吹自己的人
sick pay 病假补助
strike 罢工/打击
vice-chancellor 副校长
vote 投票
without further ado 闲话少说

第34章
辅导与建议
Counselling and Advice

背景常识

中国人对心理医生的作用还是持怀疑态度的,这一点从赵本山的小品里就可见一斑。实际上,并不是只有精神病人(the mentally ill)才需要心理医生的。西方人看心理医生,有时只是为了找人倾诉。心理医生的职业操守主要就是聆听和保密。

法律要求英国大学必须免费为学生提供心理咨询服务。校园里的心理医生通常被称为辅导员(counsellor)。他们通常都专修青年心理问题和学生生活。英国学生见辅导员的原因是各种各样的——比如感情问题(relationships)、社交生活(socialisation)、酗酒(alcohol addiction)、想家(homesickness)、学业问题(academic issues)、考试压力(exam stress)或财政困难(financial hardship)。

辅导员不但会给学生以心理上的调整,而且还会帮助学生解决具体问题。比如,专门处理国际学生事务的辅导员应该具备关于签证、移民、工作和国际旅行等方面的专业知识。

通常,辅导员是在学生会的辅导与建议中心(Counselling and Advisory Centre)工作。在有些大学里,他们则是直接隶属于校方的学生服务部(Student Services)。你可以通过学校的网站找到他们的联系方式。他们通常接受预约(appointment)和直接访问(walk-in)。离家在外,生活学习上出现困难是不可避免的。学校设立这些服务就是为了解决这些困难。毕竟,羊毛出在羊身上。学校的这些免费服务,最终都是用你的学费买单的。中国学生在各国留学生中是出了名的腼腆。其实,留学生的学费本来就比英国和欧盟学生的学费贵。所以,有麻烦时用不着跟英国大学客气。

In the Kitchen

Maggie: Hi Sunny... you don't look very happy.

Sunny: Hi Maggie... no I'm not, actually. I guess I'm just feeling the strain... you know, all of these assignments have left me a bit stressed.

Maggie: Mmm, I know what you mean. The pressure of work gets to me too. I just try to forget about it though... you know... get out and have a good time... relax at weekend... have a drink or something.

Carol: Yes... but that's not healthy. You shouldn't suppress your feelings... that just makes things worse. You should talk to someone about them.

Maggie: That's what I do... I talk to my friends in the bar or over a coffee, and we chat, and then I feel better.

Sunny: Yes, but sometimes it's too big for that. You know, sometimes I think I'm just losing my mind... I can't sleep... I burst out crying. I feel I can't get a grip on things at all.

Maggie: Oh... it sounds serious... maybe you need to call Nightline... you know the student helpline or maybe the Samaritans....

Carol: Well I think that you should probably go and seek professional advice... I mean maybe the Student Union can help you... get a counsellor for you.

Sunny: What?! I'm not crazy! I don't need psychotherapy!

Carol: Counselling isn't psychotherapy! It's just a way for you to get things off your chest and to talk about things... you know, a kind of release.

Sunny: Maybe you're right. I'll go and see the student welfare officer.

At the Counselling Session

Counsellor: Hello Sunny, nice to meet you... how are you feeling?

Sunny: I'm not really sure. OK, I suppose.

Counsellor: That's OK... let's start by trying to find the words... if I asked you to really describe your feelings when you came into the room to see me today, what words would you use?

Sunny: I don't know... "worried", maybe... "nervous", "frightened"....

Counsellor: That's very honest of you, Sunny. Not many people like to admit that they are scared, do they? Do you feel frightened a lot?

Sunny: I feel afraid all the time. When I wake up in the morning I have a feeling of dread... and all day it's like a sick feeling in my stomach... like nausea.

Counsellor: Good! I mean, it's good that you said that. Once you admit to something, you can start to deal with it.

Sunny: Perhaps... I'm under a lot of pressure....

在厨房里

玛吉：嗨，桑妮。你看起来不太高兴。

桑妮：嗨，玛吉。没有，我没不高兴。我想我只是比较郁闷，这些作业让我很紧张。

玛吉：嗯，我明白你的意思。我也经常受到学习压力的困扰。我试图忘记它，出去玩玩，享受生活。周末放松放松，出去喝点儿什么的。

卡萝尔：是啊，但这对身体不好。你不应该压抑自己的情绪，这只会火上浇油。你应该找人把这些问题谈一谈。

玛吉：我就是这么做的。我去酒吧或者喝咖啡，跟朋友聊天。说完之后就感觉好多了。

桑妮：对，但有时那样也解决不了问题。有时我觉得自己快要疯了，我失眠，莫名其妙地大哭。我觉得自己完全失控了。

玛吉：哦，听起来很严重啊。也许你应该给"夜间谈心"服务打电话。你知道的，那个学生服务热线。或者"好心人"组织。

卡萝尔：我觉得你应该去寻求专家建议。学生会应该可以帮你找个辅导员。

桑妮：什么？我又没得神经病！我不需要心理治疗。

卡萝尔：辅导不是心理治疗！它不过是让你发泄情绪、说出心里话罢了。那是一种放松方式。

桑妮：也许你是对的。我会去找学生福利官的。

在辅导过程中

辅导员：你好，桑妮，很高兴见到你。你感觉如何？

桑妮：我不清楚。还行，我估计。

辅导员：没关系。我们就以找字眼儿来开始吧。如果我要你确切地形容你走进这个房间见到我时的心情，你会用什么词呢？

桑妮：我不清楚，"忧虑"，也许吧，"紧张"，"害怕"……

辅导员：你能这样说表示你很诚实，桑妮。没有多少人愿意承认自己的恐惧，不是吗？你觉得很害怕吗？

桑妮：我总是提心吊胆的。我早上一起床就有一种恐惧感。一整天，我胃里都有一种恶心的感觉，像要吐似的。

辅导员：好！我的意思是，你能说出来很好。一旦你能面对某事的时候，你就可以着手对付它了。

桑妮：也许，我的压力太大。

Counsellor: Why? What from?

Sunny: Study. My family… they expect me to do well, and it cost them a lot of money to send me here, and they want me to do a course that I don't like… I don't like Business Studies, I like Literature and Art… it's too much pressure.

Counsellor: You seem very bright, Sunny. What year are you in?

Sunny: Third year.

Counsellor: So, even though you say you don't like your course, you've still managed to get to the third year of your course? So your marks must have been OK so far…?

Sunny: I suppose so.

Counsellor: So… what we need to do is something practical, right?

Sunny: Yes….

Counsellor: Do you need an extension for your assignments? I mean, do you need extra time?

Sunny: Actually, I think I do.

Counsellor: Right. I'll write to your tutor and I'll tell her that you have been to see me, and that because of family pressure and stuff you need more time to complete your assignments… would that help?

Sunny: Oh, thank you!

Counsellor: Right. I'll do that. However, this is not an excuse to stop doing your assignments, and I do need to see you again, because I think that there are some deeper issues that we need to deal with.

Sunny: All right, then.

Counsellor: Let's say① we'll meet up again next week at the same time….

Sunny: All right.

注释 ① Let's say 表示尝试着提议。

辅导员：为什么呢？哪儿来的压力？

桑妮：学习。我的家人，他们都对我寄予很大希望，花了一大笔钱送我来这儿，而且他们硬要我学我不喜欢的科目。我不喜欢商学，我喜欢文学和艺术。压力真的太大了。

辅导员：你看起来很聪明，桑妮。你几年级了？

桑妮：三年级。

辅导员：那么，尽管你说你不喜欢你的课程，你还是熬了 3 年？这么说来，你的成绩应该还是不错的吧？

桑妮：我估计是吧。

那么：这样的话，我们需要做的是一些实际的事情，对吗？

桑妮：对。

辅导员：你需要延长作业时间吗？我是说，你需不需要额外时间？

桑妮：实际上，我觉得我需要。

辅导员：好吧。我会书面联系你的老师，我会告诉她你来过我这儿。而且由于家庭压力等原因，你需要更多的时间来完成你的作业。这样有帮助吗？

桑妮：哦，太谢谢你了！

辅导员：好了，就这么说定了。但是，这不是停止做作业的借口。而且，我还得再见你一次，因为我觉得我们还有一些更深层的问题需要处理。

桑妮：好吧。

辅导员：让我看看，我们下星期的这个时候见吧。

桑妮：好的。

实用短语

- ◆ You don't look very happy. 你看起来不太高兴。
- ◆ Let's start by trying to… 让我们从……开始。
- ◆ If I asked you to… what words would you use? 如果我要你……,你会用什么词?
- ◆ That's very honest of you. 你这样非常诚实。
- ◆ Once you…, you can begin to… 一旦你……,你就能开始……
- ◆ Even though you say… you've still managed to… 尽管你说……你还是坚持/设法……
- ◆ Your… must have been… 你的……一定是……
- ◆ Actually, I think I do. 实际上,我觉得是的。
- ◆ This is not an excuse to stop doing/working. 这不是停止工作的理由。
- ◆ Let's say we'll… 我们要不然……
- ◆ I suppose so. 我估计如此。

词汇表

admit 承认
afraid 对…担心的
assignment 作业
be under pressure 在有压力的情况下
brave 勇敢的
bright 聪明的/明亮的
burst out crying 突然哭泣
counsellor 辅导员
cousins 表兄弟/表姐妹
deal with 处理
describe 形容
dread 害怕
expectations 期望
extension 延长/延期
feel the strain 感到郁闷

frightened 受到惊吓的
get a grip 振作/把握住
get things off one's chest 倾吐心事
healthy 健康的
honest 诚实
issues 问题
lonely 孤独的
lose one's mind 失去理智
manage 应付/管理
marks 成绩/分数
nausea 恶心
nervous 紧张的
Nightline 夜间谈心(英国的一个学生心理服务电话热线)
psychotherapy 心理治疗

release 释放
Samaritans 好心人(英国的一个学生心理服务电话热线)
scared 害怕的
seek professional advice 寻求专业的意见
sick 有病的
stressed 受压抑的
Student Helpline 学生帮助热线
Student Welfare Officer 学生福利官
successful 成功的
suppress one's feelings 压抑自己的情感
worried 担心的

第 35 章
加入一个社团
Joining a Society

背景常识

从功能和性质上来说，中英之间的学生社团是十分相似的。兴趣相投（like-minded）的人通过集会来交流或宣传自己的爱好或主张。然而，在英国的学生社团活动则更加规范。大部分学生社团从属于（be affiliated to）学生会。因此它也是具有法律责任的社会团体，享有慈善机构（charity）的身份。它的财政和管理均受到法律和社会的监督。

一个社团通常由以下几个职能组成：主席（president），由会员（members）选举产生，代表（represent）并运作（administer）这个组织；副主席（vice president），一个社团可以有不止一个副主席，负责组织不同方面的事务，比如筹款（fundraising）、发展会员（membership development）、对外关系（external relations）等等；财政官（treasurer），负责管理社团的收入（revenue）和支出（expenditure）；社交活动秘书（social secretary），负责会内交流和组织娱乐活动；委员会（committee），选举产生的一组会员，作为社团的决策机构（decision-making body），通常由主席担任委员长（chairman）；会员（members），所有拥有成员资格的人。

学生组织的资金来源主要是学生会、外来赞助（external sponsorship）和会员费。它应当有公开的章程，并定期举行民主选举。

你也可以创建自己的社团，无论你的主意有多稀奇古怪。除了一些正常的，基于体育、文化爱好的社团以外，英国学生还经常为喜欢某种酒或某个明星而结社。加入和管理一个社团不仅是交友的最佳渠道，同时也能锻炼你的领导力和组织能力。

The Freshers' Fair

Liu: I'm a bit worried about the freshers' fair. What is it exactly?

Joe: Well, fresher's week is when all the new students arrive at the uni and start to get to know the place. The fair is organised by the students union and by individual clubs and societies, and it consists of dances, gigs, food, drinks and exhibitions where different clubs and societies set up stall and try to attract new members.

Cui: Wow... that sounds exciting. What are clubs and societies?

Joe: Well, clubs and societies are a fundamental part of university life in Britain. They are set up by the students themselves and affiliated to the Students' Union. They can be anything you like, but the most popular ones are sports clubs like the Rugby Club, the Hockey Club, the Judo Club and so on or political clubs like the Socialist Workers' Party through to groups like Chinese Soc①, or Palestinian Soc... or more artistic societies like literary societies, film clubs and drama groups. There's something for everyone... and if there isn't, you can start your own club or society.

Liu: It all sounds very interesting, but you know we Chinese have to study hard. It's expensive to study here and we don't speak English as well as you do, so I think we shouldn't waste our time on social activities.

Joe: Well, that's where you're wrong... see.② The point is that if you join a good club or society you'll get in with British students and your English will improve, so will your confidence and you'll make friends. You Chinese are always complaining that you never have a chance to really get in with British students "cause③ our courses are full of Chinese...." Well, this is your chance, isn't it?

Cui: Hmm, I suppose so, but I don't think my parents would be happy about me spending all my time on social things.

Liu: I suppose it's a question of balance, isn't it? It's OK as long as we don't overdo it, and we concentrate on work④.

Joe: That's right. Degrees do not fall into your lap while you sit in the bar downing cider... balance is everything.... Any idea what clubs and socs you might be interested in?⑤

Cui: Well, I'm not really sporty, although I do like watching football, so I don't think the sports clubs would be any use. Chinese Soc? Well... that will probably be full of Chinese. I think I might be interested in one of the political societies. What do they actually do... these clubs and socs?

Joe: Well, they have meetings, they organise talks and lectures and sometimes they just meet up for a drink and a chat in the pub.

Liu: That sounds cool... I think I'll have a look round the different stalls and then make up my mind.

Cui: Yes... I'll do that as well.

新生博览会

刘：我对这个新生博览会有些担心。它到底是怎么回事啊?

乔：新生周是指新生抵达学校并开始了解这个地方的一段时间。这个博览会是由学生会、俱乐部和社团举办的。博览会包括舞蹈、晚会、吃、喝，还有俱乐部和社团搭起来的展台，用来吸引新生。

崔：哇，听起来真棒。什么是俱乐部和社团呢?

乔：俱乐部和社团是英国大学生活的基本部分。他们是学生自己建立的，并附属于学生会之下。它们可以是关于任何主题的，但是最流行的还是体育俱乐部，比如橄榄球俱乐部、曲棍球俱乐部、柔道俱乐部等等。还有政治性的俱乐部，比如社会主义工人党、中国社团，或巴勒斯坦社团等等。另外还有艺术性的社团，比如文学社、电影俱乐部和戏剧社。每个人都能找到自己喜欢的社团。如果真的没有你喜欢的，你还可以成立自己的俱乐部和社团。

刘：听起来很有意思。不过，你知道的，我们中国学生必须努力学习。我们来这儿得花不少钱，而且我们的英语又不如你们好，所以我觉得我们不应该在社会活动上浪费时间。

乔：瞧，这你就错了。参加俱乐部和社团的意义就在于，你能融入英国学生当中并改进自己的英语，还可以增加自信和交朋友。你们中国人总是抱怨说没有机会和英国学生接触，"因为课程里都是中国人"。新生博览会就是你的机会了，不是吗?

崔：嗯，有道理。但是我估计我父母不会赞成我把时间都花在社会活动上。

刘：我估计这是一个如何掌握平衡的问题，不是吗? 只要我们不做过头，并把主要精力放在学习上。

乔：对。当你坐在酒吧里给自己灌苹果酒的时候，学位是不会自己落到你身上的。一切事情都要讲究平衡。你们想好要参加什么俱乐部和社团了吗?

崔：嗯，我没有多少体育细胞，虽然我喜欢看足球，所以我估计体育俱乐部对我是没什么用了。中国社团呢? 嗯，那儿可能全是中国人。我想我可能会对一个政治社团感兴趣。它们到底做些什么呢，这些俱乐部和社团?

乔：他们聚会，组织讨论和讲座，有时还在酒吧里闲聊，一起喝一杯什么的。

刘：听起来蛮酷的。我想我得先把所有这些展台都看一圈再决定。

崔：对，我也这么做。

At the Martial Arts Stall

Rep: Hi, there. You're Chinese... do you know how to do *Kung Fu*?

Lu: Ha ha... I do, actually. We call it *Wu Shu* in China.

Rep: Wow... well, come and join the Martial Arts Soc. You could practise *Wu Shu* and learn some other cool stuff as well.

Lu: Oh yeah? Like what?

Rep: Well there's Karate, Judo, Thai Kick Boxing, Capoeira... that's like a Brazilian martial art... half dancing, half fighting and Tai Kwon do. They're all great for self-defence and for keep-fit as well.

Lu: That sounds wicked. How much is it?

Rep: Well, membership is £20 a year... that's just to cover costs... we get group membership at the SU gym and then we meet up at these times... look, here's a timetable. Judo on Monday evenings, karate on Wednesdays... oh, and this is new, look; we're going to start a *Tai Chi* class.

Lu: OK... I'll sign up. Here you are... £20.

Rep: Great! We're having a little get together tomorrow evening at the pub round the corner at eight o'clock. Why don't you come along? You can meet other club members there.

Lu: OK then. See you there.

注释

① Soc 是 Society 缩写和简称。
② well 是语气词,用在这里使语气缓和;see 这里也是语气词,表示让对方注意。
③ because 在口语中可以省略为 cause。
④ work 对学生来说有"学习"的意思。
⑤ Do you have 被省略了,原句应该是 Do you have any idea...。

在武术展台

代表：嗨，你是中国人，你会中国功夫吗？
陆：哈哈，我还真会。在中国，我们管这叫"武术"。
代表：哇，那好，参加我们武术社吧。这样你可以练习武术，还可以学些别的本事。
陆：是吗？比如什么？
代表：我们有空手道、柔道、泰拳、巴西战舞，这是一种巴西格斗术，一半是舞蹈，一半是格斗，还有跆拳道。这些用来自卫和锻炼身体都很好。
陆：听起来太棒了。多少钱？
代表：会员费20英镑一年，这些钱仅仅够支付开销。我们能从学校的健身房拿到团队会员资格。我们集合的时间是这些，给，这是我们的时间表。柔道星期一晚上，空手道星期三。哦，这是新项目，看看，我们要新设太极拳班。
陆：好，我加入。给，20英镑。
代表：太好了！明天晚上8点我们在那边拐角的酒馆有个聚会，你也来吧，到时候你能见到其他的会员。
陆：那好，回头见。

实用短语

- I'm a bit worried about...   我对……有些担心。
- What is it exactly?   它到底是什么？
- Any idea what you might be interested in?   想好你对什么感兴趣了吗？
- Well, that's where you're wrong, see.   这你就错了/你错就错在这儿了。
- The point of... is that...   ……的意义在于……
- It all sounds very interesting, but...   听起来很有趣,但是……
- Well, maybe, but...   嗯,可能吧,但是……
- Hmm, I suppose so.   嗯,我想也是。
- I suppose it's a question of balance, isn't it?
  我估计这是一个如何掌握平衡的问题,不是吗？
- That sounds cool.   听起来很酷。
- Hmmm, maybe, I'm not really sure...   也许,我不敢肯定……
- Erm, let me have a think.   让我想想。
- Well come and join the...   那就加入……吧。
- You could practise... and learn some other...   你能练习……还能学些别的……
- They're all great for...   它们对……都有好处。
- OK. I'll sign up.   好,我加入。

词汇表

artistic 艺术性的
attract 吸引
be affiliated to... 附属于
cause（because）因为
clubs and societies 俱乐部和社团
dance 舞蹈/跳舞
drama 戏剧
exhibitions 展览
fresher 大学新生
fresher's fair 新生博览会
fresher's week 新生周
get in with... 融入
get together 相聚/聚会
gig 歌舞会
hockey 曲棍球
judo 柔道
karate 空手道
keep-fit 保持身体健美
kick boxing 自由搏击
literary 文学的
member 成员
membership 会员身份
overdo sth. 做某事过头
rugby （英式）橄榄球
self-defence 自卫/自卫术
Socialist Workers' Party 社会主义工人党
sporty 体育的/有体育细胞的
stall 展台
Student Union 学生会
uni 大学（university 的缩写和简称）

第36章
闲聊体育
Talking Sport

背景常识

体育应该是英国校园里最热门的话题了。一说起英国体育,人们自然会想到曼联(Manchester United)、阿森纳(Arsenal)、大卫·贝克汉姆(David Beckham)、维恩·鲁尼(Wayne Rooney)和迈克尔·欧文(Michael Owen)。足球绝对是英国最流行的体育项目。作为一名留学生,不能亲临现场看一场英超的比赛会是一件终身憾事。不过要小心英国臭名昭著的足球流氓(football hooligans)。这里介绍几个关于足球的术语:开球(kick-off)、半场休息(half-time)、球门/进球(goal)、犯规(foul)、越位(off-side)、点球(penalty)、任意球(free kick)、角球(corner kick)、界外球(throw-in)、断球(tackle)、传球(pass)、射门(shoot)、黄牌警告(yellow card)、裁判(referee)、教练(coach)、替补(substitute)。

然而,足球并不是英国学生唯一为之狂热的运动。比如说,橄榄球(rugby)就在英国和澳洲都非常流行。橄榄球可能看上去十分野蛮,但实际上很需要在战略和战术上多动脑筋。如果你喜欢更绅士一些的运动,那就玩板球(cricket)和马球(polo),或者飞镖(dart)和斯诺克台球(snooker),这些都不会让你横冲直撞。如果你喜欢速度,那就去银石(Silverstone)赛道看一级方程式赛车(Formula One),或者在德比日(Derby Day)去爱普瑟姆(Epsom)赌马、吃草莓、喝香槟。如果悬念和优雅是你的选择,英国还有温布尔顿网球公开赛(the Wimbledon Open)。

中国学生应当多尝试那些在中国尚不流行的体育项目。在英学习的这几年可能是你一生中唯一的一次挥动板球棒的机会。既然打板球的中国人这么少,你可能轻而易举地就成为全世界板球打得最好的中国人。何乐而不为呢?

In the Uni Bar

Jane: Hi guys... you look tired... what have you been doing?
Tamer: We've been playing five-a-side with the lecturers down in the gym. Mr. Foster got a team together from the staff, and I got some students together. The teachers beat us 8: 2.
Jane: But they are all old... they must be in their 30s and 40s!
Larry: They are, but they are fit! That Mr. Foster cycles to work every day... and Mr. Walker goes running every lunchtime... and that Dr. Baker plays squash, and they both must be in their mid-forties!
Jane: Yes, but there's another thing.... you guys smoke, and the lecturers don't. And I think maybe you're a bit scared to tackle them hard as well because they are your lecturers... am I right?
Tamer: Maybe, but I bet on a proper football field we'd run rings round them! Do you girls play any sports, Alison?
Alison: Well, I'm in the uni hockey team actually.
Sarah: Yeah... and I play volleyball. We play tennis on Saturday mornings as well.
Larry: So, do you play against the teachers as well?
Alison: No. It doesn't seem to be what older women want to do. I think your teachers are just trying desperately to stave off old age!
Sarah: That, or pretend they are still young!
Tamer: Anyway, I think it would be a good idea to organise a mini-league. You know, different national groups.
Larry: I think different departments would be better. It would be really good for bonding.

Loud Drunken Singing from Another Table

Larry: Oh no... it's the rugby club having another piss-up!
Sarah: Yeah... they're always getting drunk and singing rude songs and stuff.
Tamer: Well... it's all part of the tradition, isn't it... they behave like hooligans in the bar, but they're supposed to be gentlemen outside... I mean, it's mostly middle-class students who play rugby, isn't it?
Sarah: Yeah... what is it they say? "Soccer is a game for gentlemen, played by hooligans, and rugby is a game for hooligans played by gentlemen." My flatmate told me that football is a traditionally working-class game.
Tamer: Yes. Rugby is a really rough game. It looks it anyway.
Alison: What is rugby, anyway? Is it like what they play in America?

在学生会酒吧

简: 嗨,伙计们。你们看起来无精打采的,你们干什么了?

塔墨尔: 我们跟一帮老师在体育馆里踢5人足球。福斯特老师从教职工中撮合了一支球队,我从学生中挑了几个人。老师把我们打了个8比2。

简: 但是他们都岁数大了,最起码都三四十了!

拉里: 他们是上岁数了,但是他们身体强壮!福斯特老师每天骑自行车上班,沃克老师每天午饭时间去跑步,贝克博士打壁球!而他们个个都得有四十五六了。

简: 是啊,不过还有一个原因。你们这帮人抽烟,老师们不抽。而且,我估计你们也有点儿不好意思跟他们冲撞,因为他们是你们的老师,对吗?

塔墨尔: 也许吧。但是我打赌如果在正规的足球场上,我们能让他们忙得团团转!你们女生搞什么体育活动吗,艾莉森?

艾莉森: 我是曲棍球校队的。

萨拉: 我打排球。我们星期六早上还打网球。

拉里: 你们也跟老师对阵吗?

艾莉森: 没有,岁数大的女人似乎不喜欢运动。我估计你们老师也无非是在毫无希望地延缓衰老。

萨拉: 是这样,或者就是硬装年轻!

塔墨尔: 无论如何,我认为组织一个小联赛还是一个好主意。比如,按国籍划分队伍。

拉里: 我觉得不同院系之间比赛要好一些,这样有利于交流。

从另一张桌子传来大声的醉醺醺的歌声

拉里: 哦,不,橄榄球俱乐部又来狂饮了!

萨拉: 是啊,他们总是酩酊大醉而且唱些粗俗的歌曲什么的。

塔墨尔: 有什么办法呢?这是传统,不是吗?他们在酒吧里像流氓,但出去后却像绅士。实际上打橄榄球的都是些中产阶级子弟,不是吗?

萨拉: 对,他们怎么说来着?"足球是流氓们玩的绅士运动;橄榄球是绅士们玩的流氓运动。"我的寓友告诉我,足球在历史上一直是无产阶级的游戏。

塔墨尔: 对。橄榄球是一种非常野蛮的比赛。最起码看起来是这样。

艾莉森: 橄榄球到底是怎么回事?跟美国人玩的那种一样吗?

Larry: No, no... it's only the ball that's the same shape... basically, they have no protection like they do in American football... no helmets and padding and stuff... it looks really scary.

Tamer: Yeah... rugby players get to act out their violent fantasies on the rugby field, get drunk and behave like hooligans in the bar and then go to work as doctors and lawyers on Monday morning.

Larry: Yes... whereas when football players do that they call them hooligans!

Alison: But I guess it's good... I mean, at least it controls their aggression.

Sarah: It's great... all the opportunities we have to play sports here. I mean, they even have women's rugby, football and cricket teams... did you know that?

Tamer: What are the rules of cricket, by the way?

Larry: I don't think we should even go there! You have to be English, born-and-bred to understand them.

Sarah: Or from the Commonwealth countries. Also, I've heard that in India and Pakistan they are even madder about cricket than the English!

Alison: Yeah... and in Australia and South Africa too.

拉里：不，不一样，只不过球的形状相似罢了。大致说来，英式橄榄球没有美式橄榄球那么多保护装备，没有头盔和护肩等等，看起来挺瘆人的。

塔墨尔：对，英式橄榄球队员在球场上可以发泄自己的暴力幻想，在酒吧里像流氓一样喝个大醉，然后星期一早上照常上班去当他们的医生律师。

拉里：是啊，可足球运动员有那些行为的时候却被骂作流氓！

艾莉森：但是我想这也有好处，起码橄榄球让他们的侵略性得以控制。

萨拉：我们有机会从事各项体育运动真是太好了。学校竟然还有女子橄榄球队、足球队和板球队。你们知道吗？

塔墨尔：板球都有什么规则啊？

拉里：我觉得我们根本不应该踏进那块地方！你必须是土生土长的英国人才能理解板球。

萨拉：或者是英联邦国家的人。而且，我听说印度人和巴基斯坦人对板球比英国人还要着迷呢！

艾莉森：是啊，澳大利亚和南非也如此。

实用短语

- You look tired... what have you been doing? 你们看起来无精打采的,你们干什么了?
- That Dr. Baker... 那个贝克博士……
- Yes, but there's another thing. 对,不过还有一个原因。
- It doesn't seem to be what... want to do. 这似乎是一件……不愿意做的事。
- I think it would be a great idea to... 我觉得……会是一个好主意。
- We'd run rings round them. 我们能让他们忙得团团转。
- Oh no! It's... having/doing/making ... 哦,不!是(某人)……在(做某事)……
- What is it they say? 他们怎么说来着?
- It looks it anyway. 起码看起来是这样。
- What is... anyway? ……到底是什么?
- I guess it's good. 我觉得这是好事。

词 汇 表

act out 发泄	gentleman 绅士	rude 不礼貌的
aggression 侵略性	get drunk 喝醉	run rings around 使忙得团团转
American football 美式橄榄球	gym 健身房	scary 吓人的
Australian 澳大利亚的/澳大利亚人	helmet 头盔	South African 南非的/南非人
	hooligan 流氓	squash 壁球
born-and-bred 土生土长	lawyer 律师	tackle 抢断
cricket 板球	middle-class 中产阶级	tennis 网球
cycle 骑车	mid-forties 四十多岁的	trash 垃圾
fantasy 幻想	padding 护垫	violent 暴力的
five-a-side 5人一队	piss-up 暴饮狂欢	volleyball 排球

第 37 章
义务劳动
Volunteering

背景常识

在汉语里,"慈善机构"总是让人想起救济贫苦、残疾和弱势社会群体的组织,比如中华慈善总会(China Charity Federation)和中国青少年基金会(China Children and Teenagers' Fund)。在英语中,charity 的含义要更广。任何不以盈利为目的而参与社会和经济活动的、非国家机关的组织都是一个 charity。

大的 charity 包括 Oxfam UK,CARE UK,Cancer Research UK,Save The Children UK,等等。它们主要的工作目标是国际经济发展、抢险救灾、教育科研和政治民主化等等。而成千上万的小 charities 更是遍布英国各地,功能也各式各样。现如今,没有 charity 的英国社会是无法想像的。

对于在英的留学生来说,charties 尤为重要。英国用人单位对工作经验(work experience)的重视超过学位。在校学生只能靠义务劳动来积累经验,然后再找有偿的工作。在中国,学生们义务劳动的内容大多是打扫卫生和栽树之类的,而英国的义务劳动则五花八门。虽然义务劳动应当是以道德(morality)和良知(conscience)为主要动机,不少英国学生也是抱着给自己镀金的心态去参加义务劳动的。只要最终结果能让社会公众受益,动机不纯也未尝不可。如果你打算在留学期间或之后在英国工作,你就要做好参加义务劳动的心理准备。

学生会通常有介绍义务劳动和组织志愿者的机构(volunteer organisation)。英国政府还为能持之以恒的志愿者颁发各种证书(certificates)和奖励(awards)。对留学生来说,这些都是尤为抢眼的荣耀和成就。

At the Student Union

Wang: Hello there… I've just started on my degree course here, and I'm interested in doing some kind of voluntary work while I'm here.

SU Officer: OK… what sort of area are you interested in? I mean, do you have any experience of voluntary work?

Wang: Well it isn't really common back home in China… so I was hoping you'd be able to give me some ideas.

SU Officer: OK then… well, as a union, we aim to support the student body in its volunteering and community projects by building links with the wider community. Our purpose is to help you build partnerships which benefit you as students and the community. I know that sounds like a load of jargon… it's what's written down in our mission statement, but what it basically means is that we run projects with local schools and organisations.

Wang: So what sort of projects do you run?

SU Officer: Well… we've got sports coaching with local primary schools… senior citizens' parties, meals-on-wheels, helping kids to read, painting old folks' houses and stuff… it's good to do these things, and it's also something that employers take a positive attitude to. So it looks good on a CV… especially if you've moved on to do something serious like working for the St John Ambulance, or working for an outreach group with homeless people… I mean the last one especially would be pretty gritty… you'd be coming face-to-face with some serious social problems… alcoholism and drug addiction and so on. Some employers are pretty impressed by stuff like that… but most of all, it gives you involvement in the local community and a great sense of personal fulfilment. It's really good for your language skills too.

Wang: Well, I'm not scared of dangerous situations… I mean, I am a black belt in Karate and Judo… I have trained students in *Tae Kwon Do* back in China too. So, maybe I could start off by training school kids in martial arts or something.

SU Officer: OK… look, I'll put you down for the next training workshop, shall I? Not to train you in martial arts, of course… just to get you oriented in how to deal with school kids here. We'll also have to do a police check on you—a necessary precaution, people with a criminal record normally are not allowed to work with kids—which I am sure you don't have, otherwise the government wouldn't have given you a visa to Britain. It is just a procedure. A police check is useful when you apply for jobs too. Normally you have pay to get it done, but once we recruit you, we will do it for free.

在学生会

王：你好，我刚刚开始在这儿上学，我希望能借这个机会做一些义工。

学生会官员：好的。你对哪些领域感兴趣？你有什么义务劳动的经验？

王：义务劳动在中国不是那么普遍，所以我希望你能给我指点指点。

学生会官员：好吧。作为一个组织，我们的宗旨是通过在学生和社区之间建立联系来支持学生会的义务和社区项目。我们的目的是帮你建立有利于你和社区的合作机制。我知道，这听起来像是一堆术语。这是我们使命陈词里的话，它的基本意思是，我们与本地学校和组织一起运作项目。

王：什么项目呢？

学生会官员：我们为小学提供体育教练、组织老人晚会和食品发放、帮助小孩子读书、帮老人们漆房子等等。这些是社会公德，用人单位也会对义工经历持积极态度。所以，这也是个人简历上的亮点，尤其是如果你从事更严肃一些的志愿工作。比如圣约翰救护队，或者某个帮助流浪汉的外联小组，后者尤其能显示你的品质。你会与一些严肃的社会问题面对面打交道，酗酒和毒瘾之类的。这些经历留给用人单位的印象会很深。但是最重要的是，它让你能亲身体验本地社区，并给你很大的成就感，对你提高语言能力也有帮助。

王：我不害怕危险环境，我是空手道和柔道的黑带。在中国，我还带过跆拳道的学生。所以，也许我可以从教学校孩子们学武术开始。

学生会官员：好的，那我就给你报名参加下一个培训讲座了。当然不是培训你武术，是给你介绍如何应对这里的中小学生。我们还必须给你做个警察核对，这是必要的防范措施。有犯罪纪录的人通常是不能从事涉及儿童的工作的。我肯定你没有什么犯罪纪录，不然政府也不会给你来英国的签证了。不过这是程序问题。有了警察核对对你找工作也有帮助。通常你得花钱才能办核对。但是如果我们录取你，我们可以为你免费核对。

In the Coffee Bar

[*Anna and Olive Come in Looking Dirty*]

Anna: Hi guys…. guess where we've been?

Jack: Where? You both look a mess.

Olive: We've been doing voluntary work… gardening.

Kanat: Whereabouts?

Olive: Down at the old-people's home… they needed some new flower beds and stuff, and the lawn was a disgrace… so we thought that we'd offer them some help.

Jack: Uh… what do you get out of it?

Anna: Satisfaction and a feeling of fulfilment of course… these old people don't have any families to look after them, and they love talking to young people.

Kanat: Sounds a bit daft to me.

Anna: Uuugh… you are horrible! It's a good job some of us have a social conscience and a heart!

在咖啡屋

[安娜和奥利芙一身泥泞地走进来]

安娜：嗨，伙计们，猜猜我们去哪儿了？

杰克：哪儿？你们看起来很狼狈。

奥利芙：我们去做义务劳动了，当园丁。

卡内特：在哪儿？

奥利芙：在老人院。他们需要些新的花坛之类的东西，而且那儿的草坪简直不堪入目。所以，我们琢磨着应该帮帮他们。

杰克：你们得到什么报酬了？

安娜：当然是满足感和成就感。那些老人没有家人照顾他们，而且他们喜欢跟年轻人聊天。

卡内特：听起来有点儿傻。

安娜：啊？你太没有同情心了！幸好我们中有些人还有社会良知和好心肠！

实用短语

- What kind of... are you interested in? 你对哪种……感兴趣?
- Do you have any experience of...? 你在……方面有没有经验?
- I was hoping you'd be able to... 我本希望你能……
- As a... we aim to... 作为一个……我们的宗旨是……
- What sort of... do you...? 你(做)……哪一种……?
- You'd be... with... 你将跟……做……
- Employers are pretty/quite/really impressed by... ……给用人单位留下深刻印象。
- I'll put you down for... 我给你报名参加……
- You look a mess! 你们看起来很狼狈。
- It's a good job some of us have...! 幸好我们中有些人还有……!

词汇表

alcoholism 酗酒
attitude 态度
basically 基本上
be impressed with 对…有印象
come face-to-face with 面对
community 社区
daft 愚蠢的
disgrace 耻辱
drug addiction 毒瘾
experience 经历
flower beds 花床

forge 制造/伪造
gardening 园丁工作
get oriented 找到头绪
gritty 表现品质的
have a heart 有良心
homeless people 流浪汉
horrible 令人发指的
jargon 术语
lawn 草坪
links 联系
meals-on-wheels 食品发放

old-folk 老人
old people's home 老人院
partnership 合作伙伴关系
personal fulfilment 自我成就感
primary school 小学
senior citizen 老人
social conscience 社会良知
sports coaching 体育教练活动
St John Ambulance 圣约翰救护队
training workshop 培训讲座
wider community 更广的群体

第38章
业余打工
Part-Time Jobs

◯ 背景常识

人们印象中的勤工俭学都是挣钱少、体力重的工作，比如刷盘子（wash dishes）或者在麦当劳里炸鸡（fry chicken）。但是，如果你能更自信一点儿而且想法不拘一格（think outside of the box），你就完全可以找到真正享受的工作，比如在足球场里当球童（steward）或者在花店里当个花匠（florist）。

找工作的渠道一般有三个。首先，你的大学和学生会应该有职业中心（career centre）。你所在的城市也应该有 Job Centre，一种免费的公共职业介绍中心。这些就业中心里都装备有触屏电脑（touch-screen computer）。里面储存有大量的关于本地雇主的信息。第二个渠道是直接上门问人家是否缺人手（whether have vacancies）。第三个渠道是通过朋友介绍。

发现自己喜欢的工作是一回事，得到自己喜欢的工作是另外一回事。首先，你的英语口语必须"入得厅堂，下得厨房"。如今在英国，就连遛狗的都得有良好的交流能力（communication skills）。第二，你得有一技之长（skills）。出国之前先学门手艺，比如乐器、电脑图片设计或者紧急抢救（first aid）之类的。即使这些手艺跟你将来的工作无关，它最起码能让你从一堆千篇一律的个人简历中脱颖而出（distinguish）。最后，记住不要本末倒置，不能勤工"减"学。

作为留学生，你不用付税（tax），但是你仍然需要申请国家保险号码（National Insurance Number），以便英国的税务局（Inland Revenue Services）能给你退税。留学生在上课期间每周打工不能超过20小时。英国国家规定的最低工资（minimum wage）目前是5.05镑一小时。你的雇主、就业中心和学校的职业中心都可以为你提供在劳动法律问题上的咨询。

In the Coffee Shop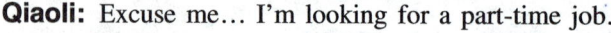

Qiaoli: Excuse me… I'm looking for a part-time job.
Duty Manager: Have you got any experience?
Qiaoli: Well, I worked part-time in a coffee shop in China.
Duty Manager: Was it a chain one… like this? Or was it more slow and relaxed? I mean, it can get pretty hectic and full-on here at certain times of the day. And it's worse when the place is full of tourists who can't speak English.
Qiaoli: I think I can cope with it.
Duty manager: All right, well we'll need to see your passport and visa first to check that you're allowed to work, and then we'll try you out for the afternoon. Luisa here will train you, and we'll see what you're like.

Later

Luisa: Right… just watch me… yes sir, what would you like?
Customer: Erm… could I get a medium Mocha and a double Espresso please?
Luisa: Sure… is that to have here or to take away?
Customer: To drink in, please.
Luisa: Right… [to Qiaoli]… the customer wants it to drink in… that means we use the proper cups… not the plastic or paper ones… this size for the Mocha and this for the Espresso… tell the person making the coffee what the order is….
Qiaoli: Erm… [shouts] a medium Mocha and a double Espresso to drink in!
Jaco: Coming up!
Luisa: Would you like anything else with that, sir? A pastry or a biscuit?
Customer: No thanks.
Luisa: OK… that'll be £3.20 altogether. You can pick up your drinks at the end of the counter.
Customer: Here you are… thanks….
Luisa: [to Qiaoli]… so as you can see, we've got a kind of production line going… I take the orders…. Jaco makes the coffee… and Jenny delivers it to the customer on the counter at the end… we're called *baristas*… it's Italian for "barperson"… a bit of a pretentious name, I know, but there you go.

At the Supermarket

Mike: Hello… could I speak to the manager, please?
Checkout girl: Why? Have you got a complaint?
Mike: No… I'm looking for a part-time job.
Checkout girl: Well you'll need to speak to the supervisor, then. He's over there….

在咖啡店里

乔立：对不起，我想找一份业余工作。
当值经理：你有什么经验吗?
乔立：我在中国时在一家咖啡店里干过兼职。
当值经理：是像这样的连锁店吗？还是更轻松和缓慢的那种？这里一天中总有一些时候非常嘈杂繁忙。要是碰上一屋子不会说英语的顾客就更忙不过来了。
乔立：我想我能对付。
当值经理：好吧，我需要看看你的护照和签证，看你是否被允许工作。然后今天下午我们试用你。路易莎会培训你。我们看看你到底怎么样。

稍后

路易莎：好，看着我。先生您好，您要点什么?
顾客：哦，我想要一杯中号摩卡和双份儿浓咖啡。
路易莎：没问题。在这儿喝还是带走?
顾客：在这儿喝。
路易莎：好的。[对乔立] 顾客要在这儿喝，这表示我们得用普通的杯子，而不是塑料杯或纸杯。这样大小的杯子是装摩卡的，而这个是装浓咖啡的。告诉冲咖啡的伙计顾客要什么。
乔立：哦。[喊] 中号摩卡和双份浓咖啡，在这儿喝。
雅各：来了！
路易莎：您还要点别的吗？糕点或饼干?
顾客：不用了，谢谢。
路易莎：好了，一共是 3 镑 20 便士。您在柜台的那头取您的饮料。
顾客：给，谢谢。
路易莎：[对乔立] 你都看见了，我们这儿有个流水线。我负责记顾客点的单子，雅各冲咖啡，珍妮把咖啡送到柜台另一边的顾客手里。我们被称作"咖啡师"，这来自意大利语，指在咖啡吧里工作的人。有点儿装腔作势，我知道，但也就这么叫了。

在超市里

迈克：你好，我能跟经理说话吗？
女收银员：什么事？您要投诉吗？
迈克：不，我想找一份兼职工作。
女收银员：那你需要见工长，他在那边。

Mike: OK... [*to supervisor*]... I'm looking for work.

Supervisor: What? Stacking?

Mike: Stacking shelves... yes... anything really.

Supervisor: OK... you'll need to fill in this application form here, if we like you, we will call you... by the way, can you do nights?

Mike: Sorry?

Supervisor: Can you work night shift?

Mike: Well during the summer holidays I can, otherwise I'm only available during the weekends, I'm afraid.

Supervisor: OK... well, if we take you, we'll start you off in the warehouse putting stuff onto pallets... then we'll move you on to the shop floor.

迈克：好吧。[对工长说] 我想找份工作。

工长：什么样的工作？摆货架？

迈克：摆货架可以，什么工作都行。

工长：那好，把这份申请表填了。如果我们相中你，我们会给你打电话的。对了，你晚上能干吗？

迈克：什么？

工长：你能上夜班吗？

迈克：放暑假的时候可以，不过其它时间我只能在周末工作。

工长：好吧。如果我们录用你，我们会让你先在仓库工作，往集装台上码货，然后再把你调到商店里来。

实用短语

- I think I can cope with it. 我想我能对付。
- We'll try you out first. 我们得先试用你。
- Just watch me. 看着我/跟我学。
- Yes, sir. What would you like? 您好,先生。您要点什么?
- Could I get a...? 我想要一份……
- Is that to have here or to take away? 在这儿喝还是带走?
- To drink in, please. 在这儿喝。
- Coming up! 来了!
- Would you like anything else with that, sir/madam? 您还要点别的吗,先生/女士?
- That'll be... altogether. 总共是……
- Could I speak to..., please? 我能找……吗?
- You'll need to speak to the..., then. 那你得找……
- During the... I can, otherwise, I... 在……期间,我可以,不过其他时间,我……
- We'll start you off in... then we'll move you on to... 我们先让你……再让你……

词汇表

barista 咖啡师
barperson 在酒吧或咖啡吧工作的人
biscuit 饼干
checkout girl 女收银员
Coming up! 来了!
complaint 投诉
counter 柜台
deliver 投递
double Espresso 双份浓咖啡

duty manager 值班经理
full-on 全面运转
get... going 使某事运作起来
have here 在这儿吃喝/不带走
hectic 忙碌的
medium Mocha 中号摩卡
night shift 晚上的工作时段
pallet 堆放货物的方形大木板
pastry 点心
plastic 塑料/塑料的

pretentious 装模做样的/不真诚的
production line 生产线
proper 正经的
shelves 货柜
stack 堆/摆放
supervisor 监督
take away 带走
try somebody out 试用某人
warehouse 库房

第39章
谦虚地展示技能
Demonstrating Skills Humbly

背景常识

说中国人与西方人相比过于谦虚,这其实是讹传。诚然(admittedly),由于西方社会高度的商业化(commercialisation),西方人只有善于推销(sell)自己才能取得事业和感情上的成功。然而,正因为如此,物以稀为贵,谦虚(modesty/humility)才恰恰是受人尊重的品质。而卖弄(showing off)则是在全世界都让人讨厌的。所以,既能推销自己又能保持谦虚才是"善之善者也"(the acme of strategy)。

在英国人的语言习惯中,既谦虚又能突出(highlight)自己的谈吐可以有以下几种方法。

第一,你可以首先恭维对方的长处,然后再引出自己的骄傲。比如,如果你想要告诉别人你会演奏一种乐器,你可以说:Hi, I heard you playing piano last night. It was great. I play the violin myself.

第二,不要故作谦虚。比如,如果一个人说"不是我自夸(not to brag)"或者"不是我吹牛(not to sound cocky)",十有八九这个人其实就是在自夸吹牛。如果你承认自己在卖弄,反而还好一些:I know this is going to make me sound quite shameless, but….

第三,当别人夸奖你的时候,如果你当之无愧,就大方地接受。在英语里,表示"您过奖了"的短语包括 I am flattered./You are too generous with your words./I take it as a compliment./Oh, stop it./You are just saying it. 如果别人明显是在"过奖"你,你就不要用这些表示接受表扬的句子了。

作为留学生,你经常会遇到别人的恭维或忽略。不要急着卖弄。生活总需要一些耐心和自我解嘲(self-deprecation)。

International Students' Night

Compere: Right, we're here this evening for an evening of food, music and dance from China, Brazil, Morocco, Japan, Russia, Spain and Turkey… Wang Shu is going to play two musical instruments… the *guqin* and the *erhu*… and I'm sure that you'll find that he's a master on both….

Wang: [*bows*] I'm not that good, really. Get your earplugs ready.

Compere: Then, Gizela from Brazil will perform a traditional samba dance….

Audience: Hooray… [*claps*]… [*whistles*]…

Gizela: [*bows, waves*] I'm not that good a dancer, really.

Compere: Calm down everyone… and after Gizela, Nadjia from Morocco will bring things down by showing you all how to paint designs on your hands using henna to do traditional North African designs and patterns.

Nadjia: [*waves her hands*]… it's nothing special, actually.

Compere: Of course it is. It's beautiful. After that, Mariko from Japan will calm us all down even more by showing us how to perform the Japanese tea ceremony the right way….

Mariko: Oh… I'm not an expert by any means…. I just know a little bit about it….

Audience: Wow… oooh….

Compere: And once she has done this and you are all relaxed, we'll turn up the tempo again with a Russian dance from Boris… he's going to do a traditional Cossack dance… you know—arms folded, squatting down and kicking his legs out… all very exciting.

Boris: Oh… I'll try my best, but don't expect too much. I'm a bit fat.

Audience: Yeah… get the Vodka out now!

Compere: And finally we'll have Francisco from Spain doing a Flamenco dance with Pinar from Turkey. You'll see how proud and dignified Spanish men are when they dance like this… and how beautiful and graceful Turkish women are… and if you ask her nicely, Pinar will do a belly dance as well… that's something that's traditional all over the Middle East.

Audience: Wow… yeah… do it now!

Francisco: [*bows*]… please, please….

Pinar: Oh… no… no….

Compere: Now, at the end of these performances, there'll be dancing for everyone with an international buffet. Right, let's get on with the show straight away… Mr. Wang Shu from Shanghai is going to play the *guqin*, and then the *erhu*….

After

Pinar: That was amazing, Wang. The music you played was so moving. Where did you learn to play like that?

Wang Shu: Oh, it was nothing special. Really. You want to hear the old guys in my home town… they are fantastic. I'm nothing compared to them.

Pinar: Well I certainly found it beautiful. I was almost in tears.
Wang Shu: Well, I'm flattered. Thanks. What about your dancing, though? Where did you learn that?
Pinar: Oh, I started late actually. They have different kinds of dance classes here in the uni… salsa, jazz, Belly-dancing. It's great for keeping fit.
Wang Shu: You're telling me!

留学生晚会

主持人：好了，今天晚上，我们有来自中国、巴西、摩洛哥、日本、俄罗斯、西班牙和土耳其的食物、音乐和舞蹈。王书将表演两种乐器，古琴和二胡。我肯定你们会发现他在两样乐器上都游刃有余。
王：[鞠躬] 我其实没那么好。把你们的耳塞准备好吧。
主持人：然后，来自巴西的吉则娜将表演传统的桑巴舞。
观众：好！[鼓掌，吹口哨]
吉则娜：[鞠躬、招手] 我真的跳得不好。
主持人：大家静一静。吉则娜之后是从摩洛哥来的娜德佳，她将给我们一些安静的节目，向我们展示如何用海娜粉在手上画出传统的北非图案。
娜德佳：[挥手] 其实也没什么特别的。
主持人：当然特别了，很美的！那之后，日本的麻里子将通过日本茶道让我们更加安静。
麻里子：噢，我不是什么专家，只是略知一二。
观众：哇……唔……
主持人：等她的表演结束，你们也彻底放松之后，我们将加快节奏，欣赏鲍里斯的俄罗斯舞蹈。他将表演传统的哥萨克舞——双臂抱团，屈膝提腿——非常刺激！
鲍里斯：哦，我尽力吧。不过别期望太高，我有点儿发福了。
观众：好哎……现在就把伏特加端上来吧！
主持人：最后，西班牙的弗朗西斯科和土耳其的皮娜将一起表演弗拉门戈舞。你将看到西班牙男人在这个舞蹈中的骄傲和尊严，还有土耳其女人的动人与优雅。而且，如果你们彬彬有礼地求她，皮娜可能还会给你们跳一段肚皮舞。这是中东地区的传统艺术。
观众：哇……好……现在就跳！
弗朗西斯科：[鞠躬] 错爱，错爱……
皮娜：哦，别这样……
主持人：在表演之后，大家可以一起跳舞，并享用国际自助餐。好了，我们开始进入表演，上海的王书先生将演奏古琴和二胡……

之后

皮娜：你的表演太吸引人了，王。你的音乐非常感人。在哪儿学的？
王书：哦，这没什么，真的。你应该听听我家乡的老人们表演，那才叫好听。我跟他们没法比。
皮娜：我觉得它很好听。我都快哭了。
王书：我受宠若惊。谢谢。你的舞蹈呢？你在哪儿学的？
皮娜：哦，我起步很晚。学校里有各种舞蹈班，莎莎、爵士、肚皮舞，对保持身材很有用。
王书：显而易见！

实用短语

- I'm not that good, really.　我其实没那么好。
- Get your earplugs ready.　把耳塞准备好。
- I'm not that good a dancer, really.　我跳得并不好。
- It's nothing special, actually.　真没什么特别的。
- Oh, I'm not an expert by any means.　我无论如何都不能算专家。
- I just know a little bit about it.　我只是略知一二。
- Oh, I'll try my best, but don't expect too much.　我尽力吧,不过别期望太高。
- I'm a bit fat.　我有点儿发福了。
- Please, please.　算了吧/没什么/错爱了。
- No, no.　别这样。
- The music you played was so...　你的音乐真是太……
- You want to hear/see the...　你应该听/看……
- I'm nothing compared to them.　我跟他们没法比。
- Well, I'm flattered.　我受宠若惊/过奖了。
- What about your..., though?　你的……呢?
- You're telling me!　不言而喻/显而易见。

词汇表

belly dance 肚皮舞
bow 鞠躬
buffet 自助餐
cheer 欢呼
clap 鼓掌
design 设计
dignified 有尊严的
earplugs 耳塞
exciting 令人兴奋的
expert 专家
Flamenco 弗拉门戈舞

flatter 吹捧
fold 折叠
get on with... 开始做某事
graceful 优雅的
hurray 好!(感叹词)
kick out 踢出
master 大师
Morocco 摩洛哥
musical instrument 乐器
North Africa 北非
pattern 图案/规律

right way 正确的做法
Samba 桑巴舞
squat down 蹲下
tea ceremony 茶道
tempo 节奏
traditional 传统的
try one's best 尽某人的所能
turn up 出席/呈现为
Vodka 伏特加
wave 挥手
whistle 口哨/吹口哨

第40章
酒吧与晚会
Pubs and Parties

背景常识

喝酒(drinking)是英国校园生活的重中之重。中英酒文化之间有很多区别。中国人喜欢边吃边喝,而英国人则喜欢饭后饮酒。中国人不提倡将不同的酒混起来喝,而英国人恰恰喜欢换着喝。不仅一晚上可以既喝啤酒(beer)、葡萄酒(wine),又喝高度酒(spirits),人们还干脆把不同的酒兑在一杯里——也就成了鸡尾酒(cocktail)。

在英国流行的啤酒品牌有:Guinness,世界闻名的爱尔兰黑啤;Strong-bow,苹果啤酒(cider);Carling,英国最畅销的淡啤酒(lager)。把 cider 和 lager 倒在一起,再加一点儿浓缩黑莓汁(blackcurrant cordial),你就得到了一杯危险的 Snakebite Black。

说到英国的高度酒,人人都会首推苏格兰威士忌(Scotch whisky)。而伏特加(Vodka)总让人联想到俄罗斯,但伏特加其实才是全欧洲最畅销的酒。英国其它的高度酒还包括:杜松子酒(gin)、朗姆酒(rum)和白兰地(brandy)。因为007而风靡世界的马丁尼酒其实是 gin 和 vermouth 的混合。不过007所喜欢的马丁尼其实还换了伏特加,而且是"摇拌而不搅拌"(shaken, not stirred)。建议中国女生们都试试加了果汁的伏特加,还有 Baileys——爱尔兰有名的巧克力奶油甜酒。

葡萄酒不能算是英国的特色。最好的葡萄酒和香槟还得数法国和意大利产的。中国人都知道葡萄酒有红、白之分。其实葡萄酒还有粉色的,被称为 rosé,在英国日渐流行。

英国法律禁止向18岁以下的人售酒。所以,如果你长得年轻,出去喝酒要携带身份证件。英国朋友之间有时喜欢买圈(buy rounds)。这表示每个人都要请其他所有人喝酒。这样喝压力比较大,很容易醉。

In a Kitchen in the Halls of Residence

Jack: Erm... I was wondering... does anyone fancy going down the pub later on... it's a bit boring here....

Soraya: Sure... I'm up for it.

Anna: Yeah... why not?

Jay: Yeah... sounds good to me... what about you, Arnur...?

Arnur: Oh, I don't know... I've got an assignment to finish before Tuesday.

Soraya: It's Friday night, Arnur! You've got the whole weekend and Monday to do your assignment... don't be so boring.

Jay: Yeah... don't be a spoilsport.

Arnur: Oh, all right then. Twist my arm.

At the Bar

Barman: Right... what can I get you?

Jay: [*to others*] It's OK... I'll get these... what are you all having?

Soraya: Could I have a gin and tonic please?

Anna: Erm... I'll have a Smirnoff Ice.

Jay: OK... what about you, Jack?

Jack: I'll have a pint of lager please.

Arnur: Pint of Guinness, Jay, please.

Jay: Right [*to the barman*] ... could I have a pint of Guinness, a pint of lager, a Smirnoff Ice and a gin and tonic... oh and a pint of bitter as well please?

Barman: OK... ice and lemon in the G & T?

Soraya: Yes, please.

Jay: Do you all want to go and grab a table? Jack... you can help me with these drinks....

Barman: That'll be 9.30 altogether, please.

Back at the Table

Jay: Listen... there's a band playing at the Student Union... shall we go and see them... two of the members—the guitarist and the drummer are students on our course... they're really great.

Anna: Oh, I don't know... what kind of music do they play?

Jay: Rock with some world music influences... you know... a bit of Latin rhythm, a bit of African, a bit Middle Eastern... it's difficult to describe... you'll like it....

Soraya: Oh, I don't know... I prefer easy listening, soft rock... you know... ballads. What sorts of music do you like, Anna?

Jack: Well, look… there's a late bar there… this place closes at 11, and it's last orders now… listen! They've just rung the bell. So we need to make up our minds.

Anna: OK… look, I'll get the last round in here… then we'll go along to the Union… OK?

在宿舍厨房

杰克： 哦，我想知道，有谁一会儿想去酒吧？这儿有点儿无聊。

索拉娅： 没问题，我去。

安娜： 好啊，干嘛不去？

杰伊： 是啊，好主意。你呢，阿那？

阿那： 哦，我没准儿。我周二前得完成一门作业。

索拉娅： 现在是周五晚上，阿那！你有整个周末和周一来写你的作业，别那么沉闷嘛！

杰伊： 说得对，别让大家扫兴。

阿那： 那好吧，真是强人所难。

在酒吧

酒保： 你们要点什么？

杰伊： [对其他人] 不用担心，我来付账。你们都要喝什么？

索拉娅： 我能来一杯杜松子酒加奎宁水吗？

安娜： 我要一瓶冰雪口味的斯莫诺夫伏特加。

杰伊： 没问题。你呢，杰克？

杰克： 我来一品脱淡啤酒。

阿那： 一品脱吉尼斯，杰伊。

杰伊： 好的。[对酒保说] 能不能给我来一品脱吉尼斯、一品脱淡啤酒、一瓶冰雪口味的斯莫诺夫和一杯杜松子酒加奎宁水。噢，还有一品脱苦啤酒，谢谢。

酒保： 好的。杜松子酒加奎宁水里要加冰和柠檬吗？

索拉娅： 是的，谢谢。

杰伊： 你们去占张桌子吧。杰克，帮我端这些喝的。

酒保： 一共是 9 镑 30 便士。谢谢。

酒桌旁

杰伊： 哎，学生会今天晚上有乐队表演，我们去看看吧。乐队里有两个成员，吉他手和鼓手，还是我们课程里的呢。他们很厉害。

安娜： 哦，我不知道。他们演奏什么样的音乐？

杰伊： 综合世界风的摇滚，一点儿拉丁，一点儿非洲，一点儿中东，很难形容。你会喜欢的。

索拉娅： 哦，我不知道。我偏爱轻松的乐曲，软摇滚、民谣。你喜欢什么样的音乐，安娜？

杰克： 不管怎么说，学生会的酒吧关门晚。这里 11 点就关门了，现在是最后一次下单。听，他们已经打铃了，我们需要当机立断。

安娜： 好吧，我来买这最后一轮。然后我们都去学生会，行吗？

实用短语

- I was wondering… 我想知道……
- Does anyone fancy going…? 有没有人想去……?
- What about you, …? 你呢,……?
- Shall we go and see them? 要不要去看看他们?
- Sure… I'm up for it. 好啊,我去。
- Yeah… why not? 对,干嘛不?
- Yeah… sounds good to me. 对,好主意。
- Oh, all right then. 噢,好吧。
- Twist my arm. 强人所难。
- Don't be so/a…! 别这么……/别当个……
- What can I get you? 你们要点什么?
- I'll get these… 我来付这些帐。
- What are you all having? 你们要喝什么?
- Could I have…? 我能不能要……?
- I'll have… 我要……
- It's kind of… 是某种……
- It's difficult to describe… you'll like it. 不好形容……你会喜欢的。

词汇表

alternative 另一选择
band 乐队
bitter 苦啤酒
drummer 鼓手
easy listening 听起来轻松的
fancy 喜欢
gin and tonic 杜松子酒加奎宁水
grab a table 找个桌子坐下
Guinness 吉尼斯(啤酒名)

guitarist 吉他手
hip hop 街舞
ice and lemon 冰块和柠檬
lager 淡啤酒
last orders 最后的下单机会
latin rhythm 拉丁节奏
lyrics 歌词
make up one's mind 下定决心
pint 品脱

rap 说唱
rock 摇滚
soft rock 软摇滚
sounds good 听起来不错
spoilsport 扫兴的人
twist my arm 扭胳膊/强迫
up for it 愿意做某事
world music 世界音乐

第41章
电影院和剧院
Cinema and Theatre

背景常识

作为莎士比亚（William Shakespeare）的故乡，戏剧与电影在英国有着极其重要的地位，尤其是在学生与知识分子中间。

说起西方电影，我们都会想到好莱坞（Hollywood）。其实，如果没有英国电影工业的贡献，Hollywood也不会有今天的辉煌。英国是众多Hollywood大师级人物的出生地，比如卓别林（Charlie Chaplin），阿加莎·克里斯蒂（Agatha Christie）和希区柯克（Alfred Hitchcock）。许多美国电影人也喜欢到英国收集灵感（inspiration），比如伍迪·艾伦（Woody Allen）和斯坦利·库布里克（Stanley Kubrick）。英国的摄影棚，比如Ealing和Pinewood，被认为是世界上最好的特技效果制作商。其作品包括《超人》（Superman）、《星球大战》（Star Wars）、《007系列》和《哈利·波特》（Harry Potter）。英国还出产了许多电影明星：苏格兰有肖恩·康纳利（Sean Connery），威尔士有安东尼·霍普金斯（Anthony Hopkins），英格兰有迈克·凯恩（Michael Caine）。女演员中，威尔士有凯瑟琳·泽塔—琼斯（Catherine Zeta-Jones），英格兰有伊丽莎白·泰勒（Elizabeth Taylor），苏格兰有……well，苏格兰女星是欠缺了一些。

伦敦的西区（West End）与纽约的百老汇（Broadway）在西方剧场艺术界并驾齐驱。伦敦近年流行的戏剧包括：Les Miserables（《悲惨世界》）、Cats（《猫》）、The Mousetrap（《捕鼠机》）、The Phantom of the Opera（《歌剧院魅影》）、Blood Brothers（《血亲兄弟》）和Mamma Mia（《我的天啊》）等等。

不少英国人对电影和戏剧的态度是非常严肃的。由于对某一作品的不同看法，朋友之间甚至可以反目成仇。所以，你将来跟朋友去看电影的时候，可能也不得不准备好为自己的审美（aesthetics）与世界观（ontology）辩护。

In the Common Room

Wang: Hey, look at this leaflet... there's some good stuff on at the Gulbenkian Theatre this weekend. Does anyone fancy going...?

Jenny: What's on?

Wang: Well, there's the Berthold Brecht play, *The Caucasian Chalk Circle.*

Lu: [*laughing*] What? That sounds a bit obscure... what's it about? Is there music in it?

Wang: Don't be a philistine, Lu! It's a modern classic, a masterpiece of German theatre. Listen, [*reads*] "the play is often regarded as part of the epic theatrical tradition. The motifs used in the play are taken from the Bible, Buddhist and Islamic stories, and the 13th-century Chinese play, *Hui Lan Ji* by Li Xing Dao. It deals with universal themes through the story of a group of peasants resolving the ownership of a farm after the Nazis almost destroy it." This is an English-language version produced by Frank McGuinness, a famous playwright from the North of Ireland.

Lu: Oh no... it sounds a bit heavy-going for me.

Joe: Yes... far too deep and meaningful for us... we're too shallow to understand all of that! Anyway, the language will be too hard! Let's go to the cinema instead.

Wang: Right, let's see... there's an Ingmar Bergman retrospective at the Arts Cinema in town. There's also the London Film Festival. Look... here's the programme... Turkish New Wave, Iranian Women's Cinema, Latin American Feminist and Voices Against Globalisation... all of this looks really good.

Jenny: No... no... listen! We need to relax at the weekend, not get depressed or think about saving the world. Anyway, do you know how hard it is to concentrate on a foreign-language film with English subtitles?

Joe: I think we should go and see the new James Bond film, *Casino Royale.* It's on at the Odeon. That's what we need... an action movie.

Wang: Is that what you're into? Mindless sex and violence?

Joe: Well yes, actually! But I also like horror films, sci-fi, comedies, war films and thrillers! Anyway, 007 is not mindless—it is a well-respected genre, and it's very ironic and tongue-in-cheek. But most of all, it's good old escapist fun! Listen to this review... "a totally new James Bond, beefed-up, raw and really human... he bleeds and he has emotions!"

Jenny: OK... the new James Bond it is! The programme starts at 7.20... plus twenty minutes of ads and stuff before the actual film. If we get there for 7.30, we'll be fine.

After the Film

Wang: That was great. I didn't think I would enjoy it, but I did. Did you see that

bit where Bond was fighting with the baddie! He was really hurt and injured... a real human, not like the other Bonds.
Jenny: Wow, yes... and what a man! Those eyes, those muscles....
Joe: Calm down, will you?

在活动室

王：嘿，看看这本册子。古尔班基安剧院这个周末上演不少好节目。有谁想去吗？

珍妮：都演什么？

王：有贝尔托特·布莱希特的戏剧《高加索灰阑记》。

陆：［笑］什么？听起来有些晦涩。什么内容？里面有音乐吗？

王：陆，别装文盲了！这可是现代经典，德国戏剧的代表作。听着，［念］"这部戏通常被认为是史诗剧传统的一部分。主题取材于圣经、佛教和伊斯兰教故事，还有13世纪的中国戏剧——李行道的《灰阑记》。它通过一群农民解决一个被纳粹摧毁的农庄的归属权问题的故事，来揭示具有普遍意义的主题。"这是由北爱尔兰著名剧作家福兰克·迈克吉尼斯创作的英语版本。

陆：哦不，听起来太沉重了。

乔：是啊，对我们这样的人来说太深奥了。我们这么肤浅是没法理解的！而且，语言肯定也很难懂！我们还是去看电影吧。

王：好吧，我看看。城里的艺术电影院在放英格玛·博格曼的回顾展，还有伦敦电影节，这是节目单……土耳其新浪潮、伊朗妇女电影、拉丁美洲女权主义，还有反对全球化……这些看起来都不错。

珍妮：不，不，听着！我们周末需要放松，而不是寻求郁闷或者思考如何拯救世界。你知道专心看一部外语对白英文字幕的电影有多难吗？

杰伊：我觉得我们应该去看那部新的詹姆斯·邦德，《皇家赌场》。正在奥迪恩电影院放映。这才是我们需要的，一部动作片。

王：你就喜欢那个？没头脑的性与暴力？

乔：说实话，我就喜欢！可我还爱看恐怖片、科幻片、喜剧片、战争片和悬念片！再说，007可不是没脑子——它是一个非常受人尊重的电影派别，而且它还非常具有讽刺和滑稽意味。最重要的是，它是经久不衰的休闲娱乐！听听这个影评："一个全新的詹姆斯·邦德，粗犷、生猛而且人性化……他会流血，他有情感！"

珍妮：好啦，詹姆斯·邦德，就这么定了！节目7点20开始，再加上20分钟的片头广告什么的。如果我们7点30到那儿，正好赶上。

电影结束后

王：这电影太好了。我没想到自己会这么喜欢它，我确实非常喜欢。你注意到邦德与坏人搏斗的场面了吗？他真的受伤了。一个真实的人，不像以前那些邦德。

珍妮：哇，对，多棒的男人！那双眼睛，那些肌肉……

乔：你俩能不能别那么激动？

实用短语

- There's some good stuff on at the… 这周……放映不少好东西。
- Does anyone fancy going? 有谁想去吗?
- What's on? 演什么?
- That sounds a bit obscure. 听起来有些晦涩。
- Don't be a philistine! 别装文盲了!
- The play/film/performance is regarded as… 这部戏剧/电影/演出被认为是……
- This is a… version, produced by… 这是由……制作的……版本。
- It sounds a bit heavy going for me. 听起来太沉重了。
- Did you see that bit where…? 你们注意到……的部分/镜头了吗?
- What a man! 多棒的男人!
- Calm down, will you? 你们能不能别那么激动?

词汇表

Arts Cinema 艺术影院
baddie 坏人
be into 对…感兴趣
beefed-up 粗犷
bleed 流血
Buddhist 佛教徒
comedy 喜剧
deep and meaningful 寓意深刻的
depressed 压抑的
emotions 感情
epic 史诗
escapist fun 逃离主义的乐趣
genre 种类(尤指艺术)
good old 当初美好的
heavy going 主题沉重的
horror 恐怖
hurt 受伤

injured 受伤的
ironic 讽刺意味
Islamic 伊斯兰的
James Bond 詹姆斯·邦德
Latin American Feminist 拉美女权主义
leaflet 小册子
London Film Festival 伦敦电影节
masterpiece 代表作
mindless 漫无目的的
modern classic 现代经典
motif 主旨
muscles 肌肉
obscure 难懂的
philistine 文盲/对文化敬而远之的人
play 话剧

playwright 剧作家
programme 节目
raw 野蛮
regard 认为/关心
resolve 解决
retrospective 回顾的
review 评价
sci-fi 科幻
sex 性/性爱/性别
subtitles 字幕
tongue-in-cheek 滑稽
universal themes 普遍主题/人人都关注的主题
violence 暴力
voices against globalisation 反对全球化的呼声
war film 战争电影

第42章
圣诞节与新年
Christmas and New Year

背景常识

对大部分中国学生来说,圣诞节是一年中最让人忧伤的时刻。看着万家团圆、灯火辉煌,而自己却独在异乡。所以,出于对你身心健康的考虑,你应该尽早安排自己的寒假。想要在英国有个 Merry Christmas,以下几个计划是你可以考虑的。

第一,去一个英国同学家过年。这应该是最理想的选择。你可以见识到英国家庭是如何用圣诞树、彩灯(fairy lights)、饰品(decorations)、礼物、长筒袜(stocking)、圣诞歌(carol)、火鸡(turkey)、填料(stuffing)、小红莓果酱(cranberry sauce)、百果馅饼(mince pie)和布丁来庆祝圣诞的。还有,到英国同学家过圣诞节,别忘了给人家的家人买礼物。

第二个选择是旅游。许多旅行社都组织圣诞游。比如,在闹鬼的(haunted)苏格兰高原城堡(castle)里过平安夜(Christmas Eve)、品威士忌、吃haggis(肉馅羊肚)、追寻尼斯湖水怪(Loch Ness Monster)就是一个不错的线路。在旅行团里,你可能会遇到不少有趣的人。他们跟你一样,也是在圣诞节"无家可归"的人。

如果你不想旅游,最起码,你也应该跟其他的留学生一起组织点儿活动。比如自己学着烤只火鸡。跟学包饺子一样,烤火鸡也不是那么容易的。

无论你做什么,总之不要把自己关起来,在家苦读就是了。如果你的英国同学知道你圣诞节还在用功,他们会说:It is Christmas, for God's sake!(圣诞节到了,看在上帝的份上!)关于这个话题的英语常识,大概只有两个关键词 Merry Christmas!和 Happy New Year!别忘了用感叹号。

Students Wrapping Christmas Presents

Wang: Can you pass me the scissors and the sellotape, Jenny? I need to cut this wrapping paper... God! I'm terrible at this; I think it needs a woman's touch!

Jenny: If you just give it here... I'll wrap it for you... you are all fingers and thumbs.

Lilly: You must be missing home, Francisco... I'll bet you'd be having really great celebrations if you were there.

Francisco: Well, yes, actually. In fact, it's not really like here in England at all. If I were at home in Spain, I would be having my Christmas dinner on Christmas Eve—not Christmas Day. In fact, it would be very late at night around midnight to welcome in the Baby Jesus.

Wang: Wow... cool... we don't really have anything like big Christmas celebrations in China. I mean, I guess Christians celebrate it as a religious festival, but for the rest of us, it's more of a shopping and present-giving season. If you go to the big shopping malls in China, you can see a big Santa Claus or Father Christmas, but most people don't know what the religious significance is.

Lilly: That's interesting, isn't it? Christmas has become so commercialised... if you were to go to a shopping mall in Singapore, where I am from, you would see some of the huge shopping centres wrapped up as presents or Christmas cakes or Christmas trees. That's because every year the government gives a prize for the best decorated building in the country.

Jenny: We also seem to have lost lots of our Christmas traditions here in England, and it has become very commercialized, but there are still some interesting ones... if you're at a Christmas office party, you have to be careful where you stand....

Francisco: Why's that?

Jenny: Mistletoe.

Lilly: Oh... I know about that!

Wang: What is it?

Jenny: Well, it's a small green plant with white berries that people hang up over a door or somewhere, and if you stand under it, someone—usually a man—might try to kiss you. Kissing under the mistletoe is an ancient tradition that goes back to pagan times when people celebrated the Winter Solstice, the shortest day of the year... it's curious that these Christian religious days are usually the same as the earlier pagan ones.

Wang: That's right! Our lecturer was saying the same thing.

Jenny: Anyway, the thing is... if you want a man to kiss you, make sure you catch his eye and then stand under the mistletoe... we have other Christmas plants too... like holly... that has red berries... and ivy, and if it's snowing and you see robins in the garden, that's even better....

学生们包圣诞礼物

王：你能把剪刀和透明胶递给我吗，珍妮？我需要剪包装纸。天哪！我在这方面太没用了，我想这该是女人的活儿！

珍妮：要是像你这样……还是我帮你包吧，你笨手笨脚的。

莉莉：你一定很想家吧，弗朗西斯科。我打赌如果你这会儿在家的话，一定欢天喜地的。

弗朗西斯科：是的。实际上，我们那儿跟在英国很不一样。如果我在西班牙家里，圣诞晚宴是在平安夜吃的，而不是在圣诞日。实际上，欢迎小耶稣是在很晚的时候，接近午夜。

王：哇……酷……在中国我们不会大张旗鼓地庆祝圣诞节。基督徒们把圣诞节当作宗教节日来庆祝，对于我们这些人来说，这就是个购物和送礼物的季节。如果你去中国的大商场，你就能看到巨大的圣诞老人，但是大多数人都不知道其宗教含义。

莉莉：有意思，圣诞节已经被商业化了。如果你去我家乡新加坡的商场，你会看到某些购物中心被包装成一个圣诞大礼包，或者圣诞蛋糕和圣诞树的样子。那是因为政府每年都会奖励装饰得最好的一栋建筑。

珍妮：我们英国似乎也丢失了不少圣诞节的传统习俗，圣诞节也变得很商业化，但是还有不少有意思的东西。如果你参加一个办公室圣诞节晚会，你得注意自己站的位置。

弗朗西斯科：为什么？

珍妮：槲寄生。

莉莉：哦，我知道！

王：是什么？

珍妮：它是一种小的结白色果子的绿色植物。人们经常把它们挂在门上或其他地方。如果你站到它下面，某个人，一般是男人，会试图亲你。在槲寄生下接吻是一个悠久的传统，这可以追溯到异教徒时期人们庆祝冬至的时候，一年中最短的一天……这其实很让人好奇，如今基督教的节日都与早先的异教徒节日吻合。

王：对！我们老师也是这么说的。

珍妮：关键是，如果你想让哪个男人亲你，首先得吸引他的视线，然后站到槲寄生的下面。我们还有其他的圣诞植物。比如结红果子的冬青，还有长青藤。如果下雪的时候你在花园里看见知更鸟就更吉利了。

Francisco: What do you do on Christmas day if you're in England?

Jenny: Well, we get up and go downstairs and open our presents, which are under the Christmas tree… if you're a child, you'll believe that Santa Claus has brought the presents… but if you're an adult, you'll know who's actually bought them! Anyway, we sit around eating and drinking… mince pies, sherry, champagne, red wine… if you don't like alcohol, it's no problem… you can have fruit juice… and we prepare a big Christmas dinner… turkey and all the trimmings.

Wang: What's that?

Jenny: Well, it's a big turkey, covered in bacon and stuffed with herbs and stuff, cooked in the oven, and it's served with little sausages called chipolatas, roast potatoes and seasonal vegetables like carrots and sprouts.

Lilly: Wow….

Jenny: Then, if you still have enough space you can have a dessert… usually Christmas pudding, mince pies and cream… cheese… fruit and nuts… port wine….

Francisco: What's this thing about the Queen's Speech?

Jenny: Well it's been a tradition since the BBC was set up that the Head of State would give a Christmas speech to the nation… something innocuous about peace and understanding in an uncertain world. It's generally older people who watch it these days. It's on at 3 pm every Christmas Day. But, if we didn't have the Queen's Speech on TV, it wouldn't be Christmas.

Francisco: New Year is a bit wild in England, isn't it? People drinking and acting crazy.

Jenny: Well it can be if you want it to be, but if you were in Scotland it would be a lot more interesting… there they call New Year Hogmanay, and they have different traditions… for instance, they have a thing called first footing… that means being the first person to cross a neighbour's threshold after midnight on 1st January. You have to take a lump of coal for the neighbour's fire, and in return you'll get a glass of whisky… an alternative way is to take your own bottle of whisky around all your neighbours' houses giving them all a tot as you go… people pass each other in the street as they go around the town or village and you get, like, impromptu parties with fiddle music and bagpipes and stuff. Of course, on 1st and 2nd January the whole country has a massive collective hangover!

Wang: I think it would have been better if I had gone to a Scottish university!

Lilly: If you'd gone to a Scottish university, you wouldn't have done any work.

弗朗西斯科：在英国你们圣诞日的时候都干什么？

珍妮：我们起床、下楼、开礼物，礼物都在圣诞树下面。如果你是小孩儿，就会相信礼物是圣诞老人送来的。如果你是成年人，你就知道其实那些都是有人买的！总之，我们就闲坐着，吃吃喝喝……百果馅饼、雪利酒、香槟、红葡萄酒……如果你不喜欢酒也没关系，可以喝果汁。我们还做一顿很丰盛的圣诞晚宴，包括火鸡和所有配菜。

王：那是什么？

珍妮：一只大火鸡，用熏肉裹着并填满了香草和其他作料，放在烤箱里烤，然后跟一种叫做奇布拉塔的小香肠以及烤土豆和应季蔬菜比如胡萝卜和甘蓝，配在一起吃。

莉莉：哇……

珍妮：然后，如果你肚子还装得下，你还可以吃些甜点，通常是圣诞布丁、百果馅饼、奶油、奶酪、水果、坚果、葡萄酒……

弗朗西斯科：女王演讲是怎么回事儿？

珍妮：自从英国广播公司成立以来，国家元首每逢圣诞节向全国发表讲话就成了一项传统。都是些无关痛痒的话，在一个不稳定的世界里保持和平和理解之类的。现在只有上岁数的人才看。每个圣诞日的下午3点播放。但是，如果没有女王的演讲，大家又感觉不到圣诞的气氛了。

弗朗西斯科：英国的新年比较疯狂，是吗？大家都喝酒胡闹。

珍妮：你想这么干也未尝不可。不过，如果你在苏格兰就更有意思了。他们管新年叫霍格玛内，还有特别的传统。比如，他们有一种说法叫第一脚，表示在1月1号凌晨第一个迈过邻居门槛的人。你必须带上一块炭，为邻居升火。而作为回报，你会得到一杯威士忌。另一种方式是你自己带一瓶威士忌在周围邻里绕一圈儿，请所有邻居喝一杯。人们在村镇街坊间走动，互相打着招呼。你会看到人们自发地集会，演奏小提琴和风笛之类的乐器。当然，1月的头两天全国人民都有集体性的酒后头疼。

王：我觉得我要是在苏格兰上大学就好了。

莉莉：你要是去了一家苏格兰大学，你就根本什么都学不进去了。

实用短语

- If you want…, make sure you…   如果你想要……,确定你……
- If it's…, that's even better.   如果是……就更好了。
- What do you do on Christmas day if you're in England? 在英国你们圣诞都干什么?
- If you don't like…, it's…   如果你不喜欢……就……
- If you go to…, you can see…   如果你去……,你可以看见……
- If you're at a…, you have to be…   如果你在……,你必须……
- If you…, someone might try to…   如果你……,某人可能会试图……
- If you still have… you can…   如果你还有……你可以……
- Well it can be if you want it to be.   你想这么干也未尝不可。
- If you really want to…, you can just…   如果你真的要……,你可以干脆……
- If you just give it here… I'll do it for you.   如果你这样……我来帮你。
- If I were…, I would be having…   如果我是……,我就将有……
- If you were to go to… you would see…   如果你去……你可以看见……
- If we didn't have…, it wouldn't be Christmas.   如果我们没有……,就觉得不像圣诞节。
- If you were in… it would be a lot more…   如果你在一个……那就更……
- It would have been better if I had…!   如果我……就好了!
- If you'd…, you wouldn't have…   如果你……,你就不会……

词汇表

a bit wild 有点儿狂野
a woman's touch 女人的巧手
all fingers and thumbs 笨手笨脚的
Baby Jesus 小耶稣
bacon 熏肉
bagpipes 管风琴
berry 梅
best-decorated 装饰得最好的
boxing day 圣诞节第二天
carrot 胡萝卜
catch someone's eye 吸引人注意的
champagne 香槟
cheese 奶酪
chipolata 小香肠
Christmas cake 圣诞蛋糕
Christmas carol 圣诞歌
Christmas day 圣诞日
Christmas eve 平安夜
Christmas pudding 圣诞布丁
Christmas tree 圣诞树
coal 煤炭
collective 集体的
commercialised 商业化的

cream 奶油
curious 好奇的
dessert 甜点
fiddle music 提琴音乐
first foot/first footing 第一脚
fruit juice 果汁
fruit 水果
hang up 挂
hangover 酒后的头疼
Hogmanay 新年
holly 冬青
impromptu 一时兴起
innocuous 无关痛痒的
ivy 长青藤
mince pie 百果馅饼
mistletoe 槲寄生
nuts 坚果
pagan 异教徒
plant 植物
port wine 波特酒
prize 奖品
public holiday 公共节假日
Queen's speech 女王演说
religious festival 宗教节日

roast potato 烤土豆
robin 知更鸟
sack 背包
scissors 剪刀
Scotland 苏格兰
seasonal vegetable 时蔬
sellotape 透明胶
serve 盛上桌
set up 建立
sherry 雪利酒
shopping mall 购物商场
significance 重要性
Singapore 新加坡
spirituality 精神实质/精神文明
sprout 豆芽
threshold 底线
tot 小杯
turkey and all the trimmings 火鸡和配菜
uncertain 不肯定的
whisky 威士忌
Winter Solstice 冬至
wrap 包裹(动词、名词)
wrapping paper 包装纸

第43章
中国春节
Chinese New Year

背景常识

  大多数英国大学里，秋季学期的期末考试是在春天进行的。对英国学生来说，圣诞节里酒足饭饱以后，一、二月份就该是学习和准备考试的时间了。对中国学生而言，我们还有春节（Spring Festival）要庆祝呢。在英国的许多中国学生都会组织不同规模的庆祝活动（celebration）。这可以是简单的会餐（group dinner），也可以是历时一周包括中国曲艺表演（art performance）和小吃的节日周。如果你提前通知你的大学，他们甚至可能给你放假。

  组织春节庆祝是一个很大的工程。不过也是一次极佳的锻炼机会。首先，你不能一个人单干。你需要召集（gather）一批能组织和会表演的人。除了中国学生以外，许多外国学生也对中国文化很感兴趣，他们也能帮你不少忙。

  然后，你需要设计节目（programmes）。在如今的英国校园和社区里，有不少擅长中国乐器、武术（Martial art）、书法（calligraphy）、哲学和烹饪的中国人和外国人。发现并动员（mobilise）这些人，一定能向你提供不少节目资源和灵感。

  设计完庆祝活动的内容以后，你需要定场地（venue）和道具（prop）。校方和学生会都很乐于给你提供场地的。他们都喜欢当地报纸报道他们是如何倡导（encourage）文化多元主义的。

  Last, but not least（最后，但不是最次要的），是钱。学校和学生会都能给你资助（funding）。当地商家也可以给你赞助（sponsorship）。或者你可以举行一些筹款活动（fundraiser）。另外，在庆祝期间卖一些中国饰品和节目单也可以补偿一些组织成本。而庆祝活动本身最好是免费的，以保证上座率（turnout）。

In the Union Bar

Su: Hi guys, I have just checked the lunar calendar, and guess what? The Spring Festival is exactly a month from now.

Mike: Really, how are you guys going to celebrate?

Ling: I don't know. It is revision period. I guess I'll probably just read fewer pages for a change.

Lee: Oh, come on, Ling, I am Korean, and even I am going to have a small party. You can't just spend the Chinese New Year like any other day. It is bad luck for starters.

James: Exactly, I think you guys need to celebrate. Su, those dumplings you made last time... yummy. Didn't you say that dumplings are the traditional food for Chinese New Year? Maybe you guys should organise a dumpling buffet or something on the New Year's Eve. You can make some money out of it, as well as promoting Chinese culture on campus.

Mike: Excellent idea, mate. I know some local ladies who practice *Tai Chi*. I am sure they will be happy to give some demonstrations. You know, you can't just eat without some Chinese entertainment.

Su: That is exactly what I was thinking. I know some Chinese students who play *erhu* and *pipa*... traditional Chinese music instruments, in case you were wondering, James.... They said they wanted to play publicly on campus before. Also, Professor Zhou, from the Department of Asian Studies—I've heard he is quite a calligrapher. I think he might be interested in doing some Chinese calligraphy demonstrations and perhaps giving a talk on the history of Chinese New Year.

James: Cool! This buffet is turning into a gala now. I am totally behind you, Su. It is going to be great.

Ling: Speaking of galas, I really don't want to miss the CCTV Chinese New Year Gala. My parents will be watching it without me this year.

Mike: Closed-Circuit Television? Isn't that for surveillance?

Su: Chinese Central TV, China's national broadcast network, you idiot. Its New Year Gala is the world's most watched TV programme. It has become an inseparable part of Chinese New Year celebration ever since its first airing on New Year's Eve 1983.

Lee: You know what? I may just have the solution to your problem, Ling. Look... [*pointing at the big screen TV at the corner of the bar*] That is Sky... satellite TV....

Su: Genius! They must have CCTV 9 here. We need to speak with the Bar Manager and see if we can use the screen to show the New Year gala.

学生会

苏：嗨，伙计们，我刚刚查了农历的日历。你们猜怎么着？还有正好一个月就到春节了。

迈克：真的，你们准备怎么庆祝？

玲：我不知道。现在是复习阶段。我猜我大概也就只能少读几页书来庆祝一下。

李：噢，别这样，玲。我是韩国人，就连我都要搞个小聚会。你不能把春节当普通日子过。对新生来说这样可不吉利。

詹姆斯：对，我觉得你们应该庆祝。苏，你上次做的饺子真好吃。你不是说饺子是传统的春节食品吗？也许你们应该在大年三十组织一个饺子自助餐什么的。你还能挣点儿钱，顺便在校园里弘扬中国文化。

迈克：好主意，哥们儿。我认识一些本地练太极的女士们。我肯定她们会乐意来表演表演。你不能只闷头吃而没有中国式娱乐。

苏：这正是我所想的。我认识一些演奏二胡和琵琶的中国学生……传统的中国乐器，明白吗，詹姆斯？她们说过想在校园里公开表演。另外，亚洲研究系的周教授——我听说他还是个不错的书法家呢，估计可能会有兴趣做个书法演示，并讲讲关于中国春节的历史。

詹姆斯：酷！这自助餐变成晚会了。我支持你，苏。到时候会非常热闹的！

玲：说到晚会，我真不想错过 CCTV 的春节联欢晚会。我父母今年没法跟我一起看了。

迈克：闭路电视？那不是监视用的吗？

苏：中国中央电视台，中国的国家电视台，你个笨蛋。它的春节联欢晚会是世界上观众最多的电视节目。自从1983年第一次播出以后，就成了中国新年庆典中不可或缺的一部分。

李：你猜怎么着？我可能正好有办法解决你的问题，玲。看，[指向酒吧一角的大屏幕电视]那是天空卫视，卫星电视。

苏：天才！他们这儿一定能收到中央9台。我们得跟酒吧经理谈谈，看我们能不能用这台电视放春节联欢晚会。

Lee: Yes, this way, you've also solved the venue problem. We can just hold your gala here, at the Union Bar. I know the Union's International Student Officer. He seems to be very keen on the idea of organising more multicultural events in the Union. I am sure he will be willing to help with booking this place.

Ling: Don't worry about the money. I will sort it out. You are lucky to have a MBA student as a friend.

James: Sound! People, let's do it.

In Su's Room

Su: OK, guys, how is everyone getting on with the Chinese New Year gala?

Lee: I have spoken with the International Student Officer. He is a cool bloke. I have already got the entire Union Bar booked for New Year's Eve, from 12 pm to 12 am.

Mike: And I have spoken to my *Tai Chi* friends. It turns out that they even do the dragon and lion dance. They have all the costumes and Chinese percussion. So, should I tell them to arrive at five pm to set things up then?

Su: That is great! I never knew we had these people around. Five pm is good.

James: I've booked some fireworks from the party shop in town. Since we need to watch the dragon dance outside, we may as well have some fireworks.

Su: That would be fun, as long as the campus security is fine with it. I've spoken to my friends who play Chinese music. They are all glad to join. Now, I am wondering if we can dig out anybody who can sing Chinese songs or Peking Opera.

Mike: What about Professor....

Su: Professor Zhou? He is a positive as well... the talk and calligraphy. His wife also has some gorgeous Chinese dresses. I am thinking, perhaps, we can have a Chinese fashion show. Mmm... I think I need some Chinese girls....

James: Anyway, how is the fundraising coming on, Miss Ling?

Ling: Quite all right! I have secured 200 from the university and the student union. This Wednesday night is Reload Party in the Union. It is going to be packed. I want to run a raffle by the door. That would give us at least 100. Also, the HSBC bank is interested in sponsoring us. I was just on the phone with the manager of their local branch. They will give us half a grand, if we print their logo on our brochures and let them set up a stand in the bar during the gala.

Su: I have no objection to that. As long as the dumplings, munchies and drinks are paid for, I am willing to shake hands with evil multinational corporations. It seems we can offer the entire gala for free, with money to spare.

James: What about publicity? How do we let people know about our gala?

Ling: Way ahead of you, there! I've contacted Information Services, and they'll send out a notice for us to the entire university via their weekly e-mail.

James: You are the best businesswoman I have ever known, Ling.

Ling: Woman?!

李：对，这样你还能解决场地问题。我们可以在这儿举办你们的晚会，就在学生会酒吧室。我认识学生会的国际学生官。他好像对在学生会组织多元文化活动很感兴趣。我肯定他会愿意帮我们订这个场地。

玲：不要担心钱的问题，我可以搞定。你们有一个学 MBA 的朋友算你们走运。

詹姆斯：万事俱备！诸位，我们干吧。

在苏的房间

苏：好，伙计们，大家对春节晚会的准备工作做得怎么样了？

李：我已经跟国际学生官说了。他是个够意思的哥们儿。我把大年三十那天整个学生会酒吧都订下来了，从中午 12 点到凌晨 12 点。

迈克：我也跟练太极的朋友们商量了。到时候她们还会舞龙舞狮子呢。所有的服装和打击乐器她们都有。那么，我是不是该让她们下午 5 点到达，做好准备工作呢？

苏：好！我不知道我们身边还有这么一群人。5 点钟可以。

詹姆斯：我从城里的晚会商店订了一些鞭炮。既然我们得在户外看舞龙，那干脆就放放鞭炮。

苏：那应该很有意思，只要校园保安没有意见。我已经跟我表演中国音乐的朋友说了，他们都乐意来。现在，我不知道我们能不能发掘几个能唱中文歌或京剧的人。

迈克：有个教授……

苏：周教授？他也同意了，演讲加书法。他太太还有不少漂亮的中国服装。我想，我们可以搞个中国时装表演。得找几个中国女孩……

詹姆斯：筹款的问题怎么样了，玲小姐？

玲：不错！我已经从学校和学生会拿下了 200 镑。这个星期三是学生会的重装晚会，到时候人会很多。我想在门口办个抽奖式有奖销售活动，这怎么说也能筹到 100 镑。另外，汇丰银行也有兴趣赞助我们。我刚刚与他们本地的经理通了电话。如果我们在宣传材料上印他们的商标，并让他们在晚会上办个展台，他们可以提供我们 500 镑。

苏：我没有反对意见。只要饺子、小吃和饮料有人付账，我心甘情愿和邪恶的跨国财团握手。这样看来，我们的整个晚会都可以是免费的，而且还能省下些钱呢。

詹姆斯：宣传问题怎么办？怎么才能让别人知道我们的晚会呢？

玲：早想在你前头了！我已经跟信息服务部联系了，他们将通过每周电子邮件把我们的晚会通知发给全校。

詹姆斯：你是我所认识的最棒的女商人，玲。

玲：女商人？

实用短语

- I've just checked... and guess what?　我刚刚查了……你们猜怎么着？
- Come on! Even I'm going to…!　别这样！连我都要……
- Excellent idea!　好主意！
- That is exactly what I was thinking.　我就是这么想的。
- He might be interested in…　他可能对做……感兴趣。
- Speaking of…　说到……
- I may just have the solution.　我可能有办法。
- Don't worry about… I'll sort it out.　别为……担心,我可以搞定。
- You're lucky to have a… as a friend!　有一个……朋友算你们走运！
- Sound! People, let's do it!　万事俱备！诸位,我们干吧。
- I never knew we had…　我从来不知道我们还有……
- What about…?　……怎么样？
- How is the… coming on?　……怎么样了？
- I have no objection to that.　我没有反对意见/我同意。
- As long as…　只要……
- Way ahead of you, there!　早想在你前头了！

词汇表

airing 播放/发表
bloke 男人/哥们儿
book 预订
broadcast 广播
calligrapher 书法家
campus security 校园保安
CCTV 中央电视台/闭路电视
celebrate 庆祝
costumes 服装
dig out 发掘
dragon and lion dance 舞龙舞狮
dumplings 饺子
entertainment 娱乐
fashion show 时装表演
fireworks 鞭炮
for a change 作为改善
for starters 首先/起码
funding 资助

fundraisers 集资会
gala 歌舞晚会
give a talk 发表演讲
grand 千/远大的
gunpowder 火药
inseparable 分不开的
logo 商标
lunar calendar 农历
multicultural events 多元文化活动
munchies 零食
on the phone with 跟…通电话
organisational skills 组织能力
packed 拥挤的
Peking Opera 京剧
performances 表演
poster 海报
project 项目
promoting 弘扬

props 道具
publicity 公众宣传
raffle 抽奖
revision period 复习阶段
satellite TV 卫星电视
sorted 解决了的
sounds like a plan 听起来是个计划(表示赞同)
spend 花(钱)
sponsorship 赞助关系
stand 展台
Tai Chi 太极拳
turnout 出席率
venues 场地
way ahead of you 早在你前面了
weekly e-mail 每周电子邮件
with... to spare 还能剩下…
yummy 好吃

第44章
谈中国
Talking about China

背景常识

作为留学生,与其他国家的同学谈论中国是不可避免的。而且,有时候,这些外国学生可能还对中国有一些不满或偏见。比如吃狗肉和强制计划生育就让许多西方人难以接受。

拿国家领导人开玩笑在英国是司空见惯的。女王(The Queen)和首相是喜剧演员(comedians)在电视上常用的笑料。而在中国文化中,政治领袖(politicians)是让人敬畏的。许多中国学生因此在遇到批评中国政府的讨论时就闪烁其词(shy away),这其实是不对的;它只会显得中国人思想封闭、政治上麻木。你越是躲避,外国人越觉得自己有道理。

相反,你应该积极融入(engage)这样的谈话中并展示(present)一个公正(fair)和真实(original)的现代中国。如果他们对中国的批评是具有偏见(biased)或被误导的(misinformed),你就应该纠正他们。如果他们确实有道理(valid),那你就应当大方地接受并面对(face up to)中国的不足。一个真正的爱国者(patriot)通过改进他的国家来爱国;一个假的爱国者通过假装他的国家已然无可厚非来爱国。如果他们只是和你开玩笑(make fun of you),你就可以自我解嘲或以牙还牙(tit-for-tat)。

温斯顿·丘吉尔(Churchill)首相曾经说过:"当我出国的时候,我有条规矩,那就是从来不批评我自己的政府。我在回国以后再把失去的(批评政府的)时间补偿回来。"本国人之间可以随便批评自己的政府,在外国人面前就要面子,这是一个即使丘吉尔也摆脱不了的人性缺点。作为一名留学生,你应该能够以更公平和客观的眼光来看待世界上的所有国家,区分"爱国主义"与"国家主义"。

Ning, Paul, Drew (Chinese), Rachel (English) and Carlos (Spanish) Having Coffee

Carlos: Hey... look at this in the paper... it says that China has failed to meet its own targets for reducing energy consumption.... They're saying that the Chinese government hopes to reduce China's energy consumption by 20% by 2010... yet the country's power consumption grew 14.9 percent in the first quarter of this year. That's disgraceful!

Ning: That's just so one-sided, that is! You foreigners only like to report bad things about China! The US is the biggest green house emitter in the world. You tree-huggers① are missing the point when you jump on the Anti-China bandwagon along with all the other Chinaphobes. Anyway, Australia has the second highest per-capita carbon emission worldwide and your government still hasn't ratified the *Kyoto Protocol*, for god's sake. So, just give us all a break, would you?

Carlos: Oh. Sorry for breathing②! I'm just telling you what was in the paper... it is the *Guardian*③ that I am reading... it just reports the facts... it doesn't have an agenda to do China down. You Chinese are so thin-skinned!

Drew: I think it's just that we don't like to air our dirty washing in public... you'll find that we Chinese are always discussing stuff like this among ourselves... Ning, don't tell me you didn't hate the grey sky in Beijing. We just don't like it when foreigners talk about it, that's all.

Rachel: Yeah... but you have to admit that these are things that people are curious and interested about when it comes to China... they don't want to slag Chinese people off... it's just that these issues are "newsworthy"... you should know that... you're doing Media Studies. You shouldn't get the hump about it or get all huffy.

Drew: That's right! Even if the *Guardian* doesn't have an agenda, it still has to dig for stories that will sell. During the 7/7 Terrorist Attack in London, I was watching BBC and CNN at the same time on my computer. They interviewed the same guy who just came out of a bombed station. The BBC used the footage where this man had already calmed down and was talking about how brave the passengers were... while CNN chose to air earlier footage where he was still trembling and crying. The BBC didn't want to show the early footage because that would damage morale. CNN wasn't interested in the later footage because they did want to make the 9/11 survivors look too cowardly in comparison. How would you like it if you saw the Chinese media saying bad stuff about your country?

Rachel: What? About Britain? We get it all the time! The War in Iraq, The Royal Family, the class system, colonialism, racism, Northern Ireland! We just take it in our stride. You know what, it sometimes worries me that the British now seems to feel so little for their country. Everything patriotic is turned into a laughing stock.

宁、保罗、德露（中国人）、雷切尔（英国人）和卡洛斯（西班牙人）在喝咖啡

卡洛斯： 嘿，看看这个，报纸上说中国没能成功达成自己的能源消耗削减目标。他们说，中国政府希望在 2010 年将能源消耗减少 20%，但今年第一季度，中国的能量消耗反而增长了 14.9%。令人汗颜呐！

宁： 这也太片面了！你们外国人就喜欢报道关于中国的坏事。美国是世界上最大的温室气体排放国。你们这些环境主义者由于加入了其他有中国恐惧症的人的反华潮流，已经开始跑题了。另外，澳大利亚的人均碳排放量居世界第二，而且你们还没批准《京都议定书》呢，看在上帝的份上。所以，你还是别烦我了。

卡洛斯： 噢，用不着这么大惊小怪嘛！我只是告诉你报纸上写了什么。我读的可是《卫报》，它只报道事实，可没有什么贬低中国的使命。你们中国人也太敏感了吧？

德露： 我想我们只是不喜欢家丑外扬。你会发现我们中国人之间还是会讨论这些事情的。宁，别告诉我你不讨厌北京灰色的天空。但是我们不喜欢外国人说我们。

雷切尔： 是啊，但是你得承认往往是这方面的事情让人好奇。他们不是有意要贬损中国人，只是这种事"有新闻价值"罢了。你应该明白，你是学传媒的，不应该对这些事耿耿于怀或小题大做啊。

德露： 说得对！即使《卫报》没有什么使命，它也还是要挖掘卖座的新闻。在 7 月 7 号伦敦恐怖袭击的时候，我在电脑上同时收看英国的 BBC 和美国的 CNN。他们采访了同一个从被炸毁的地铁站里出来的男人。在 BBC 采用的片断里，这人已经冷静下来并谈及乘客们如何勇敢。而 CNN 则采用了较早的一个片断，那时他还在一边颤抖一边哭呢。BBC 不愿意播这个早的片断，因为他们不想打击英国国民的士气。CNN 对后来的这个片断不感兴趣，因为他们不想让 9·11 的幸存者在相比之下显得太懦弱。你想想，如果中国媒体说你们国家的坏话，你会感觉怎么样？

雷切尔： 什么？英国？我们天天都挨批评！伊拉克战争、王室丑闻、社会等级、殖民主义、种族主义、北爱尔兰！我们对这些都无所谓了。你知道吗，有时候我很担心，英国人似乎已经没有国家荣誉感了。一切爱国主义的东西都成了笑料。

Paul: I think you're right actually... but China is exactly the opposite, I think China has a chip on its shoulder too often... it may be to do with history, being colonised and all.

Rachel: Yeah... I've noticed that... I mean, sometimes you get embarrassed and angry when people mention, like, the Cultural Revolution, or people show images of China connected to that like those propaganda posters, and Mao's little red book. But, in fact, many Westerners think these images of China are interesting and fascinating, not negative. The portrait of Mao was one of Andy Warhol's④ masterpieces. The original copies of Mao's Red Book are sold to Western collectors at sky-high prices on Ebay.

Drew: Maybe we just misunderstand what people are referring to... but sometimes maybe you Westerners are also seriously misinformed about China... I mean, look at the things you say about human rights, the one-child-policy, the Three-Gorges Dam, Tibet, Taiwan... there are two sides to every story....

Paul: Yes... and take what they say about the one-child policy and human rights... you know that Japanese student, Mariko? She gave this presentation condemning China for the one-child policy... said it was against human rights, but what she didn't say was that in terms of development it was necessary for China to do this... you have to have your economic needs met first. Then you can worry about individual rights.

Ning: I know, but I would really like to have a little sister of my own. We have to admit that the government made a mistake in encouraging the last two generations to overreproduce.... Western people think China going to be the world's next superpower. I think we overseas students ought to be super-citizens first—who love and hate their country for what it is.

Carlos: Wow... this is amazing, Ning! You're actually talking about this stuff in a dispassionate way. That's great... actually you make me think about my own country, Spain. We like to think we are open and critical, but there seems to have been a collective amnesia about our own civil war and the dictatorship... and it's only now that we're beginning to talk about it.

Ning: Mmm... I guess that for some things you just have to wait until the people involved are dead and gone... then it's easier to discuss things. I mean, my lecturer was saying yesterday that there are aspects of British history that are still not being discussed openly and honestly, like the pointlessness of the First World War, for example.

Rachel: Yes, but we are now free to beat ourselves up over colonialism and stuff....

保罗：你说得对。而中国恰恰相反。我觉得中国总是太注意维护自己的形象，大概是由于历史原因吧，被殖民侵略等等。

雷切尔：对，我也注意到了。有时候，当人们提到文化大革命或者跟大字报和毛泽东红宝书有关的东西时，你们总是很尴尬和气愤。但实际上，很多西方人觉得中国的这些形象非常有趣，引人入胜，并不消极。毛的画像是安迪·沃霍尔的代表作之一。易趣网上的西方收藏家们以天价收购红宝书。

德露：也许我们只是误解了人们的意思，但有些时候你们西方人也经常在中国问题上被严重误导了。比如说，看看你们在人权、计划生育、三峡大坝、西藏、台湾问题上说的一些东西。凡事都要一分为二地看待。

保罗：对啊，就拿计划生育和人权来说吧。你们知道那个日本学生麻里子吗？她做了一个谴责中国计划生育政策的演讲，说它有违人权，但是她却没说中国这样做是在寻求发展的情况下迫不得已。你得首先满足经济需求再考虑个人需要吧。

宁：但是，我倒真希望自己能有个妹妹。我们必须承认，政府当初鼓励中国前两代人多生是个错误。西方人认为中国将成为世界下一个超级大国。我觉得我们留学生首先应该成为超级公民——对自己的国家爱恨分明。

卡洛斯：哇，这太奇妙了，宁！你竟然真的能冷静地讨论这个问题，这实在是太好了。其实你使我想起我自己的国家，西班牙。我们总觉得我们非常开放并且具有批判性，但对内战和独裁统治我们却都有点儿集体失忆，直到最近我们才开始讨论这些事情。

宁：嗯，我估计对有些事情来说，只能等到相关的人都过世以后，才更容易讨论。我的老师昨天还说，英国历史的许多方面是至今还不能开诚布公地讨论的。比如第一次世界大战的无目的性。

雷切尔：对啊，但是我们现在已经能够对殖民历史一类的事情坦诚反省了。

注释

① tree-hugger　是对环境主义者 environmentalist 的戏称。
② sorry for breathing　原义为"对不起我喘气了"，表示为不应当道歉的事道歉。
③ Guardian　《卫报》，英国的一家主流报纸，常被指为左翼。
④ Andy Warhol　安迪·沃荷，美国流行激进艺术家。

实用短语

- I'm just telling you… 我只是告诉……
- It is just…, that's all. 它只不过是……罢了。
- We don't like it when… 我们不喜欢……（某人做某事）
- You have to admit that… 你得承认……
- How would you like it if…? 如果……你会怎么想？
- I think you're right actually. 我觉得其实你说的是对的。
- Maybe you're right. 你也许是对的。
- Look at the things you say about…/and take what they say about… 拿你们说的关于……的话打比方说吧。
- There are two sides to every story. 凡事都要一分为二。
- Love and hate sth for what it is. 对某事爱憎分明。
- Look at this in the paper. It says that… 看看这报纸。它说……
- They're saying that… 他们说……（通常表示公众舆论）
- That's so one-sided, that is! 这根本就是偏见！
- That really makes my blood boil! 这才让我热血沸腾！
- Sorry for breathing! 对不起我喘气了（表示不情愿、不应当的道歉）！
- I'm just telling you! 我告诉你就是了！
- You have to admit that… 你必须承认……
- Maybe we just… 也许我们太……
- Take what they say about… 比如他们对……的言论
- This is amazing! You're actually…-ing about…! 太神奇了！你真的……！

词汇表

2008 Olympics 2008年奥运会
abuse 虐待
after all 毕竟
air one's dirty washing in public 家丑外扬
be seriously misinformed 被严重误导
Chairman Mao 毛主席
Chinaphobe 盲目讨厌中国的人（反义词：Chinaphile, 盲目喜欢中国的人）
civil war 内战
collective amnesia 集体失忆
condemn 谴责
corporal punishment 体罚
Cultural Revolution 文化大革命
dictatorship 独裁统治
do down 有意贬低
First World War 第一次世界大战
for God's sake 看在上帝的份上（常表示对不合理和荒谬事物的感叹）
get all huffy 小题大做
get the hump 耿耿于怀
give someone a break 让某人休息一下/不去烦某人
have a chip on one's shoulder 小心翼翼/爱保护自己的（走路小心，怕肩膀上的筹码掉下来）
Hollywood 好莱坞
human rights 人权
image 形象
jump on the bandwagon of… 加入……的潮流
little red book 红宝书
make one's blood boil 令人激动
misunderstand 误解（动词）
Northern Ireland 北爱尔兰
one-sided 片面的
paper (the) 报纸
pointlessness 无目的性
propaganda poster 大字报
racism 种族主义
Royal Family (the) 皇室
say bad stuff 说坏话
slag off… 损某人
sorry for breathing 别大惊小怪
spoil 娇惯
superpower 超级大国
take sth in one's stride 逆来顺受/无所谓
thin-skinned 敏感/爱面子
Three Gorges Dam 三峡大坝
Tibet 西藏
tree-huggers 环境主义者（戏称，贬义）
War in Iraq (the)/the Iraq War 伊拉克战争
well-meaning 好心好意的

第45章
外国留学生
Other Overseas Students

背景常识

在不少英国大学里，留学生的人数占全体学生的一半。中国学生的人数远远（by far）超过（surpass）其他国家的留学生数量，是英国最大的留学生群体。近年来，由于欧盟（European Union）的扩大，英国高等教育对东欧国家的学生变得更加便宜。所以，波兰（Polish）和立陶宛的（Lithuanian）学生数量在飙升。由于英国在南亚的殖民历史，来自印度（India）、巴基斯坦（Pakistan）的学生也很多。然后就是西欧、北美和澳洲的学生，他们当然是英国教育的老客户了。

这样一个国际化的校园是英国教育得天独厚的优势。在国际化校园里，你只需要"读万卷书"，"行万里路"就不必了。可惜，中国留学生在英国却有一个"自闭"（self-isolation）的名声。中国学生很少跟其他国家的学生深入交往，大多只跟其他中国学生抱团。只有那些少数敢于放眼看世界的中国学生，才终能练就出色的英语，并取得学业和社交上的双重成功。

在跟外国学生交流时，除了勇气之外，还需要一些技巧。首先，要始终保持对对方的国家和文化背景表示兴趣。不要刚问完对方的国家马上就转到别的话题上。其次，不要取笑你认为奇怪的习惯和传统。第三，如果你对某个留学生的国家有一些了解，向他展示你的知识可以拉近你们的距离；不过不要把你对那个国家的印象强加（impose）给别人。比如，不是所有德国人都不苟言笑，不是所有美国人都文化贫瘠。这些典型的国家形象往往都是经过夸张的。哪个民族都不喜欢被一概而论（be pigeonholed）。孔子曰："己所不愿，勿施于人"；耶稣说：Do unto others as you would have them do unto you。

Outside the Classroom

Alison: Hi everyone... I'm looking for Room 355, am I in the right place?
Noura: I think so.
Madina: Yeah... this is it, I think, but it's locked and the lecturer isn't here yet.
Laura: Yes.
Madina: Your English sounds pretty good... where are you from?
Alison: I'm Chinese, but I went to a boarding school here in England.
Madina: Oh, right. So did I. How did you find it?
Alison: I thought it was OK, but it was hard going at first... I mean, I didn't understand anything when I arrived and they just, sort of, threw me into this class where everyone was speaking English. So it was, like, sink-or-swim. Where are you from originally?
Madina: Me? Oh, I'm from Russia, but my family lives here... I went to a boarding school as well.
Laura: Oh... which school did you go to? Did it take a while to get used to it?
Madina: I went to Clarewell, and well, yes. I mean, I feel more comfortable speaking English than Russian now. Sorry... what's your name?
Laura: Laura... my folks are from Iran originally, but I was born here... we've been back to Iran on holiday, but I don't think I could live there... I don't even speak Farsi that well, you know. [*to Mizue*] Hi, I'm Laura... what's your name?
Mizue: I'm Mizue.
Laura: Hi Mizue. Are you Chinese too?
Mizue: No, I'm Japanese, actually. Ping here... she's Chinese.
Ping: Hello.
Laura: Wow... cool... how long have you been here?
Mizue: I just got here last week... this is my first time in the UK.
Alison: Wow, really... your English is good... did you study it just at school or did you go to a language school as well?
Mizue: Oh... I actually did a summer course at a language school before I came here... it was very intensive.
Madina: God! I wish this lecturer would come... who are those guys standing down the corridor there? Are they in our group?

After Class, in the SU

Madina: So, Mizue, do you think that was very different from what you do in school in Japan?
Mizue: Gosh... yes. I never expected to have to speak so much. In Japan, the teacher teaches, the students listen and take notes, and they never ask any questions.
Laura: Really? So what do you do if you haven't understood something?
Mizue: Well we just kind of try and read up on it.
Ping: It's actually a bit like that in China too. Teaching is very teacher-centred... you

know, the teacher teaches from the front, and the students just listen... there's none of this pair work and group work... I think this is just playing around actually. It's not real teaching....

Alison: Do you really think so, Ping? I often think that back in China they like to teach like that because it's safer for the teacher! She doesn't need to think on her feet and respond to what the students need... and just gives the same boring pre-prepared lesson every week.

教室外

艾莉森：你们好。我在找355号房，是这儿吗？
诺拉：我想是的。
马迪娜：对，是这儿，我估计。但是门是锁着的，老师还没到。
劳拉：是。
马迪娜：你的英语听起来很好，你从哪儿来？
艾莉森：我是中国人，但是我在英国上过寄宿学校。
马迪娜：喔。我也上过。你觉得上寄宿学校怎么样？
艾莉森：我觉得还可以，但是最开始比较难。我刚到的时候什么也听不懂，而且他们干脆把我扔进了一个人人说英语的班里。就像是，要么学会游泳，要么被淹死。你从哪里来的？
马迪娜：我？哦，我是从俄罗斯来的，但是我家在这儿。我也上过寄宿学校。
劳拉：哦，你上的哪个学校？要很久才能适应吗？
马迪娜：我去的克来威尔，嗯，是的。我现在觉得说英语要比说俄语流利得多。对不起，你的名字是？
劳拉：劳拉。我家人是从伊朗来的，但我是在这儿出生的。我们偶尔回伊朗度假，不过我觉得我已经不能在那儿生活了，我甚至不怎么说波斯语。[对米祖] 嗨，我是劳拉。你叫什么？
米祖：我叫米祖。
劳拉：嗨，米祖。你也是中国人吗？
米祖：不，我是日本人。萍是中国人。
萍：你好。
劳拉：哇……酷……你在这儿多长时间了？
米祖：我上个星期刚刚到。这是我第一次来英国。
艾莉森：哇，真的？你的英语听起来很好。你是在学校里学的，还是上的语言学校？
米祖：哦，我在来这儿之前上了一个夏季语言课程，非常高强度的。
马迪娜：天哪！我希望这老师还能来。那边的几个人是谁？他们也是我们组里的吗？

下课后，在学生会里

马迪娜：那么，米祖，你觉得我们上课的方式与你在日本的学校有很大不同吗？
米祖：哦，那当然。我从来没想到要说这么多话。在日本，老师教书，学生听讲记笔记，他们从来不问问题。
劳拉：真的吗？那如果你没听懂怎么办？
米祖：我们只能尽量在课后自己看书。
萍：在中国也是这样，教学是以老师为核心的。老师在上面讲，学生就听，根本没有搭档练习或小组讨论。我觉得在这儿上课就跟玩似的，根本不是教育嘛。
艾莉森：你真的这么想吗，萍？我总觉得在中国大家那么爱当教师，是因为当老师更安全！她不用随机应变，只需要每周讲些乏味的事先准备好的内容就可以了。

实用短语

- Hi everyone... I'm looking for...　大家好……我在找……
- Am I in the right place?　我找对了吗?/这个地方是我要找的吗?
- Are you two Chinese?　你们两个是中国人吗?
- Who are those guys?　他们是谁?
- Are they in our group?　他们是我们小组的吗?
- How did you find it?　你觉得它怎么样?
- Which school did you go to?　你上的哪个学校?
- Did it take a while to get used to it?　它很难适应吧?
- Your English sounds pretty good...　你的英语听起来不错……
- How long have you been here?　你来这多久了?
- So, ..., do you think that was very different from...?　那么,……,你觉得……跟那区别很大吗?
- I never expected to have to...　我从来没想到……
- Do you really think so?　你真的这么想吗?

词汇表

boarding school 寄宿学校
compare 比较
corridor 走廊
Farsi 波斯语
folks 人/家里人
get used to sth. 对某事适应
group work 小组学习
guys 伙计们/男人们/人们
hard going 做起来难的

intensive 密集的
Iran 伊朗
language school 语言学校
lecture 讲座/课
originally 本来的
pair work 成对学习
play around 闹着玩
pre-prepared 提前准备
pretty good 挺好

read up on 通过读书来了解
respond to 回应
security 安全
sink-or-swim 要么游泳要么沉底（表示孤注一掷）
teacher-centred 以老师为核心的
that well 那么好
think on one's feet 随机应变
throw 扔

第46章
校园浪漫
Campus Romance

◎ 背景常识

在许多中国大学里，学生之间的浪漫关系，如果不是被禁止的（banished），起码也是不被提倡的（discouraged）。在英国，健康稳定的男女关系（relationship）被认为是对学生生活有积极作用的（positive）。结交外国男女朋友也是体验英国生活和锻炼英语的好办法。

英国的年轻人大多通过社交活动（socialising），比如在酒吧里，找到约会对象的。当一个人对另一个人产生兴趣的时候，根据风俗，他或她会给那个人买一杯饮料。然后进入聊天和交换电话号码阶段。在互相认识了以后，其中一个人会约另一个人出来（ask someone out）。青年人现在更喜欢用短信和电子邮件的方式来设定约会（date），而不是靠打电话。

在第一次约会的时候，男生也许会给女生带一束花，但是现在这已经有点儿老土了（old-fashioned）。法式接吻（French kiss）指的是有舌头接触的亲吻，但是这通常是等到两个人更熟悉了以后才发生的。西方人常说"第三次约会是个奇迹"（the third date's the charm），表示第三次约会往往是人们将感情发展到性爱阶段的时候，但现实中往往不是如此。约会的技巧已经被写成了很多书，但到头来都是纸上谈兵。

如果说追求爱情或发展关系有什么秘诀的话，那就是真诚（true）与诚实（honest）。卡萨诺瓦（Casanova，西方文化中的情圣）的精髓只能意会不能言传。爱情里没有牛顿定律。圆滑善谈（smooth and articulate）的男人并不一定总能情场得意。不少女孩儿就是喜欢笨嘴拙舌和实实在在的男生。所以，你不应该让一时的语言和文化障碍阻止你追求异国恋情。毛主席的"在战争中学习战争"和鲁迅先生的"拿来主义"在这里都是至理箴言。

In a Coffee Shop near the University

Allen: Erm… do you mind if I sit here?

Camilla: No… go ahead.

Allen: It's very crowded in here….

Camilla: Mmm… yes it is. Are you a student here?

Allen: Yes… I'm doing my undergrad in Astrophysics… I've been here for three weeks. I'm still trying to get used to things.

Camilla: Yes… It's pretty difficult, isn't it? New country and language and everything…? I'm Camilla… what's your name?

Allen: Camilla… Mine is Li Lu, but my friends call me Allen. I'm from China.

Camilla: I'm from Peru, but my father is Indonesian.

Allen: So are you studying here as well?

Camilla: Gosh, no! I couldn't afford the fees! I work in the shop next door, but I come in here just to read and stuff.

Allen: But your English is so good, Camilla… where did you learn it?

Camilla: Thanks… I studied at school in Peru; then I went to a language school here and worked in a shop.

A Bit Later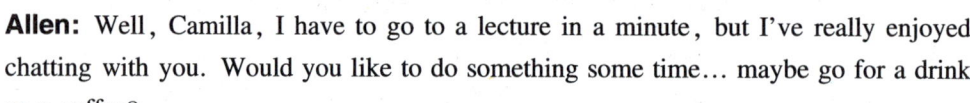

Allen: Well, Camilla, I have to go to a lecture in a minute, but I've really enjoyed chatting with you. Would you like to do something some time… maybe go for a drink or a coffee?

Camilla: That'd be nice….

Allen: Well, what time do you finish work?

Camilla: Oh… I'm afraid I'll be working until late tonight….

Allen: Well, what day are you free?

Camilla: Erm… let's see… I'll give you my number and we'll arrange a time we can meet up. It's 07949163714.

Allen: OK… it's been nice meeting you Camilla… hope to see you soon.

On the Phone

Camilla: Hello.

Allen: Hello… Camilla? This is Allen here… we met yesterday in the coffee shop.

Camilla: Oh… hi Allen… how are you?

Allen: Not bad… working hard… youself?

Camilla: Oh… you know… the boss is a slave driver!

Allen: Listen… I was wondering if you'd like to go for a drink tonight….

在学校附近的咖啡厅里

艾伦：嗯，你介意我坐这儿吗？
卡米拉：不，请便。
艾伦：这里挺热闹的。
卡米拉：是啊，是挺热闹。你是这儿的学生吗？
艾伦：是的，我上天体物理学本科，来这儿3个星期了，对很多事情还在适应中。
卡米拉：是啊，挺不容易的，不是吗？陌生的国家，陌生的语言，所有东西都是陌生的。我叫卡米拉，你叫什么名字？
艾伦：卡米拉，我的名字叫李路，但是朋友们叫我艾伦。我是从中国来的。
卡米拉：我来自秘鲁，我父亲是印度尼西亚人。
艾伦：那么，你也在这儿上学吗？
卡米拉：啊，没有！我可付不起这儿的学费！我在旁边的商店工作，我只是来这儿看看书而已。
艾伦：但是你的英语非常好，卡米拉。你在哪儿学的？
卡米拉：谢谢。我在秘鲁上学时学的。后来我在这儿上的语言学校，又在商店里找着了工作。

一会儿

艾伦：噢，卡米拉，我得马上去上课了。很高兴跟你聊天。你愿意有时间……也许一块儿喝杯咖啡什么的？
卡米拉：好啊。
艾伦：那，你什么时候下班？
卡米拉：哦，我恐怕会工作到很晚。
艾伦：那，你哪天有空呢？
卡米拉：嗯，我把我的电话号码给你吧，这样我们可以安排时间见面。我的电话是07949163714。
艾伦：好吧。遇见你很高兴，希望很快再次见到你。

电话里

卡米拉：你好。
艾伦：你好，卡米拉。我是艾伦，我们昨天在咖啡馆见过的。
卡米拉：噢，嗨，艾伦，你好吗？
艾伦：还不赖，努力学习呢。你呢？
卡米拉：噢，你知道的，我们老板跟个奴隶监工似的。
艾伦：哦，不知道你愿不愿意今晚出来喝杯酒。

Camilla: I'd love to.

Allen: Great! I mean, that's cool… look, why don't we meet at the 101 Bar, say about nine?

Camilla: Great. See you there.

That Evening

Camilla: Hi Allen.

Allen: Hi Camilla… I'm glad you came. Can I get you a drink?

Camilla: Sure… could I have a Bacardi Breezer? Apple please….

Later

Allen: You know, the first thing I noticed about you was your eyes…?

Camilla: Really? What about them?

Allen: Well, they're deep and mysterious and sexy….

Camilla: Ha! You said you wanted to sit at my table because the place was full!

Allen: Come on! Give me a chance! You didn't expect me to walk up to you and say, "your eyes are dead sexy," did you?

Camilla: Haha… noo… but I could tell you fancied me….

Allen: How's that?

Camilla: Well, because you went red and started stammering. You seem a bit more confident now, though… hehe… Dutch Courage?

Allen: Hey… I don't need any Dutch courage… anyway, I can tell, you're thinking about kissing me….

Camilla: Ha! Dream on! China boy!

Allen: Well, we'll see…. What sort of music do you like, then, Camilla?

A Week Later

Camilla: Listen, Allen… I think we are going a little bit too fast… I don't think I am ready to… you know… have sex… I mean, I have a boyfriend back in Peru, and when I came here he said it was OK… I am free and single. I can do what I want. But I don't feel comfortable with this…. We need some time… OK?

Allen: That's OK… but you should have told me before.

Camilla: I know. Look, I am really sorry. I really like you too, Allen. I think you are really sweet. I just needed more time to think things over.

卡米拉：我愿意。
艾伦：太好了！我是说，酷！你看咱们9点在101酒吧见面怎么样？
卡米拉：好的。在那儿见。

晚上

卡米拉：嗨，艾伦。
艾伦：嗨，卡米拉，很高兴你能来。我给你买杯喝的吧？
卡米拉：好，我能来一瓶百加得冰锐吗？苹果口味的。

稍后

艾伦：你知道吗，我最先注意的是你的眼睛。
卡米拉：真的吗？我的眼睛怎么了？
艾伦：嗯，它们深邃而且神秘、性感。
卡米拉：哈！你还说是别的地方没位子了才想跟我坐一块儿。
艾伦：别这么说嘛！这不是找机会吗？你总不能让我走到你跟前直接说"你的眼睛很性感"吧？
卡米拉：呵呵，是不好，但我知道你喜欢我。
艾伦：怎么知道的？
卡米拉：嗯，因为你脸红了而且结结巴巴的。你现在看起来倒是自信了点儿，呵呵，有酒壮胆儿吧？
艾伦：嘿嘿，我才不需要靠酒壮胆儿呢，我敢说，你现在想吻我。
卡米拉：哈哈！做梦去吧，中国男孩儿！
艾伦：好啊，我们走着瞧。那么，卡米拉，你喜欢什么音乐呢？

一周之后

卡米拉：嗯，艾伦，我觉得我们有点儿太快了。我还没准备好，你知道吗，发生性关系。我的意思是，我在秘鲁有男朋友，当我来这儿的时候他说他无所谓。我是单身，有自由做任何我想做的事，但是我还是觉得不对劲。我们需要一些时间，好吗？
艾伦：可以，但是你该早点告诉我。
卡米拉：我知道，我很抱歉。我是非常喜欢你的，艾伦。我觉得你是个好人。我只是需要一些时间来把事情考虑清楚。

A Month Later

Allen: Camilla... I just want to tell you that I really like you, but... I... can't go on like this.

Camilla: What do you mean?

Allen: Don't get me wrong. It is not like I am not having fun just hanging out with you... I just need... you know... a real girlfriend. You wanted me to wait and I waited, but I don't think it is fair... to either of us.

Camilla: Yes, I understand... you are right... and I am glad you are being so mature about this. Maybe it'd be better if we stopped going out... and you moved on.

Allen: Thank you... we can still be friends, you know....

Camilla: Oh... grow up!

一个月之后

艾伦：卡米拉，我想告诉你我真的很喜欢你。但是，我，不能总这样继续下去。

卡米拉：你什么意思?

艾伦：别误会我。并不是我不喜欢跟你在一起，我只是想要，你知道，一个真正的女朋友。你让我等，我等了，但是我认为这不公平，对我们两个来说。

卡米拉：是的，我明白，你是对的。我很高兴你在这个问题上能如此成熟。也许我们最好不要再约会了，而你应该重新开始。

艾伦：谢谢。我们还可以做朋友的，你知道。

卡米拉：噢，成熟点儿吧！

实用短语

- ◆ Do you mind if I sit here? 你介意我坐这儿吗?
- ◆ It's very crowded in here. 这地方太挤了。
- ◆ What day are you free? 你哪天有空?
- ◆ I was wondering if you'd like to go… tonight. 我不知道你今晚愿不愿意去……
- ◆ Would you like to do something some time? 你愿意有空干点儿什么吗?
- ◆ Maybe you'd like to meet up again. 也许你愿意再见面。
- ◆ Why don't we meet at…? 我们在……见面怎么样?
- ◆ What time do you finish work? 你什么时候下班?
- ◆ I'd love to… 我愿意……
- ◆ Dream on! 做梦去吧!
- ◆ What sort of music do you like? 你喜欢什么音乐?
- ◆ The first thing I noticed about you was… 我最先注意到的是你的……
- ◆ I think you are really sweet. 我觉得你非常可爱。
- ◆ I've really enjoyed chatting with you. 跟你聊天很高兴。
- ◆ I don't think we should rush into things. 我觉得我们不应该这么快。
- ◆ I don't feel comfortable with this. 我觉得不对劲。
- ◆ We need some time… 我们需要更多的时间……
- ◆ You should have told me before… 你该早点儿告诉我……
- ◆ Don't get me wrong. 别误会我。
- ◆ It is not like I am not having fun… 我并不是不喜欢……
- ◆ We can still be friends. 我们还可以做朋友。
- ◆ Grow up! 成熟点儿吧!

词汇表

Astrophysics 天体物理学
Bacardi Breezer 百加得冰锐
crowded 拥挤的
dead sexy 非常性感
Dutch Courage 酒胆
free and single 自由且单身的
free 有时间的
go red 脸红
have sex 发生性关系
in a minute 一会儿
Indonesia 印度尼西亚
mind 介意
mysterious 神秘
Peru 秘鲁
slave driver 奴隶监工
stammer 结结巴巴
think over 考虑
walk someone home 送某人回家

第47章
学生性健康
Student Sexual Health

背景常识

中国的家长和学校在与青年人就"性"这个问题的交流上总是模糊腼腆的（reluctant）。实际上，性健康与刷牙洗脸一样，都是个人卫生（personal hygiene）的一部分。对性知识的缺乏导致了不少海外中国学生的悲剧。而缺乏与性健康相关的语言能力，更使得中国学生在遇到此类问题时，不敢于向英国校方和社会求助。

避孕套（condom）仍然是目前最可靠的避孕措施（contraceptive）和预防性病（Sexually Transmitted Disease, STD）的手段。大多数学生会和学生健康中心都为学生免费提供避孕套。学生不需要任何手续就可以匿名领取。在有医嘱（doctor's prescription）的情况下，女生们可以得到免费的避孕药。英国国家健康部（National Health Service）下属的医院为女生提供免费的紧急避孕药（emergency contraceptive pills）。紧急避孕药通常在无避孕性行为（unprotected sex）后24小时内有效。学生会还为缺乏性经验的女生提供润滑剂（lubricant）。

如果你遇到关于性的问题，前面第34章里提到的学生会辅导员依然是你求助的主要对象。

在英国大学里，有不少公开的同性恋（homosexual）和双性恋（bisexual）学生。大部分学生会都设有"同、双、变性学生官"（Lesbian, Gay, Bisexual and Transsexual, LGBT Officer）。英国政府和法律禁止基于性取向的歧视行为（discrimination）。另外，英国的流产（abortion）法也十分复杂。许多医生和诊所都不愿意进行流产手术。其实跟中国一样，英国社会同样在传统与自由之间不断摸索和争辩。留学生活的一大挑战就是在经历了东西方各种文化背景以后如何建立起自己独立的道德信仰。

Jessie and Julie Are Chatting

Jessie: Listen, Julie... there's something personal I need to talk to you about. I don't know how to put this... but I think I'm pregnant.

Julie: Oh... erm... gosh... how did that happen? Didn't you use contraception?

Jessie: Eh? How do you think it happened? We just got carried away in the heat of the moment. You know what I mean?

Julie: Sorry, I know what you mean... it just took me by surprise. Look, are you sure you're pregnant? It's not just that your period's late?

Jessie: No... I've been to the Student Health Centre, and they did a test. It just confirmed the home pregnancy test that I did.

Julie: So, what are you going to do?

Jessie: Well the nurse talked to me about different options... I mean, I could always go through with it and have the baby but, with my studies, I don't think that's an option. The nurse said they could arrange a termination.

Julie: What? An abortion?!

Jessie: Yes. Why not?

Julie: Well, it's just that here there's still a little bit of stigma around that sometimes. I guess some people object to it on religious or moral grounds.

Jessie: Look. I'm not going to let a little mistake disrupt my studies and ruin my life... I'll just have to make sure that I'm extra careful in future.

Camilla and May Are Chatting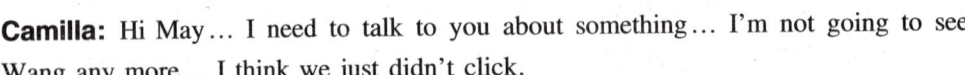

Camilla: Hi May... I need to talk to you about something... I'm not going to see Wang any more... I think we just didn't click.

May: Oh... I'm sorry to hear that... what happened? Have you split up?

Camilla: Oh, I don't know. Maybe it was just a culture clash. I think he thought I liked him more than I actually did. I mean... I don't know what it is, but he really kept coming on strong with me, and I only wanted to be friends... at least, I didn't want to be as "friendly" as he wanted to be... haha.

May: What do you mean?

Camilla: Well, when I kissed him on the cheek, erm... he thought it meant we were like boyfriend and girlfriend! You know, an item!

May: Well the thing is, we're not used to public displays of affection in China... I mean, we don't usually kiss each other in public.

Camilla: It wasn't a "kiss" kiss, May—only a peck on the cheek. It wasn't like I snogged him or gave him a French kiss!

May: Yes... it's difficult... I mean, in China if we hold hands in public it's considered daring, so I think he just got the wrong end of the stick. Poor Wang! I think he really loves you!

杰茜和朱莉在聊天

杰茜： 朱莉，我有些个人问题想跟你谈谈。我不知道该怎么说，我估计我怀孕了。

朱莉： 噢，哦，天哪，怎么发生的？你没有采用避孕措施吗？

杰茜： 哦？你以为是怎么发生的？我们是一时冲动。你明白我的意思吗？

朱莉： 对不起，我明白。我只是太吃惊了。你肯定自己怀孕了吗？不是你的月经来晚了？

杰茜： 不是。我已经去过学生健康中心了。他们给我做了检查。那也不过是确认了我自己做的怀孕检查结果罢了。

朱莉： 那你准备怎么办？

杰茜： 那个护士跟我谈了几种选择。我可以硬着头皮把孩子生下来，但是考虑到我的学习，我觉得这不太可能。那护士倒是说她可以帮我安排流产。

朱莉： 什么？流产？

杰茜： 对啊。为什么不呢？

朱莉： 因为流产在这儿有时是个很有争议的话题。我想有些人出于宗教或道德原因反对流产。

杰茜： 听着，我是不会让这个小错误干扰我的学习，并毁掉我的一生的。我只要今后加倍小心就是了。

卡米拉和梅在聊天

卡米拉： 你好，梅，我有事儿要和你商量。我不会再见王了，我觉得我们之间没有感觉。

梅： 哦，很抱歉听见你说这个。发生了什么事？你们分手了？

卡米拉： 我不知道。也许是文化差异吧。我认为他有点儿得寸进尺了。我是说，我也不知道具体是怎么回事，但是他总是过于热情。我只想做朋友罢了，最起码，我没想过像他对我那么"友好"，哈哈。

梅： 你这么说是什么意思？

卡米拉： 当我亲他的脸的时候，他以为我们是男女朋友了！是一对儿了！

梅： 其实，在中国我们是不习惯公开亲热的。我是说，我们通常不在公共场合接吻。

卡米拉： 那也不是真的接吻，梅。只是碰一下脸，我又没狂吻他或给他法国式接吻！

梅： 这，这很难把握。在中国手牵手都是胆大的了。我觉得他就是误会了。可怜的王！我想他是真的爱上你了！

第47章 学生性健康

Camilla: Love? That's pretty strong... I think you mean "like"... or "have feelings for"... love is something really serious in my culture; you can't just love someone after a couple of weeks. There's no such thing as "love at first sight". That's just infatuation or obsession.

May: Yeah... I guess we have to be careful with the words we use.

At the Student Health Centre

Fernando: I've got a bit of a problem, doctor. I've got this terrible searing pain every time I pass water.

Doctor: Right... let's have a look. Could you just drop your trousers, please? Right... when did you last have sexual contact with anyone?

Fernando: One week ago....

Doctor: And what's your sexuality? I mean, are you heterosexual or homosexual?

Fernando: I'm straight.

Doctor: All right. I'm going to need to do some tests for STDs. Now... I need to ask you... do you want an HIV test? You aren't in a high-risk group, but there's always a risk in unprotected sex.

Fernando: OK then.

Doctor: You'll need to come back for the results in three days. In the meantime, I'll give you these general antibiotics as a precautionary measure. You must refrain from sexual intercourse until you have the all clear... is that understood? Also, I don't want to give you a lecture, but I need to stress the importance of using a condom when you have sexual intercourse. They are not expensive, and they could save your life. Anyway, you can pick some up for free here. All right?

Fernando: Yes, doctor.

Outside

Fernando: God... the doctor told me off... can you believe it?

Jeff: Well, it's your own fault, Fernando.

Fernando: I bet he wouldn't have had a go at you... he'd be scared of being accused of prejudice. The PC brigade would have been straight onto him!

Jeff: What? Because I'm gay?

Fernando: Yeah... you guys are at more risk than anyone from STDs and AIDS!

Jeff: Come on Fernando, you don't really think that. You're just stressed out because of these tests... and it's not a question of being politically correct... it's a question of respect and tolerance. Being gay is not a psychological disorder, you know. Anyway, come on, tell me... who gave you the clap?!

卡米拉：爱？不至于吧。我认为你的意思是指"喜欢"，或者"有感觉"。在我的文化里爱情是非常严肃的，不能说才一两个星期就爱上谁了。一见钟情根本就不存在，那不过是冲动或沉迷而已。

梅：对，我想我们是得注意用词。

学生健康中心

费尔南多：医生，我有麻烦了。我现在小便时总有疼痛感。

医生：哦，让我看看。请你把裤子脱了。哦，你最近一次与别人发生性接触是什么时候？

费尔南多：一个星期前。

医生：你的性取向是什么？我是说，你是异性恋还是同性恋？

费尔南多：我是异性恋。

医生：好吧。我得给你做性病检查。我得问你，你要做艾滋病检查吗？你不在高危人群之列，但是没有保护措施的性生活总是危险的。

费尔南多：那好吧。

医生：3天后回来取结果。同时，我给你开点儿普通的抗生素作为应急治疗。你在没有康复之前不能有任何性行为，明白吗？另外，我不想对你老生常谈，但是我不得不向你强调在性交时使用避孕套的重要性。它们不贵，却可以救你的命。而且，你还能在这儿拿到免费的。明白了吗？

费尔南多：明白了，医生。

外面

费尔南多：天哪，那医生把我训斥了一通。你相信吗？

杰夫：这是你自己的错，费尔南多。

费尔南多：我肯定如果换了你，他是不会训斥的。他会担心被指责为有偏见。那帮"正义人士"马上就会把他盯上的。

杰夫：为什么？因为我是同性恋？

费尔南多：对啊。你们同性恋得性病、艾滋病的几率更高！

杰夫：算了吧，费尔南多，你不是真的这么认为吧。你只是因为这些检查有点儿紧张罢了。而且，这不是一个立场问题，而是一个尊严与容忍的问题。同性恋不是精神病。算了，高兴点儿，告诉我，谁把你传染上的？

实用短语

- Look, are you sure you're...? 你肯定你是……?
- It's not just that...? 不是……吧?
- So, what are you going to do? 那你准备怎么办?
- Do you mind my asking...? 你介意我问问……?
- When did you last have...? 你最近一次……是什么时候?
- Listen... there's something personal I need to tell you about. 我要跟你谈一些个人问题。
- I don't know how to put this, but... 我不知道该怎么说,但是……
- I need to talk to you about something. 我需要跟你商量些事情。
- Well the thing is, we're not... 问题是,我们不……
- Yeah... I guess we have to... 对……我估计我们是得……
- I've got a bit of a problem, doctor. 医生,我有麻烦了。
- I don't want to give you a lecture, but... 我不想老生常谈,但是……
- All right. I'm going to need to do some... 好了。我需要进行一些……
- Now... I need to ask you... 现在……我得问你……
- You'll need to come back for... 你得回来……
- You must refrain from... 你必须避免……
- Is that understood? 明白了吗?
- I need to stress the importance of... 我必须强调……的重要性。
- Well, it's your own fault... 这是你的错……
- Come on... you don't really think that. 算了吧……你不是真的那么认为的吧。
- It's not a question of... it's a question of... 这不是……的问题,而是……的问题。

词汇表

abortion 流产
AIDS 艾滋病
all over someone 亲热地缠着某人
antibiotics 抗生素
click 点击/有反映/有感觉
come on strong 来势凶猛
condom 避孕套
contraception 避孕措施
culture clash 文化冲突
daring 敢于/大胆的
disrupt 干扰
drop one's trousers 脱下裤子
French kiss 法式接吻
gay 同性恋(尤指男的)
get carried away 想入非非
get the wrong end of the stick 误解
give a lecture 讲大道理
go through with sth 经历/挺过去
have a baby 生小孩
have a go 借题发挥
have feelings for someone 喜欢某人/对某人有感觉
have the all clear 被批准
heat of the moment 一时冲动

heterosexual 异性恋的
high-risk group 高危人群
HIV 艾滋病毒
hold hands 牵手
home pregnancy test 家用怀孕测试
homosexual 同性恋的
hug 拥抱
infatuation 冲动
item 物品
kiss on the cheek 亲脸
love at first sight 一见钟情
obsession 着迷/执着
on religious/moral grounds 由于宗教和道德原因
pass water 小便
peck on the cheek (a)在脸上轻碰
period 月经
personal 个人的
politically correct 政治上正确/场面上过得去
precautionary measure 以防万一的措施
pregnant 怀孕了的

prejudice 偏见
psychological disorder 心理疾病
public displays of affection 公开暴露亲热举止
refrain from 忍耐不做…
respect 尊严(名词)/尊重(动词)
ruin 毁掉
searing pain 尖锐的疼痛
sexual contact 性行为
sexual intercourse 性交
sexuality 性
snog 狂吻亲热
split up 分手
stds 性疾病
stigma 有争议的问题
straight 异性恋的/直接的
student health centre 学生健康中心
taboo 禁忌
tell off 训斥
termination 流产
the clap 传染(隐讳的说法)
tolerance 容忍
unprotected sex 无保护的性行为

第48章
成年学生
Mature Students

背景常识

通常,在本科阶段,入学时年纪高于21岁的学生被认为是成年学生。有些学校的成年学生的划分年龄还要高一些。成年学生的划分方式通常没有年龄上限(upper limit)。在研究生阶段,各学校定义成年学生的方式差别(vary)很大。但无论如何,接受终身教育(life-long learning)在英国是非常普遍的。成年学生大约占全英国学生人口的四分之一(a quarter)。

根据(according to)英国目前的(current)移民法,持有全职(full-time)学生签证的人的配偶(spouse)与子女(dependent)可以陪同此人一起前往英国。在此人上学期间,其配偶可以从事有偿工作,其子女可以接受免费基础教育。

作为一个成年学生有不少好处(benefits)。成年学生在住宿分配和奖学金评选上通常都享有优先权(priority)。大学和学生会甚至还会为成年学生的配偶提供工作机会,并提供免费家政服务(childcare)。有些学生会还从留学生中组织志愿者到当地小学里帮助英语不好的成年留学生子女来适应英语课堂和教学方式。

把全家带到英国去上学将是一次有趣而富于悬念(thrilling)的经历。你唯一需要注意的就是住宿申请和确保你的家人在语言和习惯上做好在英国生活的准备。英国大学的学生服务机构和学生会会全力保证你全家人生活愉快(well-being)。学生会的国际学生官、成年学生官(mature student officer)和福利官(welfare officer)都是你可以求助的对象。

In the Student Union

Welfare Officer: Hello, how can I help you?

Joe: Well... I've got a bit of a problem... I'm a mature student, and my wife and son are here with me. The problem is that I've been allocated a single room in halls, and there's nowhere for my wife and son. I told them months ago that we needed family accommodation, but it looks like they've messed up.

Welfare Officer: OK... well look, where are you living at the moment?

Joe: Actually, we're living in one room in a B&B down near the station.

Welfare Officer: Why don't you let me give the accommodation office a call. If you just take a seat in the waiting room, I'll try to get back to you as quick as I can....

15 Minutes Later

Welfare Officer: Right, I've spoken to Mr. McCardle at the Accommodation Office, and he says that they do, in fact, have alternative accommodation available for you... it's a privately-rented flat on the other side of the campus... it's actually being sub-let through the university accommodation office. If you go over to the Accommodation Office, Mr. McCardle will see you, and he'll take you over to the flat.

Later

Joe: Well everything seems satisfactory... it seems very nice.

McCardle: All right... well here's the contract which you need to sign, and we'll need you to do all the financial bits today as well, if possible. The rent is payable one month in advance by direct debit... so here's the direct debit form, if you could just fill it in and sign it. This is a twelve month contract, and you will be given one-month's notice to quit.

Joe: OK... right....

McCardle: Now, you'll also need to pay £250 deposit. We will return this if everything is in order when you leave.

Joe: Well, I'm going to need to go to the cash machine to get that. I don't normally carry amounts like that on me.

McCardle: Oh... OK... in that case, maybe we should go back over to the main building. Now, while we're at it, Mr. Zhou... your son... how old is he?

Joe: He's four.

McCardle: Well in that case, you might want to tell your wife that the university operates a day nursery. It's on-campus and is set within its own gardens... it's very good... especially if your wife wants to work while she's here. Oh... and it's totally free of charge of course. Will she want to work Mr. Zhou... your wife?

在学生会

福利官： 你好，我能帮你什么？

乔： 我遇到点儿麻烦。我是一个成年学生，我妻子和儿子跟我一起来的。问题是校方给我分了一个单人间，我妻子和儿子没有地方住。我几个月前就跟住宿办公室说过我要一套家庭公寓，但看起来他们弄错了。

福利官： 好的。你现在住在哪儿？

乔： 实际上，我们现在住在车站附近的一家旅馆里。

福利官： 我给住宿办公室打个电话。你在那边的休息室等一等，我会尽快给你回复的。

15 分钟以后

福利官： 好了，我已经跟住宿办公室的麦卡德尔先生谈过了，他说他们确实还有别的选择，是一个私人的公寓，在校园的另一边。它其实是通过学校的住宿办公室转租的。如果你去住宿办公室，麦卡德尔先生会见你的，他会领你到那个公寓去。

稍后

乔： 一切都很令人满意，非常好。

麦卡德尔： 那好。这是你需要签的合同。我们需要你今天把财务问题也解决了，如果可能的话。每个月你可以通过定期银行转账预付房租。这是银行转账单，请把它填好并签字。这是一年的合同。如果你要提前退房，你得提前一个月告诉我们。

乔： 好的。

麦卡德尔： 现在，你需要付 250 镑的押金。如果房子一切完好无损，你走的时候，我们会退给你的。

乔： 我得去提款机才能拿到钱。我平时身上没那么多现金。

麦卡德尔： 哦，那好。这样的话，我们也许应该回到主楼去。既然我们说到这儿了，张先生，你儿子多大了？

乔： 4 岁了。

麦卡德尔： 这样的话，你可以告诉你的妻子，学校有托儿所。托儿所就在我们学校自己的花园里，非常不错，尤其是如果你的妻子要在这儿工作的话。哦，对了，它还是免费的。你的妻子想工作吗？

Joe: I don't know... I'll need to ask her. We've budgeted for her not working so, if she does I guess it'll be an added bonus.

McCardle: Well, tell her to go to the universty's part-time job notice board... it's very helpful.

Joe: Thank you very much. This is a big weight off my shoulders. You can't imagine how stressful it is being a mature student from overseas.

McCardle: Oh, believe me Mr. Zhou. I can. We deal with many students in your position, and remember... we're a university, so we operate in a spirit of collegiality. If you have any difficulties with your accommodation, we are here to help. All right?

Joe: Of course. Thank you!

乔：我不知道，我得问问她。我们是按她不工作计划开支的，如果她工作，那就是额外收入了。

麦卡德尔：叫她去学校的业余工作通知栏看看，那个非常有用。

乔：谢谢。这样我心里的一块石头就落地了。你没法想象作为成年留学生压力有多大。

麦卡德尔：相信我，张先生，我想象得到。我处理过很多你这种处境的学生。而且，记住，我们是一个大学，所以我们是有集体责任感的。如果你在住宿上有任何困难，我们就是为你服务的。可以吗？

乔：当然。谢谢。

实用短语

- The problem is that…   问题是……
- It looks like…   看起来……
- Why don't you let me…?   让我来……吧?
- I'll try to get back to you as quick as I can.   我会尽快答复你的。
- The rent is payable one month in advance/in arrears.   房租每月预付/后付。
- You'll also have to pay…   你还得付……
- You might want to tell your wife…   你可以告诉你的太太……
- Will she want to…, your wife?   你的妻子要……吗?
- I guess it'll be an added bonus.   我猜那将是额外的收入。
- This is a big weight off my shoulders.   我心里的石头落地了/肩上的担子轻松了。
- You can't imagine how…   你没法想象……
- Oh, believe me, Mr. Zhou, I can.   相信我,张先生,我可以。

词汇表

added bonus 额外的好处
allocate 分配
B&B 旅馆
budget 预算
cash machine 提款机
collegiality 集体感
day nursery 白天照顾/托儿所
direct debit 银行定期付款

family accommodation 全家住宿
get back to 回复
in order 就绪的
mature student 成年学生
mess up 弄乱(动词)
notice to quit 退房通知
privately-rented 私人出租的
rip off 被坑/被宰了

satisfactory 令人满意的
set within 放在…之内
shoulders 肩膀
spirit 灵魂/心灵
sub-let 转租
weight 重量/压力
while we're at it 既然说到这了,(我们就顺便…)

第49章
游历英国
Travelling in the UK

背景常识

如果你会开车,那么约几个朋友共同公路旅行(road trip)应该是最好的旅游方式了。中国的驾驶执照(driving licence)在英国依然可以短期使用。不过你要记住,这个国家的车是靠左行驶的。

英国铁路(the British Rail)不可靠(unreliable)是出了名的(notorious)。然而,与中国相比,英国毕竟是弹丸之地。即使是晚点的(delayed)旅程也不至于让人觉得太漫长。英国火车上几乎没有卧铺(sleeper)或通宵线路,因为根本用不着,从格拉斯哥(Glasgow)到朴次茅斯(Portsmouth)也用不了一天。

或者你可以参加旅行团。旅行团一般都以大巴(coach)为交通工具。这样旅行的优势在于你可以在路上结交一些朋友,而且不用自己安排食宿。缺点(downside)是你不能自己选择景点和逗留时间。

在英国国内旅游,一般没有必要乘坐飞机,除非你要去爱尔兰。大部分去爱尔兰旅游的人都坐船。渡轮(ferry)是非常舒适和便宜的。而且你还可以欣赏到爱尔兰海岸的风光。

大部分学生在旅行时住B&B。B&B是bed and breakfast的缩写。"床与早餐"也基本概括了这类旅馆的服务范围。你会睡在一个有4到6张床的房间里,早上起来有一顿免费早餐,便宜而温馨(homely)。hostel也是旅馆,和B&B差不多,不过要大一些,可能还包括酒吧。hotel(酒店)就不用介绍了吧?一个字,"贵"。

这里我们就不介绍英国的旅游景点(attractions)了。英国著名的花园、城堡、教堂、山峦和湖泊数不胜数。想要进一步了解,你还是买本旅游指南(tourist guide)吧。

In the Common Room

Lucy: Hi Julie… I'm thinking of travelling around the UK during the Easter break… have you got any suggestions?

Julie: Well, lots of overseas students want to go to Scotland because they've heard that it's wilder and more romantic than, say, the South of England… but that's only part of it… I mean the Highlands are mountainous and remote, and Edinburgh is a lovely city, but the place can get really packed with hordes of tourists during the tourist season… off season is quieter.

Lucy: Oh… where else are good places to go… apart from Scotland?

Julie: Well, if you like to get away from it all, and you want to do a day trip with your friends there are miles and miles of rolling green countryside in Britain… and it's actually quite easy to get to. I mean, here in London, the easiest way is to hop on the Tube and travel to the end of the Central or the Metropolitan lines and you're already in beautiful little picture-postcard villages.

Lucy: It does sound quite easy… what if I want to go somewhere further away?

Julie: Well, there's a good rail network… although it is a bit on the expensive side. If you book well in advance, you can get some good bargains. However, it's more expensive if you want to travel at short notice, and a lot of people say that rail travel has actually become more expensive and less efficient since the service was privatised in the nineties.

Lucy: What about cheaper forms of travel?

Julie: Well, you could go by National Express or Stagecoach… these are the main inter-city coach companies, and they run several coaches per day between all the major towns and cities in Britain. Coach travel has always been cheaper than rail travel, and now air travel, say from London to Edinburgh or Inverness can actually be cheaper than full-price rail travel.

In the SU Bar

Aslan: You know, I was thinking… the vacation is coming up, and we all want to go away somewhere, so we might as well hire a car and share the driving? I mean, four of us could split the cost of a normal saloon.

Amy: That's a good idea, actually.

Lucy: Yes, but I can't drive.

Jack: Hmm… well you could pay extra… haha!

Aslan: No… listen… I'm serious… by the time we'd bought individual tickets and all of that, I'm sure a car would be cheaper and more convenient… we wouldn't need to worry about getting from railway stations to other places, and all of that.

Jack: I've got an International Driving Licence... who else has?

Amy: I haven't, but I can get one.

Aslan: Don't forget to drive on the left!

Jack: OK... I'll have a look on the web for the cheapest car rental... and we'll take it from there. I'll make sure I get the best deal with unlimited mileage and no damage waiver.

在活动室

露西：你好，朱莉，我想在复活节期间周游英国，你有什么建议吗？

朱莉：很多留学生去苏格兰，因为他们听说那里比南英格兰更加原始和浪漫。但也不全是，我是说，苏格兰高地的确是山峰耸立，远离尘嚣，爱丁堡也是一座非常有意思的城市，不过在旅游旺季那里可是人满为患，淡季的时候要清静得多。

露西：哦。除了苏格兰还有什么好地方吗？

朱莉：如果你想彻底休闲，而且想跟朋友郊游一天，英国到处都有绿油油的田野，而且交通便利。在伦敦，最简单的办法就是跳上中央线或都市线地铁一直坐到头，你就已经到了风景如画的美丽村庄了。

露西：听起来是很容易。如果我想走远一点儿呢？

朱莉：你可以坐火车，不过要稍微贵一点儿。如果提前预定能买到一些便宜票。但是，如果你临时决定旅游，那就贵了。很多人都说，自从90年代铁路私有化以后，车票越来越贵，效率也越来越低了。

露西：还有什么便宜的旅游方式吗？

朱莉：你可以乘国家特快或长途大巴，这些都是城市间主要的长途汽车公司。他们每天都在英国的各大城市间跑好几趟。长途汽车一直都比火车便宜。而且，现在从伦敦飞往爱丁堡或伊凡内斯的机票比全价的火车票还便宜。

在学生会酒吧

阿丝兰：我在想，假期快到了，大家都想出去玩，不如干脆租辆车一起开。我们4个人可以分摊一辆普通轿车的费用。

埃米：这确实是个好主意。

露西：但是我不会开车。

杰克：那你就多付点儿钱好了，哈哈！

阿丝兰：我是认真的。等我们各自买好票什么的，我肯定一辆车要便宜和方便得多。我们不用担心从火车站到其它地方之类的事情。

杰克：我有国际驾照。还有谁有？

埃米：我没有，但是我能办一个。

阿丝兰：别忘了在路左边开车！

杰克：好。我上网看看最便宜的汽车出租，我们从那儿再做进一步的打算。我保证咱们能拿到最优惠的价格，无限公里数，不会有损坏责任。

实用短语

- ◆ That's only part of it.　但也不全是。
- ◆ The place can get really packed.　那里可能人满为患。
- ◆ We might as well…　我们不如干脆……
- ◆ wilder and more romantic　更加原始和浪漫
- ◆ the best deal　最好的价格/最好的买卖
- ◆ cheaper and more convenient　更便宜方便
- ◆ … can actually be cheaper than…　……能比……便宜。
- ◆ … has always been cheaper than…　……一直比……便宜。
- ◆ cheaper forms of travel　更便宜的旅行方式
- ◆ … has actually become more expensive and less efficient.　……更加昂贵,效率反而更低了。
- ◆ somewhere further away　更远的地方
- ◆ not much harder　不那么难
- ◆ the easiest way　最简单的办法
- ◆ the cheapest car rental　最便宜的汽车出租

词汇表

at short notice 临时决定的
car rental 汽车出租
damage waiver 事故责任豁免
day trip 一日游
Easter break 复活节放假
efficient 有效率的
get away from it all 远离喧嚣
Highlands (the) 苏格兰高地
hire 租
hop on 跳上(交通工具)

hordes 群
international driving licence 国际驾照
mainline station 干线车站
might as well 干脆不如再…
mountainous 有山的
nineties 90年代
off-season 淡季
picture-postcard village 风景美得能做明信片照片的村庄

privatise 私有化(动词)
remote 遥远的
rolling countryside 无边的农田
saloon 轿车
split the cost 分摊费用
take it from there 到那里再决定
tourist season 旅游季节
unlimited mileage 无限里程

第50章
告别英伦
Leaving the UK

背景常识

天下没有不散的筵席,早晚(sooner or later)你要跟英国道别(say farewell)。除了眼泪、道别晚会(goodbye parties)和毕业典礼(graduation ceremony)以外,还有不少事情需要你操心。比如,取回你的住宿押金。如果你要赶清早的飞机,你还要妥善安排如何归还你的钥匙。撤销你的银行账户并安全地把钱转移回国。如果你有工作,还得跟你的雇主交代好你的剩余工资、人事和税务情况。另外,跟你的院系秘书安排好毕业以后的个人行政问题,比如你接收毕业证书的地址和加入校友俱乐部(alumni club)等等。

如果你还没有对未来的安排打算,现在也正是时候考虑这个问题。是要回国工作,还是继续在世界另外某个角落继续上学?你甚至可以留在英国工作几年,如果你能找到符合移民法标准的工作的话。

对许多来英留学的中国学生来说,在英国的时间可能是他们一生最具传奇色彩的(legendary)时期之一。为你曾经生活、阅读、行走、畅饮过的地方拍些照片。收集老师、朋友们未来的联系方式。买些象征英国和你所在大学的纪念品(souvenir)。有一天,你的家人甚至孩子都可能看到这些物品,并感叹你所有的奋斗、付出与成就。留学不仅仅是苦读,在整个这一本书里我们都在鼓励读者们勇于尝试、敢于交流、善于展现。如果要把这一本书里的精髓和道理都能用一句话概括出来的话,那就是"纵横四海,匪我欲知天下,乃欲天下知我(Studying abroad is not just about knowing the world, but also about letting the world know me)。"

Four Days Before Departure

Jack: Listen, we need to close our bank accounts, arrange shipping and see the landlord to get our deposits back before we go home.

Anna: Yes... and we need to think about coming back for the graduation ceremony.

Jack: Gosh... yes... I'd forgotten about that. Right, let's work this out. The graduation ceremony, that's in September, isn't it? We'll need to fill in the forms so that they know we're going. Then, tomorrow morning we'll go down to the bank and tell them we want to close our accounts. Then in the afternoon we'll have to arrange to ship our books and clothes and heavy stuff back. We can call up our landlords after that. We'll need to get everything sorted out by Friday, ready to leave on Saturday.

Anna: Do we need to ship stuff? I mean, can't we just take it on the flight with us? Check it in?

Jack: If you want to pay a fortune in excess weight charges, be my guest! There are plenty of agents there who ship stuff to China.

Anna: You know, Jessie had problems getting her deposit back because she hadn't cleaned her flat before she left, so we need to make sure that there's no grease on the cooker or the tiles and no scum marks on the bath. If we do it on Friday, we can hand the keys over on Saturday morning, get our deposits back and go to the airport.

Jack: And we need to insist on cash because we'll have closed our bank accounts by then.

Saying Goodbye

Jack: Tomorrow is our last day here. We're both leaving on the same flight tomorrow afternoon.

Julie: Oh no..., it's been so nice knowing you. You've been such good fun to be with... oh I'm really going to miss you both....

Jack: Yes... we've learned so much in our time here... not just academic stuff, but you've taught us so much about Britain and everything... and everyone has been so nice... and so friendly.

Julie: Oh stop... you're making me cry!

Fernando: Hey... I'm really gonna miss you guys... look, let me give you my email address... you must keep in touch.

Anna: Yes... we will... definitely, and if you come to China you must stay with my family.

Fernando: Thanks. You must come to Spain some time too.

Jack: Oh, guys... I've had such a good time here... I'll remember it for the rest of my life. It's been fantastic meeting you all and getting to know you. Hey! Let's go out on the town tonight... we'll go for a curry or a pizza or something, then we'll go down the pub one last time, all right?

Fernando: Yes... definitely, and we'll say goodbye properly.

离开英国的前4天

杰克： 我们得撤销银行账户，安排行李运输，还要找房东把押金要回来。

安娜： 对。还得考虑回来参加毕业典礼。

杰克： 天哪，是啊，我都忘了。我们安排一下。毕业典礼，那是在9月，对吧？我们得填这些表，这样他们才知道我们会出席。那么，明天早上我们去银行，告诉他们我们要关闭账户。然后，下午我们去寄书、衣服之类的重物。那之后，我们再给房东打电话。我们得在星期五前把这些事办完，星期六出发。

安娜： 我们需要寄东西吗？我们不能把它们带上飞机？托运不行吗？

杰克： 如果你愿意付一大笔超重费的话，随便你！往中国寄东西的公司多着呢。

安娜： 你知道吗，杰茜在取押金的时候遇到点儿麻烦，因为她没有打扫她的公寓。我们得确保炉子上和瓷砖上没有油渍，而且浴室里没有脏东西。如果我们星期五打扫，那就能在星期六早上交钥匙，拿回押金并赶往机场。

杰克： 我们得要现金，因为我们的银行账户到那时就关闭了。

说再见

杰克： 明天是我们在这儿的最后一天。我们明天下午乘同一班飞机走。

朱莉： 哦，不。有幸认识你们真是太好了，跟你们在一起是那么的开心。哦，我真的会很想你们的。

杰克： 是啊。我们在这里学了这么多东西，不仅是学习上的，你还教了我们很多关于英国和其他的事情。大家对我们都这么好，这么友善。

朱莉： 哦，别说了，你让我快哭了！

费尔南多： 嘿，我真会想念你们的。我把我的电子邮件地址给你。我们一定要保持联系。

安娜： 对，我们会的，一定。而且如果你们到中国来，一定要来我家住。

费尔南多： 谢谢，你们有空也一定来西班牙。

杰克： 哦，伙计们，我在这儿的日子太好了！我这辈子都不会忘记。能遇见并了解你们实在太奇妙了。嘿！咱们今晚去城里吧，一起去吃咖喱或比萨饼什么的，然后最后再去一次酒吧，怎么样？

费尔南多： 对，一定的，而且我们可以好好道别。

实用短语

- I'd forgotten about that. 我都把那事忘了。
- If you want to... be my guest! 如果你要……，随便你！
- We'll need to get everything sorted out by Friday. 我们在星期五前必须把这些事都办完。
- We'll have closed our bank accounts by then. 我们到时候已经把账户关了。
- It's been so nice knowing you. 认识你们太好了。
- You've been such good fun to be with. 跟你在一起是那么有趣。
- I'm really going to miss you both. 我真的会很想你们。
- We've learned so much in our time here. 我们在这学到了不少东西。
- Everyone has been so nice... and so friendly. 每个人都这么友好，这么和善。
- I'm really gonna miss you guys. 我真的会想你们的。
- Let me give you my email address... 让我给你我的电子邮件地址……
- You must keep in touch. 我们必须保持联系。
- We will... definitely. 我们一定会……。
- If you come to China, you can stay with me. 如果你来中国，你可以跟我住。
- I've had such a good time here. 我在这儿的时光非常美好。
- It's been fantastic meeting you all and getting to know you. 能遇见并了解你们实在太奇妙了。

词汇表

agent 中介/公司（agency 和 agent 都有公司的意思，前者尤指机构，后者指人）
bath 洗澡（指坐在浴缸里洗澡，不是淋浴）
check in 经检查后带进/随身携带
close 关闭
cooker 炉子
excess weight charges 超重费用

forward 向前/转发
get one's deposit back 拿回押金
good fun 非常有意思的
graduation ceremony 毕业典礼
grease 油渍
insist on 执意做…
promise 答应
scum marks 脏痕迹

seating preferences 对座位的倾向
ship 运输（动词）
shipping 运输（名词，不仅仅指水路运输）
sort out 解决
tiles 瓷砖
VAT claim 增值税报关

英语国际人 知性英语·自信表达

"英语国际人"丛书将帮助你突破语言障碍,成功应对多话题、深层次的英语交流。
丛书第一辑包括:

商务英语情景口语 100 主题
小 16 开,定价 39.00 元,附赠 mp3 光盘
100 个场景、200 篇对话展现原生态的外企口语。作者 Amanda Crandell Ju 多年从事商务活动。她用地道的语言、丰富的词汇,生动描绘了各种真实场景中的沟通方式。对于涉外及商务人士来说,本书具有相当的实战性和针对性。

生活英语情景口语 100 主题
小 16 开,定价 38.00 元,附赠 mp3 光盘
作者 Carol Rueckert 是资深的英语教学专家,又深入英美社会生活多年。她用 100 个场景、200 篇对话细致展现了当下英美的风土人情,以及英语国家普通百姓的沟通方式。同时,本书汇集了大量英美最新的口语表达法。

留学英语情景会话 50 主题
大 32 开,定价 29.00 元,附赠 mp3 光盘
对话采自英国校园各个角落,原汁原味,风趣实用,与留学生活息息相关。作者 Martin Boyle 在伦敦大学多年从事留学生教育,是雅思考官。作者于戈毕业于伦敦大学和威尔士大学,曾任英国国家学生会国际学生官。

英语畅谈中国文化 50 主题
小 16 开,定价 25.00 元,附赠 mp3 光盘
本书以机智幽默的对话将中国文化的方方面面娓娓道来。基于对中西方文化的透彻了解,作者特别关注那些令西方人不解的中国文化习俗,其智慧点拨让阅读本书成为一种享受。

英语畅谈世界文化 100 主题
小 16 开,定价 25.00 元,附赠 mp3 光盘
本书以世界各国的文化标志作为谈资。对话部分视野开阔、趣味盎然,有丰富的固定搭配和短语帮助你掌握口语表达法。作者 Nick Stirk 毕业于英国贝尔法斯特大学和剑桥大学,在中国著名高校执教多年。

英语畅谈青春文化 50 主题
小 16 开,定价 25.00 元,附赠 mp3 光盘
本书选取全球青年都热衷于讨论的时尚话题。作者 Jessica Robertson 和 Liz Carter 出自美国常青藤高校。对话部分因不同观点的撞击而生动活泼、引人入胜,同时汇集了大量最新的美式口语表达法。

英语畅谈时事热点 50 主题
小 16 开,定价 25.00 元,附赠 mp3 光盘
本书选择当今世界的热点话题作为谈资。对话部分信息丰富、观点独特,有丰富的固定搭配和短语帮助你掌握口语表达法。作者 Graham Paterson 曾作为工程师走遍大半个世界,后作为口语专家在中国执教。

图书在版编目（CIP）数据

留学英语情景会话 50 主题 /（英）博伊尔（Boyle, M.），
于戈著. —北京：外文出版社，2007
（英语国际人）
ISBN 978 – 7 – 119 – 04905 – 2

Ⅰ. 留… Ⅱ. ① 博… ② 于… Ⅲ. 英语-口语 Ⅳ. H319.9

中国版本图书馆 CIP 数据核字（2007）第 165344 号

英语国际人
留学英语情景会话 50 主题

作　　者	Martin Boyle　于　戈
选题策划	蔡　箐
责任编辑	王　欢
装帧设计	红十月设计室
印刷监制	冯　浩

ⓒ 2008 外文出版社

出版发行	外文出版社
地　　址	中国北京西城区百万庄大街 24 号　　邮政编码　100037
网　　址	http://www.flp.com.cn
电子信箱	info@flp.com.cn　　sales@flp.com.cn
电　　话	（010）68995964/68995883（编辑部）
	（010）68320579/68996067（总编室）
	（010）68995844/68995852（发行部/门市邮购）
	（010）68327750/68996164（版权部）
印　　制	北京外文印刷厂
经　　销	新华书店/外文书店
开　　本	小 16 开　　　　　　　　字　数　187 千字
印　　数	00001 – 10000 册　　　　印　张　16
版　　次	2008 年第 1 版第 1 次印刷
装　　别	平
书　　号	ISBN 978 – 7 – 119 – 04905 – 2
定　　价	29.00 元

外文社图书　版权所有　侵权必究
外文社图书　有印装错误可随时退货